Praise for

I am delighted to welcome this exceptional book on causal AI, written by Judith Hurwitz and John Thompson, which bridges the gap between conventional methods of business analytics and modern techniques of causal analysis and machine learning. Business leaders and data scientists who are trained in pre-scriptive statistics, simulation, and optimization techniques will be happy to discover how critical problems in their field, commonly left to intuition or contentious judgment, can now be systematically conceptualized, articulated, and solved using simple techniques of causal artificial intelligence. These include predicting the effects of potential interventions, finding explanations for unexpected outcomes, testing the validity of one's assumptions, and combining data from several sources. The lucid exposition of this book and the variety of practical examples provided promise to make business analytics the new beneficiary of the causal revolution.

—Judea Pearl
UCLA chancellor professor emeritus in computer science,
recipient of the A.M. Turing Award

As the authors describe in detail, the vast majority of AI today is based on statistical association rather than causality. Under many circumstances those results aren't sufficiently clear-cut to drive action. The world will eventually move toward causal AI, and this book will provide a head start.

—Thomas H. Davenport
distinguished professor at Babson College;
author of *All In on AI, Working with AI,* and
The AI Advantage

Causal Artificial Intelligence

Causal Artificial Intelligence

The Next Step in Effective Business AI

Judith S. Hurwitz

John K. Thompson

I dedicate this book to Warren, my partner in life.

—Judith S. Hurwitz

For my readers in the analytics community.

—John K. Thompson

Contents

Foreword

Dear Reader,

It is with great pleasure and enthusiasm that I introduce you to this exceptional book on causal AI, written by the brilliant Judith Hurwitz and John Thompson. As I embarked on my journey through its pages, I found myself intrigued by the depth of knowledge, clarity of explanations, and practical insights it offers. "Causal Artificial Intelligence: The Next Step in Effective Business AI" is a true gem for those seeking to comprehend the intricate world of causal artificial intelligence.

In today's rapidly evolving technological landscape, the concept of causal AI has emerged as a source of radical innovation and a catalyst for transformation. It holds the key to unlocking the true potential of artificial intelligence, empowering us not only to predict and classify but also to understand the causal mechanisms that underlie complex systems. Through the lens of directed acyclic graphs (DAGs) and structural causal models (SCMs), pioneered by the eminent Prof. Judea Pearl, this book guides us on a remarkable journey of discovery.

One of the book's greatest strengths is its accessibility, making it a perfect companion for those who are eager to grasp the essence of causal AI but lack a formal background in the field. Whether you are a seasoned professional in the realm of business analytics or someone just stepping into this fascinating domain, Judith Hurwitz and John Thompson expertly demystify the core concepts, rendering them comprehensible to a wide audience. Their ability to translate complex theories into practical applications is commendable, making "Causal Artificial Intelligence" an invaluable resource for both novices and experts alike.

As you delve into the pages that follow, you will encounter crucial topics that lie at the heart of causal AI. Exploring the realms of explainability, you will discover how causal models offer an unparalleled understanding of why certain decisions are made by AI systems. In a world increasingly driven by algorithms, the book masterfully examines the biases that can be inadvertently embedded within these systems and provides valuable insights into mitigating such biases, ensuring fairness and equity in algorithmic decision-making.

Another significant facet the book illuminates is the vital aspect of robustness in AI systems. Through a meticulous exploration of DAGs and SCMs, you will gain a deep understanding of how to construct models that are not only accurate but also resilient to unforeseen perturbations and uncertainties. This robustness is crucial in building trustworthy and reliable AI systems that can be confidently deployed in real-world scenarios.

The book strikes a perfect balance between theory and practice. While it delves into the fundamental principles and theories that underpin causal AI, it never loses sight of the practical applications and real-world implications. The numerous case studies and examples provided throughout the book reinforce its relevance and enable you to connect the dots between theory and its practical implementation.

I have no doubt that this exceptional work will become an indispensable resource for professionals in business analytics roles. The knowledge imparted within these pages has the potential to revolutionize the way we approach artificial intelligence, enabling us to harness its power responsibly and ethically. Whether you are a data scientist, a decision-maker, or simply an enthusiast seeking to expand your understanding, this book will serve as an invaluable guide on your journey to master the intricacies of causal AI.

In conclusion, I would like to express my deepest appreciation to Judith Hurwitz and John Thompson for writing this remarkable book. Their passion for the subject matter is evident, and their ability to distill complex ideas into clear and relatable explanations is truly remarkable. Each chapter takes you on a journey, unraveling the intricacies of causal AI and imparting knowledge that is both insightful and actionable. Prepare to embark on a transformational voyage, unlocking the power of causal AI and embracing a future where we not only predict and observe but truly understand.

Enjoy the journey!

Sincerely,

Paul Hünermund

Assistant Professor of Strategy & Innovation

Copenhagen Business School

Preface

In my view, causal AI is the next stage in the evolution of software because it is focused on being able to understand the causes and effects of events. As we discuss in this book, what has caused a marketing campaign to achieve the revenue objectives? Is the problem the campaign itself, or are there underlying issues that are impacting results? Is the cause of the disappointing marketing campaign because of a sudden competitive threat? Is there a problem with the company's reputation? What would the impact on revenue if the product price was reduced by 10 percent? Would a different type of marketing campaign result in better results? The underlying casual technology needed to address these problems is complex, and the approach is instrumental for business leaders to understand the potential impact. Therefore, unlike some earlier evolutions of AI, the value of a causal AI approach can have a direct and profound effect on business outcomes.

A plethora of books and articles already address causal inference—a field that must recognize Judea Pearl as a pioneer and visionary in causality. So, why write yet another book on the topic? The reason is straightforward—this book is written for technology-focused leaders who are not developers but are responsible for bringing new technology into their companies to gain a competitive edge. In writing this book, I have spent count-less hours speaking with leaders in the field and reading many articles and books. The goal of this book is to provide an under-standing of why the field of causal AI is so important. It has the potential to truly transform how we use artificial intelligence to digitally transform business.

My journey through the complex world of software started more than 35 years ago. My experience in technology began when I joined a financial services company and was tasked with introducing emerging technology to various business units. The goal was to evaluate how the technology could help transform the competitiveness of the business. From that beginning, I went on to spend many years as a developer, strategy IT consultant, industry analyst, thought leader, and writer. Most recently, I joined Geminos Software, a causal AI company, as their chief evangelist. I credit my ability to begin to understand this amaz-ing and complex technology to the insights and wisdom of the Geminos team.

While I have spent years delving into some of the most com-plex technologies, I have always put solutions in perspective by focusing on the needs of the business organization. No matter what position I have been in, I always asked some variation of the same questions: What is the purpose of a software platform, and how does it help the business flourish? Why is the technology important?

Since I have always focused on those key issues, it is not sur-prising that I have paid particular attention to some of the most complex emerging technologies. During my pursuit of learning and understanding the value of new offerings, I have coauthored 10 books and dozens of customized e-books all focused on explain-ing complex technologies to both business and technical audi-ences. My goal has long been to bridge the gap of how business and technology leaders must collaborate to be able to succeed. I have always believed that customers will not buy technology that they do not understand. Topics of the books I have coauthored include service-oriented architecture, big data, machine learning, and cloud computing. My two most recent books focused on cognitive computing and augmented intelligence. Both books have informed my journey to an exploration of causal AI.

As with any emerging technology, causal AI will evolve over the coming decade. The goal of this book is to provide guidance and an understanding for a business audience of the foundation of this important technology. As a participant in the world of emerging technologies, I felt it was the right time to put causal AI in perspective.

—Judith Hurwitz
May 2023

While writing this book on causal AI, generative AI burst onto the market with great excitement, fanfare, and disruption. I was asked by more than a few people who knew that I was involved in writing a book on causal AI if I should put this book on hold and focus my current efforts on generative AI. As with all reasonable suggestions and questions, I considered the change in direction. My conclusion was that while generative AI is transformative in relation to how people are employed, how work will be executed, the impact on productivity, and more, generative AI is not a new field of AI. Generative AI is an extension of, and a new way of combining, neural networks, unsupervised learning, supervised learning, reinforcement learning, and much larger models than we have seen before, but it is not a new field of AI, not the way causal AI is. Hence, my conclusion was that while my day job is dominated by determining how to design, leverage, govern, deploy, and use generative AI in an enterprise environment, this book on causal AI was still needed to raise the awareness of the power, value, and transformative nature of causal AI.

My main motivation for writing this book was to put an original book into the market that takes the dialogue relating to causal AI in a new direction—a direction that begins to draw the business, technical, and analytical communities into the dialogue.

In my research to expand my fundamental understanding of causal AI and the stage of development of this completely new field of AI, before the writing process began, I read nearly 100 pieces of original writing. All of the books, research papers, most of the blogs, and more, on causal AI immediately dove into the details of the calculus and related math underlying causal AI. I refreshed my understanding of calculus that I learned in graduate school. My knowledge of calculus was extended, sharpened, and revived, but I knew that this type of writing was a barrier to broadening and deepening my understanding of causal AI. I also knew that if it was a high barrier for me, then it was a complete showstopper for most people.

I knew that the audiences that I felt needed to know about causal AI were not, for the most part, going to wade through even a 10th of what I had read. I became excited about the opportunity to be among the first people in the field of data, analytics, and AI to develop and carry the message forward that causal AI was being developed, was a powerful new tool, and would be a significant advance in our arsenal of tools in our quest to document, model, and understand our world in a more complete manner.

I wrote *Building Analytics Teams* (BAT) after having built multiple analytics teams over the previous 37 years as a technologist and an AI practitioner. One of my goals, and my primary objective, in writing BAT was to help people from all walks of life who have more than a passing interest in being part of the fields of data, analytics, and AI to understand the real-world environment, the environment in the majority of enterprise-class organizations, and the real constraints and opportunities that are at play in working in the field of analytics. I wanted to help new college graduates to understand what working in analytics really looked and felt like. I wanted new managers to have a "how to" book on how to design, build, manage, and grow, their analytics teams, and I wanted, most of all, to help analytics professionals to not make the same mistakes that I made. I wanted to make their lives and journeys better. In BAT, I accomplished that goal.

My primary goal in writing this book is to help draw the business, technical, and analytical communities into an exploration of the emerging field of causal AI. I want those practitioners to buy and read this book to understand what is coming next. I want them to engage with the content to fire their imaginations about what they can do with causal AI and how causal AI is an entirely novel and new approach to AI that expands their toolset and puts the power of AI in the hands of the business users. In that respect, putting the power of AI in the hands of business users, causal AI has some similarities to generative AI, but only at a conceptual level.

I recognized that causal AI was a completely new field of AI, and I wanted to be part of the evolution, to be a messenger that raises the awareness of this impressive new area. I knew, and know, that once causal AI moves beyond the research phase into the early adopter phase, there will be a flurry of activity enabling early-mover companies to build and maintain a defensible and significant competitive advantage. This book is a call to action for those early-stage enterprise-class innovators to take notice of causal AI and to begin their process of investigating the potential of this technology and approach.

One of the early epiphanies that I experienced in researching the topic was that the underlying causal approach could be applied to any process. Historically, the causal approach was applied to agriculture, healthcare, and specialty use cases such as dog breeding. But, as I looked back in time, all the way to ancient Greece, and then forward again to ages like the Renaissance and the Reformation, it was clear that philosophers, mathematicians, and academics of all types were touching on causality and slowly but consistently adding to the global corpus of knowledge related to causality.

This aggregation of knowledge reached an acceleration point in the past century, and causal AI gained a dedicated and devout following that drove the development of casual AI to a new level. Once I realized that the field of causal AI was racing forward, I wanted to write this book.

So, why did I write this book, or atleast my part of the book? I wanted to contribute to the understanding, adoption, and use of this incredible new toolset and technologies that we refer to as causal AI.

I hope that you enjoy reading and learning about causal AI as much as I did.

—John K. Thompson
May 2023

Introduction

Why this book, and why now?

We have spent decades exploring, researching, writing, and working with the most important emerging technologies. We have seen hundreds of innovative and novel technologies come and go, each promising to turn human knowledge into packaged solutions that are easy to understand and implement. The history of technology solutions has proven repeatedly that there are no simple solutions to complex problems. However, each technological solution takes us a step further to addressing the core issues. For the past 10 years, the focus of AI and advanced analytics has been on analyzing massive amounts of data to understand the answers to difficult problems. Big data was the silver bullet that offered some success but did not go far enough. In fact, often beginning with big data created correlations that sent businesses in the wrong direction.

One of the problems with leveraging complex technology solutions is that they are multifaceted, interconnected, and complex. It is possible that the data scientist can understand all the ins and outs of the underlying math and technology, but to be successful, the data team must work in collaboration with IT and business to anticipate customer needs and to plan for what's next. In most cases, business leaders do not understand emerging technologies, the data, or the underlying math; hence, they don't know what questions to ask to determine if the technology is well suited to solving their specific operational challenges. We have seen this knowledge gap and mismatch in understanding multiple times. Therefore, one of our primary goals in writing this book is to bridge the knowledge and communication gap between data scientists and the business leaders so that a door can be opened to facilitate a conversation and create a venue for collaboration.

However, there is no silver bullet. Many companies are either adopting or evaluating artificial intelligence-based solutions to automate processes and to determine what specific changes can be implemented to improve their businesses. The promise of AI is tantalizing—organizations can use algorithms to analyze their data in context to anticipate changes in customer requirements and prepare for the future. In competitive markets, it is imperative to understand what is happening within the industry and how to ensure that revenue can grow. When looking into the future, organizations need to be able to understand the impact of decision-making. What happens if a product price is reduced by 10 percent? Will this cause more customers to buy? If revenue suddenly decreases, does management understand why this has happened and what to do to change things? Are customers leaving because of a quality issue with a new supplier or because of an emerging competitor? Understanding the cause and effect from processes and data is the goal and the reason that causal inference is suddenly becoming such a critical approach.

How is causal inference different from other types of artificial intelligence? Simply put, causal inference and the resulting causal AI solutions focus on the assumptions we make about the world and specifically business and the underlying processes that are executed each day. The goal of causal inference is to be able to understand the "why" in the story of the data.

We wrote this book because we believe that causal AI is going to open the door to solving many critical problems in business, engineering, manufacturing, and science. While the idea of causal inference as a topic has been around for centuries, it is only now becoming the lynchpin of addressing the most complex problems facing us today. One of the benefits of causal AI is that it assumes that there is a hybrid group of professionals who collaborate to find the cause and effect from data. This hybrid team consists of data scientists, subject-matter experts, data experts, technologists, business managers, and executives.

This book is intended to provide guidance to all the members of this hybrid team. For example, for the data scientist, we will provide deep technical information as well as the type of information needed to collaborate with subject-matter experts. For the subject-matter expert, we will provide explanations that help to converse with the data scientists. These teams need to be able to work with experts who understand the business data within their organizations so they can be part of the process. Business executives and managers must be able to direct the hybrid team based on the direction that the organization wants to take and the problems that need to be solved. You will therefore be able to select sections that apply to your knowledge level.

We have been working in the intersection of business and technology for decades. We have both written numerous books and have been part of the management team of several companies. Our goal with this book is to bring an understanding and context for this important transition in artificial intelligence.

We are in an interesting and complicated transition in the evolution of artificial intelligence. While the focus of many traditional AI solutions is on data engineering, there is an interesting and revolutionary trend emerging. This revolution is called *causal AI*. This is a sophisticated technology, but it is also a transformational technology.

To summarize the main point to be made, causal inference is the science of *why*, as explained so very well by Judea Pearl in *The Book of Why*. Dr. Pearl states, "Some tens of thousands of years ago, humans began to realize that certain things cause other things and that tinkering with the former can change the latter." His point is that while we can't know all the answers, we can ask why events happen and the cause and effect of a business situation we are trying to solve. As Dr. Pearl accurately sums up the promise of causal inference, "The ideal technology that causal inference strives to emulate resides within our own minds."

We hope you enjoy the book and that the content fires your imagination to learn more about causal inference and causal AI.

1

Setting the Stage for Causal AI

The ability to understand information in the context of solving complex problems is not new. From the earliest days of artificial intelligence, scientists and mathematicians have tried to find new ways to understand the world through models and data. The promise of artificial intelligence (AI) is to reach the point where machines could think and provide answers to some of the most challenging problems of our world. There are a huge number of sophisticated analytics tools that provide significant help in understanding what has occurred in the past and predict a possible future from that data. However, one element that has been missing from the analyses is understanding the cause and effect of the observed and unobserved interactions. The dynamic of understanding why events happen and what can be done to change the outcomes is the power and opportunity of causal AI.

This chapter will put causal AI in perspective and set the stage for our exploration of the evolution of the field of AI.

Why Causality Is a Game Changer

Why is there a sudden explosion in interest in causal AI? The answer is both complex and simple. Causal AI enables us to move beyond the predictive modeling capabilities of traditional AI to understand and predict causal relationships between variables in a system. Here are some of the most salient topics that outline the value of causal AI:

- **Understanding causality:** Traditional AI models can make predictions based on observed correlations between variables but cannot tell us why a particular outcome occurred. Causal AI, on the other hand, can identify the causal relationships between variables and help us understand why a particular outcome occurred. Causality and understanding the dynamics of causality can be particularly important in fields such as healthcare, where understanding the causal relationships between risk factors and health outcomes can help identify new interventions and treatments.

- **Identifying interventions:** Causal AI can help us identify interventions that can change outcomes. For example, causal AI provides a graphical technique to pinpoint the most relevant variables needed to understand specific objective or estimate the consequences of a given intervention. The goal of causal AI is to help an organization assess the possible cause and effects of various policy actions. Causal AI has the potential to enable a team to have a common understanding of a problem so that they can work together to determine why a situation has occurred and establish a plan to arrive at the best next actions.

- **Predicting counterfactuals:** Causal AI can predict the effect of a particular variable on an outcome of interest in an alternative scenario. This is especially useful when the variable of interest is not directly observable or measurable, as it allows the estimation of the causal effect on the outcome. For example, it can help predict what would have happened if a particular intervention or policy had not been implemented.

- **Avoiding bias:** Traditional AI models can be biased if they are trained on biased data or if they do not account for all relevant variables. Causal AI, on the other hand, can help avoid bias by identifying and accounting for all the relevant variables in a system. This can help ensure that the predictions and decisions made using AI are fair and unbiased.

- **Improving decision-making:** Causal AI can help make better decisions by providing a deeper understanding of the causal relationships between variables. This can be particularly useful in fields like business, where understanding the causal relationships between different variables can help businesses make more informed decisions and achieve better outcomes. Causal AI provides us with a deeper understanding of the causal relationships between variables in a system and can help us identify interventions, predict alternative choices and actions, avoid bias, and make better decisions.

The next generation of artificial intelligence can benefit from a deeper level of collaboration between data experts, business leaders, and subject-matter experts. While AI has long been used to solve complex problems, in this new era of expanded AI, hybrid teams of business and analytics professionals can include an examination of why problems happen and what alternate approaches can help a business move forward to gain a sustainable and measurable advantage when faced with increasingly sophisticated and aggressive competition. Therefore, we are in an interesting and complicated transition in the evolution of artificial intelligence. While the focus of many traditional AI approaches focuses on data and feature engineering, there is a revolutionary trend emerging. Causal AI uses causal inference as the underlying math of cause and effect. The focus of causal AI is on business outcomes. Causal inference is the science of why, as explained so well by Judea Pearl in *The Book of Why*: "The ideal technology causal inference strives to emulate resides within our own minds. Some tens of thousands of years ago, humans began to realize that certain things cause other things and that tinkering with the former can change the latter."[1]

While it is time-consuming and challenging to examine all the possible answers, we can easily ask why events happen and what are the primary the cause-and-effect factors of a problem we are trying to solve.

We have many years of experience working with business and technology leaders who are grappling with some of the most complex problems that our current and traditional technologies are designed to solve. We have seen hundreds of emerging technologies come and go that promise to turn human knowledge into packaged solutions that are easy to understand and implement. The history of technology has proven repeatedly that there are no simple solutions to complex problems. However, each technology takes us a step further to addressing issues. For the past 10 years the focus of AI and advanced analytics has been on analyzing massive amounts of data to understand the answers to difficult problems. Big data was the silver bullet that offered some success but did not go far enough.

One of the biggest stumbling blocks to making AI and advanced analytics solutions work effectively is the complexity of the underlying technologies. Typically, business leaders want to be able to visualize the outcomes from the data buried inside applications and from both internal and external data sources. Business managers and leaders want to not only understand what the data tells them about their current situations but what actions they can take to protect and advance their future goals and objectives. Business leaders look to data scientists who employ statistical and computational techniques to determine insights from big data. Many data scientists use correlation and machine learning techniques to identify patterns and anomalies to predict outcomes. Increasingly, business leaders are beginning to understand that there is tremendous potential to leverage AI to solve complex business problems. The greatest potential for AI is to create a way to abstract the complexity from the underlying technology so that data scientists, subject-matter experts, data specialists, and business leaders can collaborate to solve business problems. Therefore, one of our goals with this book is to bridge the gap between the data scientist and the business leader so that it opens the door to use the power of causal AI and traditional AI to create a competitive advantage.

However, there are no silver bullets or simple answer. Many business and technology leaders are either adopting or evaluating AI-based solutions to automate processes and determine how to improve their businesses. The promise of AI is tantalizing—organizations can use algorithms to analyze their data in context to anticipate changes in customer requirements and prepare for the future.

In competitive markets, it is imperative to be able to understand what and why situations are happening within the business. How can leadership within a business ensure that revenue can grow? When looking into the future, organizations need to be able to understand the impact of the decisions they make. What happens if a product price is reduced by 10 percent? Will a lower price cause more customers to buy? Will the price increase entice more new customers to buy? If revenue suddenly decreases, does management understand why this has happened and what can be done to change the current course of business? Are customers leaving because of a quality issue triggered because the business began using a new supplier or because of an emerging competitor? Understanding the cause and effect from processes and data is one of the primary reasons why causal AI is emerging as such a critically importatnt approach across the fields of academia and business.

The most common techniques that have been used by data scientists are correlation-based techniques that are common in the field of traditonal AI. While correlation and causality are related approaches, they are not the same. In brief, correlation is a technique for establishing the statistical relationship between variables. In contrast, causality refers to how one variable has an impact on other variables. In the case of causality, one variable might have a direct impact on a second variable, there could be an indirect effect, or there could be a confounding effect. Causal AI is the art and science of understanding the myriad of relationships between variables that drive relevant causes and effects in a system that we are seeking to understand and manage.

Understanding the difference between correlation-based statistical analysis and causality-based analytics is key to being able to employ and deploy the power of causal AI. Therefore, in the next section we will explore the broad area of analytics. Applying a causal AI approach to analytics will help guide organizations to focus on the assumptions and knowledge that we have about how the world works. If we can answer the complex questions about why an issue occurs, we can adapt our approach to solve problems. The goal of causal AI is to be able to understand the story of the data.

Causal AI in Perspective with Analytics

Analytics is one of the most widely used, and often misused, terms today. The discussion of analytics is widespread. The term *analytics* often refers to dashboards and historical reports. In addition, analytics includes collections of data, information, applications, and analytical models related to work with descriptive statistics. Analytics encompasses work products resulting from predictive, prescriptive, simulation, and optimization projects and programs.

There are many different perceptions and assumptions about what it means to conduct an analytics project. One group may assume a focus on a historical dashboard, while others creating a simulation model might work in the operational area of the business. To make matters worse, there is likely to be a different vision for how to approach analytics. Typically, organizations and departments will be trying to solve very different problems depending both on the problems they need to address and on the stage of their projects. Approaching analytics in the context of causal AI requires a common understanding of the types and approaches to analytics.

At a conceptual level, correlation-based AI and causal-based AI approaches have the same roots; they come from the same family/branch/category of advanced analytics. So, before we move forward with our discussion and description of causal AI, let's define the broader term *analytics* to ensure that we have a common understanding as we move forward in our dialogue.

Analytics is one of the most widely used, and often misused, terms today. The discussion of analytics is widespread. Routinely, we talk about analytics with academics, researchers, government officials, university administrators, scientists, business executives, subject-matter experts, data scientists, and more.

The term *analytics* is employed when referring to dashboards and historical reports. Also, analytics is used when referring to collections of data, information, applications, and analytical models related to work in and with descriptive statistics. And the term is deployed when referring to work related to and the effort/products resulting from predictive, prescriptive, simulation, and optimization projects and programs.

So, it is not surprising to see confused expressions on people's faces when someone talks about analytics. One person is talking about a historical dashboard, while others are trying to convey how a simulation model might work in the same operational area of the business. It can be frustrating for people not to be able to connect on a topic in which they are all deeply interested.

We have found that beginning a discussion by defining the analytical maturity model or framework to be used in the ongoing dialogue helps in reducing confusion and ensures that everyone in the conversation has a clearer understanding about what is being said or what others are trying to convey given the wide range of definitions individuals hold in their minds about the term and areas of analytics.

Analytical Sophistication Model

Various analytical maturity models have been developed, including one by the staff at Gartner. Using an approach similar to Gartner's, we have created an extended sophistication model to clarify and further define *analytics enablers*, *analytics*, and *advanced analytics* (see Figure 1.1).

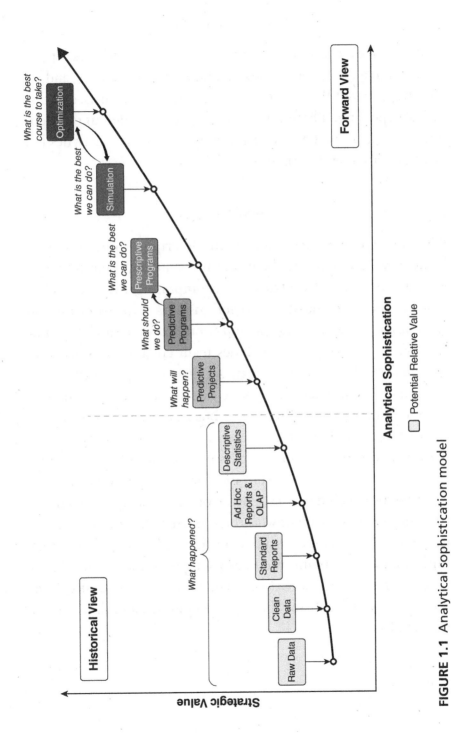

FIGURE 1.1 Analytical sophistication model

Analytics Enablers

In this model, the initial categories to the left of Descriptive Statistics (e.g., Raw Data, Clean Data, Standard Reports, and Ad Hoc Reports & OLAP) are related to data, dashboards, and historical reporting. These categories are not included in our definition of analytics. These categories are enablers of analytics but not analytics in and of themselves.

Analytics

In Figure 1.1, analytics begins with Descriptive Statistics. Analytics, as we are defining the term in this model, extends to, and ends at, the vertical dotted line encompassing Predictive Projects. Descriptive statistics provide insights into historical and current data and are valuable and useful tools in analytics projects and work. When an analytics team creates an exploratory data analysis (EDA) to investigate and gain a deeper understanding of a problem space, descriptive statistics play an integral role in examining and outlining how a business scenario operates in the real world and how that operation is described through data. An EDA and the descriptive statistics used provide a view into the factors that are at work and the relationship of those factors.

Analytics includes prescriptive projects as well. Organizations begin to experiment with their journey into more sophisticated analytics via prescriptive projects. These projects may illustrate that an organization has an appetite for advanced analytics, and it may show that this type of work is too costly, complicated, and difficult for the organization to embark upon as a sustained activity.

Advanced Analytics

Beginning at the vertical dotted line in the diagram and continuing to the right, all of the subsequent areas (i.e., predictive programs, prescriptive programs, simulation, and optimization) are encompassed in the category of advanced analytics. For the purposes of our discussion, all of AI, including both families of correlation and causal AI, exists in the portion of the analytical maturity model that is to the right of the vertical dotted line. In our discussion, advanced analytics and AI are synonymous.

Scope of Services to Support Causal AI

Causal AI must be viewed as part of the overall computing infrastructure for businesses. Therefore, it needs to be a consideration in the approaches to managing data and cloud services.

The hybrid cloud is a critical asset when moving to causal AI. One can argue that analytics can be managed locally. However, in the complex world of advanced analytics and more specifically causal AI, you have to assume that relevant data will come from a variety of sources—some will be third-party data sources managed in a public or private cloud. Other data may be generated by the Internet of Things (IoT) devices at the edge of the network. Creating a federated data approach that takes into account the fact that there are myriad data sources needed is critical to the success of advanced analytics in the context of causal AI.

In any discussion of advanced analytics, the scope of the data is critical to successfully approaching causal AI. For the past decade, data scientists have assumed that if you can collect enough data to create a model, you can make well-informed decisions.

However, one of the distinctions between a data-first approach and a model-first approach is the ability to anticipate the type and scope of the data needed to understand relationships between variables and the data that supports establishing causal relationships. Being successful with causal AI requires the ability to discover the relevant data whether it is internal or external. Some of these data sources may be extremely large, and it would be impractical to move that much data to an internal data center.

Some of the early experiments with causal AI have failed because the business simply did not collect enough of the right data to answer why a problem occurred and what approaches will help to understand appropriate next actions. The data that you will need to create a causal AI solution will be varied. For example, there is considerable data that may be stored in data lakes. There will be data from systems of record as well as third-party data sources that are relevant to market trends. In some situations, your organization may have correct information, but there is simply not a large enough corpus of data to make relevant decisions. If an analytics team using a small data set draws conclusions from that data, the answers may be incorrect.

Keep in mind that building a causal AI model and solution is an iterative process requiring incrementally adding data that corresponds to variables and relationships modeled. For example, what data might you discover that is relevant to understanding a complex problem? If you were going to try to determine (in an agricultural setting) the optimal time to plant crops, you would need a variety of data ranging from the chemical construct of the soil, the changing weather patterns, and the past planting history. You might also need to understand what crops are selling better in a changing economic environment. If one of these factors is ignored, the resulting analysis will be useless. Data discovery and incrementally adding newly discovered data is critical to building effective causal AI solutions.

The hope has been that if we are able to analyze this data, we will be able to understand our world and understand how to transform our businesses. However, harnessing and making sense of data is not simple. As with any emerging technology innovation, moving from the idea of managing data to the reality of discovering solutions to complex problems is harder than anyone could have imagined.

There are many practical techniques for analyzing massive amounts of data that has helped organizations in many ways. Tools are available that help bring together many different types of structured and unstructured data to better understand the meaning of information, which has been a tremendous help to businesses. Data warehouses and data marts, for example, have enabled organizations to analyze business data to help make decisions, such as tracking transactions and managing operational data.

The Value of the Hybrid Team

While taking advantage of a team of professionals when successfully managing a data-focused project is critical to any project, there are requirements when approaching causal AI. We will cover the process of collaboration in a causal AI project in Chapter 5. Many early AI projects have failed when data scientists work in isolation from representatives from different areas of the business. It is particularly important in causal AI to involve subject-matter experts very early in the design process. These professionals understand the content and details of the operation that will become instrumental in creating a model that matches the problem as well as having hands-on experience with the most important data sources. Business strategists will help focus the team on the most important business problems that the company needs to address.

The Promise of AI

While AI was conceived of more than 60 years ago, it has been slow to realize true benefits for industry and business. The promise of artificial intelligence for decades has been the ability of machines to mimic the capacity of the human brain to understand the context of data and make quick decisions even when all the data you need is not available. One aspect of cognition that sets humans apart from machines is that humans typically maintain a mental model of our environment. Creating mental and computing models is one of the key processes to transforming data into a meaningful understanding of phenomena that we seek to explain or understand. A goal of AI is to be able to predict the behavior of individuals. It is no wonder that the best minds in artificial intelligence haven't been able to build reliable and accurate models of similar complexity to those that are inherent in the human brain.

It is now possible to develop sophisticated models; deploy those models in a range of operational environments; and treat, integrate, and ingest numerous types of data to produce reliable, scalable, and accurate results. However, none of these approaches go far enough to understand why events happen and how predictions are made. The value of causal AI is that it provides a technique for helping organizations to leverage the power of AI and advanced analytics so that organizations understand why events happen and how to come up with better solutions.

Traditionally, AI has been thought of as one large category. However, the reality is that to be successful, there needs to be a more nuanced and multifaceted approach to AI. Commercial firms, regulators, and academic organizations—to name a few— are interested in and eager to work with a new class of AI. This new category of AI needs to provide for transparency in data transformation, model development, and, most importantly, the interpretation of the results produced by AI systems. This is one of the primary reasons why we see that causal AI and causal inference are moving out of research labs and the halls of academia into the commercial market.

Almost since the beginning of time, humans have been searching for the reasons why things happen. Once statistics became associated with correlation, there was an effort to disregard the power of causality. However, with the requirement to understand why an event has happened, what it means, and how to change outcomes—causality has emerged as a transformative trend.

As we develop a broader and deeper view of causality throughout the book, we will provide definitions and employ a business-oriented use case so that data scientists, subject-matter experts, data analysts, managers, and business leaders can have a common vocabulary to understand causal AI and how it is important to implement business solutions that will help the organization move forward.

Understanding the Core Concepts of Causal AI

As we move through the chapters in this book, we will get into more and more detail about how causal AI works and the elements that are important to understand. In this next section, we will provide an overview of the key concepts that are required to understand causal AI.

Explainability and Bias Detection

As AI has evolved over the last several decades, models have become more sophisticated, and, in some cases, multiple models are implemented in an analytics pipeline where the models interact and influence the results of the overall pipeline and the individual models. Monitoring and understanding multiple models is challenging and can be difficult to discern the influence of any one model on the overall results or outcomes.

In addition to ensembles of models running simultaneously and, in some cases, in parallel, certain analytical techniques in traditional AI rely on algorithms that are very difficult to examine, discern, and understand why certain results or outcomes are produced. Algorithms such as neural networks belong to a class of analytical technical that are referred to as *black boxes*. These class models have been given this label because the designs of the resulting models and processes running within the models are so complicated that it has been nearly impossible for humans to understand how the input variables are combined to reach the ultimate conclusions.

Academics, researchers, and commercial technology companies have been working to develop solutions to provide explainability solutions for neural networks. Over the past 5 years, we have seen solid progress made on providing clear explanations of how neural networks process data and why those models generate the outcomes and results that are seen. It will be a few years before we see and can use explainability technology that will be acceptable to government regulators and governance professionals.

A black-box model executes its analytical process based on how it interprets the data. The black-box model will not be able to provide business managers with an explanation about how the model makes decisions as to why a campaign did not work. As a result, data business managers cannot explain to shareholders or government regulators why certain business decisions were made. This traditional approach to AI lacks two important factors that are imperative for business success: explainability and fairness or identification of bias.

Explainability It seems logical, and it is mandated by national laws and regulations around the world, that if you are using machine learning techniques to help your organization make decisions based on analyzing data, you should be able to defend the results of your analysis. One of the problems with many approaches to deep learning is that they are built with complex neural networks that have hidden logic that humans find difficult to understand. This becomes a problem when a model is being used to make decisions that impact the fairness of actions taken by an organization such as decisions about who to hire or when a policy discriminates against a specific group of people. To address this issue, explainable Artificial Intelligence (XAI) is a set of processes and methods that allows human users to comprehend and trust the results and output created by machine learning algorithms. XAI is used to describe an AI model, its expected impact, and its potential biases.

Moving from a black-box model to an explainable model requires that the team begin by modeling to define and understand why the problem exists and how it might be addressed (see Figure 1.2). For example, why are we losing customers suddenly? What approach to marketing a product will produce the best results? What is the right dose of a medication for children under the age of 10? When an organization begins by defining the problem, it is much easier to select the variables that are needed to understand a problem before applying data. This method is designed to ensure that a model can be explained and understood.

Detecting Bias in a Model One of the risks of any technique or approach to modeling that is difficult to examine and explain is that it is difficult to detect and correct for bias. The consequences of these risks can cause an organization to be sanctioned or fined by regulatory authorities and to face a backlash from customers and activists. Bias in data can happen when an organization selects data that has not been reviewed and examined for inherent, historical patterns that may subtly but inadvertently perpetuate past inequities. Bias can creep in when data is selected that is out of step with the problem being addressed or not aligned with the current expectations of management, government regulators, and the public. For example, the data may include information about the age of individuals in the data set that can introduce bias. Therefore, in a black-box model, it will be impossible to see that the results are biased against either younger or older individuals. Imagine that a model is used to help an organization select the best candidates to hire for a job. If the model includes data about the candidate's race, age, or sex, the selection process might be inadvertently biased.

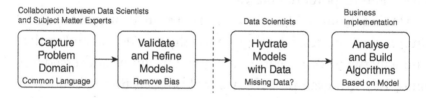

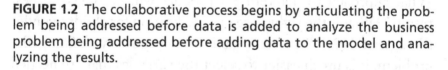

FIGURE 1.2 The collaborative process begins by articulating the problem being addressed before data is added to analyze the business problem being addressed before adding data to the model and analyzing the results.

Directed Acyclic Graphs

A directed acyclic graph (DAG) is the most common type of graphical modeling approach used to illustrate causal relationships between variables in a causal model. In a DAG, a solid forward-facing arrow indicates a subsequent variable is directly affected by the previous variable. A DAG provides process guidance as an intuitive way to represent causal relationships between variables. A DAG can represent either a direct or indirect effect, which means the sequencing of the model processing through the nodes can move only in a forward direction; there are no recurrent looping cycles. Just as in the real world, time travels only in a forward motion.

Let's examine a few examples of how variables impact and interact with each other. In this example of a causal model, one variable is warm weather; a second variable is the consumption of ice cream; and the third variable is drownings. Clearly, people eat more ice cream in warm weather, so there is a direct forward relationship between warm weather and ice cream. Likewise, there is a direct relationship between warm weather and more people drowning because people will swim in warm weather. If, in our casual models, we create a backward relationship or loop that indicates that the variable ice cream is the cause of warm weather, which is clearly wrong and misleading, and impossible, we have created a model that is invalid and is not representative of the real world and the causal relationships that naturally occur in daily life. To continue with our example, if we created a backward loop between the variable of drowning and the variable of ice cream, we would also have created an illogical conclusion. Clearly, this is a simple example that would be obvious to refute. In more complex situations, however, it will take work to understand the complex relationships and causal strengths of relationships between variables.

Structural Causal Model

A structural causal model (SCM) is a type of DAG that is designed as a mathematical framework. Once a DAG is created as a graphical model, the SCM process translates each variable or node into a mathematical equation. For example, in a complex supply chain, the SCM calculates the amount of time required to deliver a part delivered by the supplier to the customer. Therefore, moving from the graphical model of the DAG to the more precise mathematics of the SCM requires a definition of the three common types of variables. These variables include explanatory, outcome, and unobserved. In other words, there are variables that simply explain what a variable is (i.e., a metal component needed by a customer in the manufacturing process). An outcome variable is intended to evaluate the effectiveness of a process defined in the graphical DAG. The outcome variable can be calculated to determine if there is a bottleneck in a process that could impact a supply chain. As the name implies, an unobserved variable is one that is not easily identified in the DAG. For example, it may appear that everything is working well with a supply chain. However, customers are leaving the company. The unobserved variable might be lack of trust in the company or a new competitor who is doing a better job in building customer relationships. SCMs are powerful because they both indicate causal relationships between variables and can make predictions about how these relationships would change if conditions changed.

Observed and Unobserved Variables

An observed variable is a variable that can be directly measured in an experiment such as the relationship between smoking and lung cancer. If someone has lung cancer, the doctor may ask the patient if they are a smoker. If they are not a smoker, it is likely they have a form of lung cancer that isn't associated with smoking, and the treatment will be different. In contrast, an unobserved variable cannot be seen from observing a patient, for example. There are diseases such as heart disease that can be hereditary. Simply asking a patient about their lifestyle or observing their fitness level would not indicate to the doctor if the patient has underlying risks of getting lung cancer.

Counterfactuals

Merriam-Webster defines the term *counterfactual* as "contrary to fact" and "relating to or expressing what has not happened or is not the case." An example of a counterfactual conditional statement is "If kangaroos had no tails, they would topple over."

Counterfactuals are the alternate scenarios that are ingested into our causal models. Counterfactuals enable causal models to illustrate the wide range of options and alternate paths that we might want to consider. Therefore, counterfactuals are a core concept in causal AI because they help the team understand what would happen if a situation were different. Counterfactuals refer to a hypothetical scenario where the team can ask questions such as, "What would have happened if a causal relationship between two variables didn't exist?" For example, what if we had two suppliers of our products rather than one? Would we have had more sales of our new product? Would we have had better customer satisfaction if we had been able to ship products in a week rather than in three weeks? In other words, counterfactual analysis would have let us imagine a different outcome. Being able to use statistical and various machine learning algorithms to estimate causal relationships can allow the team to anticipate the impact of change in business models or actions.

Confounders

In a causal graph, a *confounding* variable is a variable that influences multiple variables and can lead to a spurious or false association.

In a causal AI system, a variable will be classified as either a cause or an effect. A cause, as the name implies, is a variable that directly influences another variable. In contrast, an effect variable is influenced by one or several variables. However, a confounder variable occurs in situations where a variable can be both a causal and an effect. Confounders are extremely important to identify in causal AI and make it difficult to identify the causal relationships between variables.

Having a confounder (also called an *observed covariate*) will likely distort the results of a model and can bias the results of the analysis. A common example would be the fact that lung cancer is caused by smoking and many low-income patients have lung cancer. Would we conclude that having less money means that a patient will have lung cancer? Of course not. However, if you look at this confounder and use it as fact, then you will likely add bias to your modeling. When creating a model, it is imperative to use statistical models such as regression analysis to remove this bias.

Colliders

The existence of a collider in a causal AI model often leads to counterintuitive and inaccurate conclusions. Colliders are also known as backdoor paths. A *collider* is a variable that has pointers to several different variables in a causal diagram or DAG. This causes confusion in understanding the actual relationships between variables. If a variable is not the cause of two conflicting variables, there is a disconnect that can lead to an erroneous conclusion and bias. Therefore, a collider is a variable in the DAG that is impacted by several different variables. These variables are not directly related to each other; therefore, these variables might lead to inaccurate conclusions. If we remember the situation where warm weather leads to an increased consumption of ice cream as well as more drowning deaths, we can't draw the conclusion that ice cream causes people to drown. This would be a collider if we tried to draw a direction relationship between the variable representing ice cream consumption and drowning.

Front-Door and Backdoor Paths

In a causal model, it is important to indicate front-door and backdoor paths to understand the cause and effect of a problem. For example, if a company wanted to determine the causal effect of customer satisfaction on sales, a typical question might be "Will increasing our customer satisfaction increase our sales?" The causal diagram would be drawn as shown in Figure 1.3.

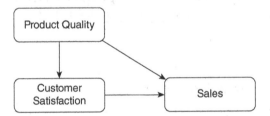

FIGURE 1.3 Causal model demonstrating the relationships between Product Quality, Customer Satisfaction, and Sales

This causal model demonstrates the different types of paths that can exist within a DAG. There is a direct causal relationship between Customer Satisfaction and Sales, which results in a front-door path between the two variables. Causal analysis would be straightforward if not for the existence of a backdoor path: Product Quality is a common cause of both Customer Satisfaction and Sales, which can be considered a confounder in this specific context. Front-door and backdoor paths are sometimes presented in a written format, as shown here:

Front-door path: Customer Satisfaction -> Sales

Backdoor path: Customer Satisfaction <- Product Quality -> Sales

The conclusion that can be drawn from our causal analysis is that to accurately determine the causal effect of customer satisfaction on sales, the company would need to control for product quality as part of their analysis. This would close the backdoor path present in the causal model and eliminate the confounding source.

Realistically, it is likely that there would be multiple other variables that would cause both customer satisfaction and sales, such as price, giving rise to more backdoor paths that would need to be closed in a similar fashion. One of the main goals of a DAG is to help identify backdoor paths that confound the relationships between variables.

Correlation

Correlation is the widely accepted statistical method for understanding the relationship between data sets. Typically, correlation assumes that you can use past outcomes to estimate future outcomes. While this may seem logical, there are some fallacies in correlation. The downside of correlation is that it only shows you results based on data but does not explain the cause of the results from that data. Typically, correlation relies on finding patterns and anomalies in data. In theory, this makes perfect sense. By applying analytics of data with machine learning techniques, correlation does a better job of using these patterns to predict outcomes. Causality, on the other hand, is designed to model relationships between a cause and an effect found in data. Unlike correlation, causal AI understands what happens and why.

Causal Libraries and Tools

Causal libraries are software tools packaged to perform key tasks in a causal AI solution. Because these methods are open-source, they provide developers with well-designed frameworks to apply methods without having to resort to proprietary approaches. These libraries abstract the complexity for leveraging causal methods such as identifying causal relationships and analyzing and visualizing data. These libraries are very important in creating DAGs. One of the most popular libraries is PyWhy, which is a Python-based library that includes an abstracted interface to a variety of existing inferences (causal methods). This library was jointly developed by Amazon and Microsoft. There are many other libraries and tools that aid developers in creating solutions. In Chapter 7 we will provide a detailed examination of the tools and libraries available to support causal AI applications.

Propensity Score

A propensity score is used to reduce bias and the effect of an observed confounding variables. The propensity score is a statistical tool that indicates differences in outcomes based on approaches to problem solving. For example, a propensity score will help understand the effect of different groups of people receiving treatment with a medication based on observed characteristics such as age or medical history.

Augmented Intelligence and Causal AI

As Judea Pearl in the introduction to *The Book of Why* stated, "Data does not understand causes and effects; humans do. . . . In the age of computers, this new understanding also brings with it the prospect of amplifying our innate abilities so that we can make better sense of data, be it big or small." The power of causal AI is not just its ability to model and analyze data but in its approach to augmenting the power of the human brain to understand the world.

Despite the speculation about the ability of machines to think, they cannot. While machines are adept at ingesting massive amounts of data, they do not have the essential causal powers of the human brain. The answer to the proposition that machines can mimic and replicate the power of human cognition is augmented intelligence. Only humans can understand the context of data to make intelligent decisions. The ability to model a business problem based on the variables that define it is a human and more importantly team process. Could a machine replace the process of modeling a problem and then understanding the counterfactuals that will change outcomes? The only way this would be possible is to have the AI environment ingest all of the data and context needed to understand and solve a problem. Such a machine would be able to anticipate changes and new data needed as circumstances change.

In reality, humans have to identify key variables and relationships based on an understanding of the issues. Data specialists must identify sources and determine if they are accurate or biased. In the context of causal AI, augmented intelligence can play an important role in helping humans identify and understand causal relationships. Humans have an ability to understand changes in the world and make decisions based on what they see and experience. It is human to ask the question, "What if things were different?"

Summary

Causal AI is the implementation of solutions based on causal inference. The power of causality comes from its ability to model a business problem based on the collaboration between team members who understand the business, the data, and the strategy. In this chapter, we provided the foundational information about what is and how it is a critical element to determining how to take actions to improve future outcomes.

In many ways, causal AI is not new. Rather, it takes advantage of the foundations of data management innovations over the past decades. It also leverages the tools and services of AI and machine learning techniques. The power of causal AI is that it goes beyond predicting outcomes and instead can identify the underlying causes of an outcome. Augmenting the power of human intuition and knowledge with the overwhelming power of cloud scalability is the benefit of causal AI.

Note

1. Judea Pearl and Dana Mackenzie. *The Book of Why*, Basic Books, 2018.

2

Understanding the Value of Causal AI

One of the purposes of this book is to review the foundational aspects of causal AI and to explore and explain why causal AI is important for business leaders, subject-matter experts, data scientists, and analytics professionals to understand the value of this important evolution the field of AI. While causal AI is a technically sophisticated approach, it will have profound implications for making better business decisions. Casual AI helps managers and leaders understand how to analyze the primary causes of a problem, the effects of those factors on outcomes, and the options available to solve perplexing problems in the most efficient and effective manner possible.

In this chapter, we will discuss the principles of causal AI, its origins, and how it has evolved through improvements in infrastructure, networks, languages, data, and analytics. At this stage of development in causal AI, we have the ability to create sophisticated models and methods that can help organizations drive value from large and diverse data sets. This emerging approach is focused on understanding the cause and effect of problems and coming up with ways to transform how businesses can continue to improve outcomes.

Defining Causal AI

Judea Pearl, the father of causal inference, summed up the power of causality in his seminal book *Causality: Models, Reasoning, and Inference*:

> *The next revolution will be even more impactful upon realizing that data science is the science of interpreting reality, not of summarizing data. The foundation of causal inference is an intellectual discipline that considers the assumptions, study designs, and estimation strategies that allow researchers to draw causal conclusions based on data.*[1]

Why is causal AI so important to business? For organizations to be able to understand how to deal with change and uncertainty, they will need the power to understand the cause and effect of business challenges. We believe that causal AI is the beginning of the next revolution in artificial intelligence. Traditional approaches to AI typically involve using data to create models that can perform specific tasks. This approach typically involves using statistical methods and machine learning (ML) to analyze and interpret data. To create models, data scientists train ML algorithms on large sets of data to identify patterns and anomalies to make predictions. The models created by machine learning algorithms are only as good as the quality and relevance of the data used to create the models. If biased data is used or data isn't clean, the model will be inaccurate. In contrast, causal AI begins by defining a problem that needs to be solved.

Why is this important? We are at a stage in the evolution of analytics where management teams understand that they need to exploit enormous amounts of data to make better decisions. These managers recognize that they are spending significant amounts of money on their data science and analytics teams. Leaders and managers want to deploy this power to solve business problems so that they can gain a competitive advantage. While much of the focus over the past several years has been on the concept of digital transformation, there isn't a clear understanding of what this means. We believe that causal AI is the key to creating digital transformation for organizations. At the end of the day, businesses want to understand why a problem has occurred, what it means, and what they can do to change outcomes. Achieving these business outcomes requires that teams go beyond traditional AI and traditional analytical approaches.

In causal AI, we first focus on creating models that reflect business challenges and then combine those models with relevant data. This contrasts with the statistical-based correlation approach, where AI begins by gathering data to create a model. Once the model is created, the correlation-based approach identifies a subset of data that indicates correlations that exceed the required threshold and then builds and trains models on that data.

Causal AI turns the process of model creation on its head. Since causal AI is intended to solve real-world problems, it is important to understand that you first must consider the knowledge that may be either in a database or even in the heads of experts. Depending on the size and complexity of your organization, it may have a formalized knowledge database or a knowledge graph. It is rare to have a greenfield operation with no deep processes and knowledge.

One of the most important aspects of causal AI is integrating the critical subject-matter understanding into the model. One of the optimal approaches to incorporate this information is to leverage a knowledge graph as a data resource. A knowledge graph is a structural database that stores information about the entities (nodes) and the relationships between them (edges). One of the benefits of a knowledge graph is that it can represent complex information about domains such as finance, manufacturing, healthcare, and agriculture. An example of a knowledge graph might be an airplane manufacturer that purchases components from many suppliers. Each supplier of component parts must adhere to a specification so that when the airplane manufacturer receives these parts, they fit together as intended. Therefore, if your company is that airplane manufacturer and you want to begin to create a causal model, you need to incorporate elements of the knowledge graph into your model. While the knowledge graph gives you an understanding of what you know about your business, it will not enable you to ask causal questions. But leveraging the knowledge graph is imperative so you are not starting from scratch.

The goal of a causal AI approach is to be able to understand why a problem has occurred and then to be able to look at potential solutions. In essence, the goal is to understand the cause and effect of a problem. For example, why are customers not renewing their contracts? While you will be able to take advantage of the data in the knowledge graph to understand how the contracting process works in your company, it will not tell you why there has been a change in customer behavior. Why are product deliveries suddenly taking twice as long as they were only six months ago? While each of these questions makes sense, they are not simple. There is a lot of information buried in these questions. For instance, what is the nature of the contracts? Are the existing contracts too complicated for customers to understand? Are competitors changing their contract language so they are simpler compared to your contracts? Do you have data to be able to answer questions about the nature of your contracts with customers? Without sufficient data, you will not be able to answer causal questions.

Therefore, it should not be surprising to realize that the causal modeling process will come before ingesting data because you first must understand what data you need to answer complex questions. The most appropriate intervention may be to simplify contract language to encourage customers to renew. However, the intervention may be more complicated. The issue may be related to emerging competitors that are offering more attractive pricing and product quality. This knowledge of the underlying business and technical issues will require the deep insights of the subject-matter experts. These experts understand the details of how the business works but also will have insights into variables that are not obvious and therefore cannot be observed. For example, there may be a new federal government regulation that is impacting sales. Subject-matter experts will have an understanding of the new regulation and how it could impact the business in the future.

The Origins of Causal AI

The most popular current view and approach to using practical causal inference was developed by Judea Pearl, a developer of Bayesian networks and a professor at UCLA. He is the author of many important books on causality including the aforementioned *Causality, Models, Reasoning, and Inference* and the popular *The Book of Why*.[2] His many writings define and explain causal inference and demonstrate how this approach provides a more accurate measure of understanding data than traditional statistical analytical methods. Pearl's greatest contribution to causal AI is his development of a modeling framework. In 2011, Pearl won the Turing Award for his fundamental contributions to artificial intelligence.[3]

Why Causality?

Causal inference, as we indicated in Chapter 1, is the foundational AI technology that is used to create AI solutions. Causal inference itself comprises a branch of statistical analysis that extends the capacity of probabilistic reasoning by incorporating elements of hypothesis testing to infer directional relationships between variables. Casual AI, a solution built from causal inference underpinnings, is an AI-based approach that is intended to explain and manage the cause-and-effect relationships within a business or discipline. Rather than beginning by selecting data sources used to create models, causal AI begins by understanding a business problem by understanding variables that define a problem and how a set of variables impact other variables. You can use casual AI to interpret the solution given the AI machine learning model and the algorithm. The power of causal AI is that it provides a common language for a hybrid team of professionals to collaborate to solve complex problems.

Causal AI has its roots in Bayesian networks. Like causal AI, Bayesian networks look to understand relationships between variables. Therefore, it is not surprising that causal AI leverages the core elements of Bayesian networks. In *Causality: Models, Reasoning, and Inference*, Pearl states,

> *Bayesian networks were developed in the early 1890s to facilitate the tasks of prediction and abduction in artificial intelligence systems. In these tasks, it is necessary to find a coherent interpretation of incoming observations that is consistent with both the observations and the prior information at hand.*

A Bayesian network is a probabilistic statistical graphical that uses quantitative data and is especially useful when there is a limited amount of data on a topic. For example, what is the probability that customers will purchase items primarily from online stores based on available data? A traditional Bayesian model might be used to take a snapshot of 2 years of data and predict that this trend will continue. Causal AI uses a directed Bayesian model because it represents variables as nodes and the causal relationships as directed edges. This model represents the different variables as nodes or points, and the causal relationships between them as directed edges or arrows. Directed Bayesian models are used in causal AI because they are useful in reasoning about complex causal relationships between variables.

With causal AI, the team is able to better understand the underlying mechanisms that cause the relationship between variables. However, to understand this data from a causal perspective, it would be important to add more contextual data.

A History Lesson

For centuries people have searched to understand why events happen. Why do people get sick? Why are there floods and famine? Humans are innately driven to understand the causes of these types of events and what they can do to fix problems. Ironically, with all of the technology innovations over the decades, we haven't found a way to clearly express the cause and effect of events.

In the 1840s, there was a well-accepted theory called Miasma that diseases such as cholera and bubonic plague were caused by pollution, or what was called bad air. Therefore, since the cause of disease was caused by bad air, the cure was to close windows. John Snow, an English physician who had treated many cholera victims, was unconvinced that this theory was correct. Instead, he was convinced that

(continued)

(*continued*)

contaminated water was the source of diseases such as cholera. In his essay in 1849, "On the Mode of Communication of Cholera," he detailed his theory. Subsequently, he was able to prove his theory during the cholera epidemic of 1854. By talking to residents of a London neighborhood where there was a significant cholera outbreak, he was able to determine that, in fact, the cause of the outbreak was contaminated water. He conducted an experiment. He removed the handle from the pump of the local well, which meant that residents couldn't use the water supply. (Figure 2.1 shows a replica of the original pump.)

Snow wrote:

> On proceeding to the spot, I found that nearly all the deaths had taken place within a short distance of the [Broad Street] pump. There were only ten deaths in houses situated decidedly nearer to another street-pump. In five of these cases the families of the deceased persons informed me that they always went to the pump in Broad Street, as they preferred the water to that of the pumps which were nearer. In three other cases, the deceased were children who went to school near the pump in Broad Street. With regard to the deaths occurring in the locality belonging to the pump, there were 61 instances in which I was informed that the deceased persons used to drink the pump water from Broad Street, either constantly or occasionally.[4]

Snow was able to definitively illustrate the power of understanding cause and effect. Why tell this story? It is a clear example of why cause and effect is at the heart of how we need to approach decision-making.

FIGURE 2.1 A replica of the Broad Street water pump.

(Source: Jamzze / Wikimedia Commons / CC BY-SA 4.0)

Expressing Relationships

One of Pearl's most important contributions, which turned causal inference from a theory into a practical approach to creating applications, is what is called a *structural causal model* (SCM). An SMC model basically codifies the ability to express the relationship between the state of a world or situation being addressed and how the available variables related to the data used to explain and iterate on a problem being analyzed.

Pearl describes an SCM as a set of variables, including the following:

- **Explanatory variables (or nodes)**: An explanatory variable is what you manipulate or observe when changes are applied to a situation. For example, if a student is given a large cup of coffee before an exam, will they do better on the test? It is essentially a response variable.

- **Outcome variables**: An outcome variable, also called a *dependent variable*, is the result of the action of one or more independent variables. For example, if the student drank a large cup of coffee, did their test score improve, and by how much?

- **Unobserved variables**: Unobserved variables are those that the developer would not see and therefore are more difficult to account for in the causal model. For example, the student drinks coffee to be more alert during the exam. The unobserved variable is that the temperature in the room is very high and uncomfortable for the student. Therefore, drinking hot coffee in that room may have a negative impact on performance. This unobserved temperature factor can totally change an outcome.

The Ladder of Causation

In addition to the development of the causal model, Pearl also provided a three-layer framework for understanding causality. It puts causal inference in context for understanding how to use this powerful concept to solve problems.

One of the best ways to understand the meaning and value of causal AI is to understand Pearl's framework, inspired by Alan Turing, "who proposed to classify a cognitive system in terms of the queries it can answer."[5] In *The Book of Why*, Pearl took this foundation to develop his framework for causal inference, which he called the "Ladder of Causation." The three rungs of the ladder indicate increasing levels of causation from passive forms of observation to the ability to understand and make judgments based on cause and effect from models and data.

In brief, the Ladder of Causation demonstrates how we can move from observing an event to understanding outcomes and then finally to answering the question about why a situation happened. Figure 2.2 illustrates the ladder and, starting from the lowest rung and moving up, its stages:

- **Association**: The ability to see or observe
- **Intervention**: The ability to do or make a change
- **Counterfactuals**: The ability to imagine or infer and understand based on observation

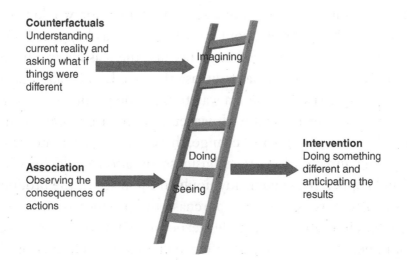

FIGURE 2.2 The Ladder of Causation indicates the stages of Pearl's view of causality.

Rung 1: Association, or Passive Observation. Pearl places traditional machine learning methods at the lowest rung of causality because they allow predictions based only on passive observations. At its simplest level, association is about how two observed entities are related. This rung of the ladder relies on observing statistical relationships between variables that are used to train a model. Like Turing, Pearl talks about association as the imitation that is prevalent in the way an animal observes the world. Even traditional machine learning depends on imitation rather than learning. The way data elements are related to each other can be inferred directly from observing data using correlation, conditional probabilities, and conditional expectation. Therefore, association is a traditional statistical approach to analyzing data.

Rung 2: Intervention, or Taking Action. The intervention rung involves not only passively observing (e.g., the tree has green leaves) but understanding the impact of change (e.g., why the leaves on the tree have turned). An intervention would begin to answer the question about why a change has happened. Did the leaves on the tree turn brown because the seasons are changing or because the tree has a disease that needs to be addressed? If a tree is diseased, is there a way to treat the problem to return the tree to a healthy state? However, if leaves are falling off the trees because of a seasonal change, there is no need to intervene. Applying interventions to a business situation could be what would happen if the company doubled the price of the product. Will customers continue to purchase the product, or will they look for alternatives that are less expensive? The obvious answer might be, of course, the customers will look for a cheaper product. However, there are more variables and factors that would need to be considered to answer this seemingly simple question. For example, what if all competing products were priced high? What if there were inflationary factors that meant that prices had to be raised so that the company would not go out of business? Could a lack of product inventory lead to a price increase that discouraged customers from buying it? In other words, we have to take into account factors such as economic conditions and customer behavior. To determine this with traditional machine learning, the company would look at statistical correlation from large data sets of customer purchases to decide the answer to the question. While observation and statistical analysis from big data will give us some answers, it will not help us understand the impact of the conditions described in the intervention.

Therefore, gaining insights into the situation requires the ability to include changing conditions. This requires a creating a causal model that includes variables such as information about the product, such as its components, competitors, supply chain variables, economic conditions of the supply chain, and even details about how customers purchase products.

In the real world that we all live in, interventions are something that we do all the time without much thought. For example, why did my headache go away? Perhaps it was because I took a pain reliever or because I ate some food after missing lunch. An intervention helps us to begin to understand the cause of a problem by looking at the cause and effect of making a change, e.g., taking the pain reliever or eating food. Since associations are purely observational, they are not model based. In contrast, an intervention will require a model to understand the context and relationships between variables. With rung 2, it will be possible to build a model that can indicate the relationship between the observed variables. But in many situations, there simply is not enough information to make a decision that will impact sales.

There may be underlying conditions that are not easy to identify that are causing the business problem.

Rung 3: Counterfactuals, or Imagining What If.   There is a good reason why counterfactuals are on the top rung in the Ladder of Causation. A counterfactual is used to determine a hypothesis of what would occur if a new condition were applied to a situation. Counterfactuals are the foundation of establishing causal relationships.

The power of rung 3 is that it incorporates both associations and interventions. Therefore, if we begin by answering counterfactual questions, we can also find the answers to how variables are related from observation and how interventions are understood. The counterfactual approach is the process of imagining what might happen if the facts were different. What if we had priced our product differently than any of our competitors? How would we be able to continue to make a profit? If we first observe that two variables have a relationship, it is possible to begin to understand the context for a problem. For example, if there is a dip in sales and a supply chain issue, are these problems related? There may, in fact, be a correlation between the variables that can be calculated. What if we hire a new supply chain vendor or even several supply chain vendors in various geographical markets? Will that intervention mean that sales will improve?

Counterfactuals are an important foundation in many fields ranging from scientific experiments (what would happen if we gave a child an adult dose of a drug?) to litigation (what would the jury conclude about whether a defendant was the direct cause of an accident or were there extenuating circumstances?) and marketing (why did my marketing campaign fail to generate the expected level of sales?).

The top rung of the ladder of causality brings us to the notion of what would happen under various conditions. Therefore, imagining is the highest form of reasoning by examining what alternative scenarios would be if conditions were different. This approach gets at the heart of the fundamental question of "why." The goal of this counterfactual approach is to articulate the cause and effect of relationships in models and data.

Why Causal AI Is the Next Generation of AI

Over the decades there has been a huge amount of progress made in artificial intelligence and machine learning. New algorithms have been developed that enable computer scientists to automate well-defined tasks, even when the underlying data changes. One of the techniques of machine learning is to use sophisticated algorithms that analyze massive amounts of data to create models.

Traditional AI is based on the ability to ingest and analyze data using statistical correlation-based algorithms. However, as we will discuss in a subsequent section, it is much harder to predict the behavior of people across markets than one would have thought. This is primarily because AI and machine learning algorithms and models are designed to ingest vast amounts of data to generate the model. Many of these techniques are also used in causal AI. Both deep learning and "ground truth" are key techniques that are important to understand in the context of causal AI.

Deep Learning and Neural Networks

Typically, data scientists select the data sources that they believe will address the problem. A common approach used by data scientists is deep learning techniques. Deep learning is a subset of machine learning that uses artificial neural networks with multiple layers to learn and make predictions or decisions based on input data. Deep learning can be used to identify causal relationships between variables in complex systems. Deep learning models can be trained to identify patterns in large data sets and make predictions, which can be used to infer causal relationships between variables. However, because deep learning models are typically black boxes, it can be difficult to interpret how the model determined its predictions to understand the underlying causal mechanisms.

Neural Networks

Neural networks work well in situations where there are large amounts of data and predictable patterns. For example, face recognition is a well-known way that neural networks can be accurate. The model can be trained on millions of images so that the resulting model will know details about a face. In extreme situations, the neural network will be able to identify a specific individual. Neural networks can be used to recognize images and speech, and ground truth is often used to train the network to identify the correct object or spoken word. For example, a neural network can be trained to recognize faces in images, with ground truth data consisting of labeled images that show where the faces are located. Neural networks have been very effective in reading a medical image. The model can be trained to recognize certain conditions such as a suspicious spot on a patient's lung.

Overall, neural networks and ground truth are effective when there is a large amount of data available and patterns or relationships in the data can be learned by the network. They are particularly effective in tasks that involve pattern recognition or classification, such as image or speech recognition, natural language processing, and medical diagnosis. However, if data scientists work in isolation from subject-matter experts, they may not understand the nuances and complexity of a situation and may not have enough data to solve a problem. In the case of diagnosing an abnormality in a patient's lungs, the model will likely not take into account underlying problems that are specific to the patient and cannot predict the right treatment plan. When there is a well-founded understanding of business data, it is much easier to create a logical model. The concept of collaboration between data scientists and subject-matter experts is the core of understanding augmented intelligence—the process of collaboration between humans and machines defined by the hybrid team.

Establishing Ground Truth

Another important requirement for the accuracy of models is establishing ground truth. Ground truth refers to a set of objective and accurate data that serves as a benchmark for evaluating the performance of a model. In casual AI, ground truth consists of what the data science team knows to be accurate. In this way, it provides a way to test and validate the model to see if the model indicates causal relationships. For example, if the organization needs to understand the factors resulting in customer churn for a service, the data engineering and data science teams will collect all relevant factors that may be involved in understanding this problem. Data experts can collect information on pricing, customer service quality, product features, and customer demographics. In this example, the ground truth will be a data set about the current state of customer behavior. This ground truth data now becomes the basis for creating the casual model.

In the context of causal AI, ground truth plays a critical role in helping to establish causal relationships. Without accurate and complete ground truth data, it is difficult to identify and validate causal relationships between variables. For example, if an AI system is tasked with identifying the causal relationship between smoking and lung cancer, it will need access to ground truth data on the smoking habits and health outcomes of a large population over time to draw accurate conclusions.

The Business Imperative of a Causal Model

Although we are talking about causal models as frameworks for the next generation of AI, creating models is something that we do instinctively when we try to figure out solutions to difficult problems. It is common in a business planning session, for example, to go to a whiteboard and plan a new strategy for selling to customers. While this type of brainstorming is useful, to be successful we need to be able to codify processes so that we can execute on the strategy. Causal models are tightly related to augmented intelligence because they bring together all the key constituents that are involved in decision-making to determine the elements of the model. In this way, the team now has a common language for subject-matter experts, data scientists, and executives to communicate regarding causal inference. This allows technical teams to better align their applications with the needs of the business and generate demonstrable value. Unlike other approaches to AI, which begin the development process by first analyzing a corpus of data, causal AI applies data only after the model is created. Training causal models with data allow users to quantify relative causal strengths (weights) and the importance of variables. These weightings provide insight into the most important causes relative to a particular outcome, supporting future decision-making. One of the profound benefits of a causal analysis-based approach is that it helps to infer probabilities that an event will occur under conditions that are constantly changing based on new factors, such as a change in market dynamics or the health of a patient. Causal AI is a powerful tool to help hybrid teams understand the business problem being addressed and then creating solutions that help explain why an event happened and how to go about figuring out approaches that will help solve problems. In Chapter 3, we will provide a further discussion of the elements of a causal model.

Understanding Cause and Effect in a Marketing Campaign

Here, we will provide an example of how causal AI is used to understand the effectiveness of a marketing campaign. Throughout subsequent chapters, we will use this example to demonstrate how causal AI works in the business world.

There are many situations where the business needs to understand changes in their markets to understand and then adapt their businesses. One of the most complicated aspects of a business is to find an optimal way to sell products and services to prospects to grow revenue and keep existing customers upgrading to new offerings. Executing effective marketing campaigns are at the heart of business success. But understanding the dynamics of effective marketing is complicated in light of economic and business changes. Take the example of online stores and the changing buying habits of customers. What is the likelihood that customers will accelerate their purchases from online stores? Will customers move back to physical stores after a pandemic has receded? Creating a causal AI model can help the business compare online sales with sales in physical stores over time. The casual AI model will then track these variables and other variables that are specific to

(continued)

(*continued*)

online sales to determine the changes in observed behavior that will impact online purchases. For example, a subject-matter expert may understand that when physical stores begin to reopen after a pandemic, people will be less likely to continue purchasing products online at the same pace. Applying a causal AI model will help the organization better understand how to refine their approach to marketing.

In another scenario, a CEO has mandated that sales performance needs to be improved by 30 percent in the coming quarter. While the company has maintained profitability by cutting costs, sales growth has been slower than expected. With this mandate, the marketing organization needs to create a new, innovative, and aggressive marketing campaign. In this case, the goal of the campaign is to convince existing customers to upgrade to a new enhanced product and to close deals with new customers.

The marketing team relied on existing data from past successful marketing campaigns to create a new online marketing campaign. However, the campaign did not achieve the anticipated outcome. Sales increased only slightly with existing customers who upgraded. However, few new customers expressed an interest in buying the products. Was the campaign held at the right time of year? Were prices too high? Was the campaign itself not well targeted to potential buyers? It is not easy to assess why such a campaign failed. There is a myriad of reasons to explain what might have gone wrong. However, the business being successful requires more than a lucky guess. It requires a systematic model-based approach to correct the problem so that the company can increase sales. For example, the problem may be that the lists used for the campaign are outdated or there is a new competitor on the market that has undercut the product price. Was the campaign initiated at the right time of year? Understanding why the marketing campaign failed and fixing what went wrong can be the difference between success and failure.

How does causal AI help an organization understand why the marketing campaign failed and how the organization can determine alternative approaches that may turn a marketing approach into a successful campaign. One of the benefits of a causal AI approach is that it enables the team to explore "what if" scenarios (called *counterfactuals* in causality). For example, what would happen if we cut the price of the product by 30 percent? You can't come up with a conclusion based on looking only at the data. We must be able to put that data in context with changes in market conditions. What if there is a deep recession and customers can't pay the price of the new offering? What if there is a new competitor in the market that offers a more innovative product that may cost more but does a better job? What if there is a defect in the current product offering? Counterfactuals or what if scenarios are the foundational construct for how we understand the impact of interventions. It is important to not just rely on past results to make assumptions about the future. For example, in the past 2 years marketing campaigns that had good results by offering discounts before a major holiday worked well to increase sales. However, does this conclusion still make sense? Modeling an environment based on the knowledge

(continued)

(continued)

of subject-matter experts can make the difference between success and failure. Experts who understand market dynamics such as pricing trends, emerging competitors, and changes in customer preferences need to be part of the process of determining what actions to take to make the right decisions.

Just creating a marketing campaign alone will not result in sales. For example, in creating a causal model for a marketing campaign, it will be important to have variables that represent issues such as customer requirements that will make them more likely to purchase a product. It will be important, for example, to have adequate customer support and great product quality to encourage customers to purchase a product. In addition, the model must take into account the competitive situation such as an emerging vendor with new technology. All the factors shown in Figure 2.3 are focused on the end goals: increased sales and revenue.

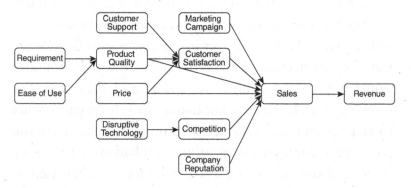

FIGURE 2.3 An example of a simple causal model of a marketing campaign.

The Importance of Augmented Intelligence

Augmented intelligence is intended to bring together the benefits of AI with the knowledge and understanding of professionals to solve business problems. As we will discuss in detail in Chapter 5, the optimal way to move forward with causal AI is by creating a hybrid team of professionals. Leveraging causal AI in organizations requires that the hybrid team identifies the important variables, creates a causal structure, and then uses that model to understand the causal effects. The power of causal AI is that it provides a framework for augmenting the ability of teams to solve business problems, determining what are the important factors in solving a problem, and then applying tools and libraries to reach conclusions.

Let's examine a simple example when managers want to understand the strength of the existing customer base. What products have customers purchased over the past decade, and how much did they pay? Obviously, these are straightforward questions that can be easily answered. However, it is much more complicated to understand why customer buying patterns are changing and what is the cause of those changes. Why have customers suddenly stopped buying the company's most popular products? Is there a change in the supply chain that the company has relied on for a decade? Are there competitors with new innovative product offerings at a lower cost?

Understanding the cause and effect of changing business conditions requires a hybrid team that understands existing customer data, data about supply chain issues, and competitive threats. The team needs to be able to gain insights to answer the following types of questions:

- What are the sources of this information?
- Are these data sources trustworthy?

- Are the data sources inadvertently biased?
- What data exists about pricing trends?
- How can the company deliver products to customers in a timelier manner?

The bottom line is that we need to understand whether the sources of data help an organization address the problem so that the business can understand why a problem is happening and how to use a causal approach to understand what would happen if a set of outcomes were different. It is often the case that models derived from the data will not reflect the problem that the business needs to address. To work, this process requires the creation of a hybrid team.

The Importance of Data, Visualization, and Frameworks

Given the importance of managing data in causal AI, it is worth spending time on the issue of identifying the data to support a model and what it means to have the right data to support a model. It also is useful to consider the significance of visualization and the use of frameworks or libraries to implement the causal inference model. All these topics will be discussed in more detail in subsequent chapters.

Getting the Appropriate Data

One of the biggest challenges for AI in general is the need to be able to explain what is happening inside the solutions. One important distinct advantage of causal AI models is that they are graphical so the models themselves indicate the relationships between variables and the strengths of those relationships. Because of the transparency of the causal AI model, it is much easier to train the model to see if the data produces the anticipated results. If the data does not match expectations, it may be that the data sources are biased, and therefore the outcome of the model will be flawed. In Chapter 6, we will delve into explainability and bias in data.

Useful data will come from a variety of sources. Some of the data might come from a pre-existing knowledge graph, which is a data structure that organizes information to capture relationships and connections. That information can be retrieved, integrated in a model, and analyzed. Other data sources will come from subject-matter experts who will evaluate data. It is imperative that a data engineer take on the task of collecting, cleaning, transforming, and organizing the raw data from the sources identified by experts within the organization. The role of the data engineer is to ensure that the information is accurate, consistent, and accessible. At the same time, data specialists will work with cybersecurity experts to ensure that important data maintains the right level of security and privacy.

Data experts in the organization collaborate with subject-matter experts to evaluate the data sets that will be consumed into the model. These professionals will be able to determine if the selected data includes the right type of data. They will also be able to determine if that data set is correct. Does the data set include out-of-date information? Are there mistakes or missing data elements? Is the sample size being used to provide results large enough to produce accurate results? In the scenario of identifying reasons for customers not renewing their service contracts, confounding variables could lead to unreliable or false outcomes. A confounding variable like poorly worded contract language could cloud the actual reason, which are the challenging economic conditions that prevent customers from affording continued service. Determining the appropriate data to include in your model is not simple. Being successful requires an iterative process to avoid bias in the outcomes. Having the ability to visually understand what is happening inside a model ensures that you are accurately predicting causal relationships. For example, once you create the model based on what you already know from your knowledge graph and the new sources of third-party data, you still must test and validate that your model is providing you with the answers you are looking for.

The causal AI approach helps teams put data in context with the business problem they are grappling with. Beginning by modeling a problem, it is possible to understand not just what the data tells you but to interpret data to explain why a problem has happened. By augmenting machine intelligence with human knowledge, organizations can be empowered to solve complex situations that cannot be addressed without a collaborative approach. Causal AI helps organizations understand why a change in a business has happened and helps explain what it means and how to address it to have a better impact on outcomes. For example, why does a drug help certain populations but is ineffective with other groups? Why did a marketing campaign fail to increase sales of a new product? Why is an existing product selling better than a new product? What has changed in the sales process that has caused a revenue disruption?

To truly understand the answer to why an event or condition happened, you must understand the root cause of that situation. The idea of root cause is a critical element in understanding why problems occur. Why does a critical element in a manufactured product begin to suddenly fail on a regular basis? Understanding this and quickly remedying the situation requires an understanding of the underlying cause of the problem and then intervening to solve it.

An article, published in 2020 in *Stanford Social Innovation Review* by Sema K. Sgaier, Vincent Huang, and Grace Charles, explains,

> [I]t is imperative that decision makers also consider another AI approach—causal AI, which can help identify the precise relationships of cause and effect. Identifying the root causes of outcomes is not causal AI's only advantage; it also makes it possible to model interventions that can change those outcomes, by using causal AI algorithms to ask what-if questions. For example, if a specific training program is implemented to improve teacher competency, by how much should we expect student math test scores to improve? Simulating scenarios to evaluate and compare the potential effect of an intervention (or group of interventions) on an outcome avoids the time and expense of lengthy tests in the field.[6]

While causality and causal inference is not a new topic, it is now moving out of academic and research environments into the commercial realm. Causality is a type of correlation (take a look at Chapter 3). However, unlike correlation, which provides a statistical understanding of data, causality is intended to understand why a problem happens. Therefore, it is not surprising that the watchword for causality is that correlation does not equal causality. What does this mean? While correlation will show us the relationships between variables, it does not help explain the cause and effect of a problem. Causal AI is an approach specifically intended to explain cause and effect from data. Causal AI is designed by modeling a problem that an organization needs to understand to make better informed decisions. Therefore, causal AI models clearly define goals and trade-offs to help automate decision-making.

Applying Data and Model Visualization

Creating a graphical representation of variables and the related data helps the team better understand outcomes from the analysis. Using causal graphs such as DAGs and SCMs, it is much easier to identify causal relationships between variables. A visual model can also quickly indicate where there is bias or a backdoor.

In addition to understanding the cause and effect by applying causal models to data, it is important to have ways to visualize outcomes. This is especially important when models are large and complex. Being able to visualize data helps subject-matter experts understand some of the hidden nuances within the data. Through interactive visualization, it is possible to look at a set of data points and analyze how a change in data could impact outcomes.

While using correlation techniques can lead to inaccurate conclusions, combining correlation with data visualization allows data scientists to see relationships within complex data. Data visualization can quickly demonstrate when a correlation is incorrect. Visualization helps to provide context for the data so that it can be applied to understand causal relationships in a model.

Since these correlation-based approaches create models from the data, those models are only as good as the data used to create them. One current example of this type of problem with predicting outcomes from data is the inaccuracy of election polling data. Typically, polling estimates are based on correlating past trends in data without considering external factors that can impact results. Combining data visualization with a causal model will prove to be a better approach since it combines the ability to understand the context of data based on cause and effect.

Applying Frameworks After Creating a Model

The process of putting causal AI into practice has the potential to transform businesses. The model creation involves subject-matter experts and data scientists working together to address the business problem to be able to understand why a situation has occurred and how it can be addressed. We will discuss this process in greater detail in Chapter 5. One of the values of causal AI as it emerges as a business imperative is that it brings together business decision-making and AI-based modeling.

Once a model has been designed at the business level (see Figure 2.3 earlier in the chapter), the data science team begins to use a set of frameworks or libraries to implement the causal inference model. One of the benefits of the commercial approaches of causal AI is that many of the emerging open-source frameworks or libraries help developers implement causal inference models more quickly. Many vendors have developed these language-based (e.g., Python) frameworks that have been put into the public domain. This means data scientists can access sophisticated libraries (many are open-source) as a starting point for building models. These frameworks are designed so that they can be integrated with popular deep learning frameworks including Tensor-Flow and PyTorch. Many of the implementations of these frameworks also include the ability to integrate data from a variety of sources.

Getting Started with Causal AI

Beginning the process of implementing causal AI in the real world begins by assessing the problem you are grappling with. The following is a suggested list of issues to consider when getting started:

- What are you trying to understand, and what is the problem you are trying to explain? Why are events happening? If you have a campaign to grow sales by 30 percent, what is the relationship between an increase in spending on ads and growth in sales?

- What information do you already have, such as a knowledge graph, written information from subject-matter experts, or codified data sources? These should be part of the process of getting started.

- Detail what subject-matter experts understand about an area and how those variables are related to each other.

- Begin building a dynamic model with knowledge graphs, source data, etc. Once you have tested this initial model, you can begin to address your questions, such as the causes of the situation you are addressing.

- Once you have the initial model built that you are testing with data, you will begin tuning the model by adding more data sources that may make better sense of your causal questions.

One of the most important capabilities of causal AI is that it involves an iterative process. Once the model is designed, the programming is completed, and data is added, the hybrid team now tests the data against the model to ensure that the data is consistent with the problem being addressed. The various elements of this process are detailed throughout the rest of the book.

Summary

In this chapter, we provided you with an overview of what causal AI is and why it is important to a hybrid team of subject-matter experts, strategists, and data scientists to collaborate through a common language. The common language is through first modeling a problem and then providing data and testing results. As we have shown, the ability to show cause and effect is critical to decision-making. Teams need to be able to question what would happen if an approach to a problem were different. Would the outcome change if we changed the price of a product? Would a marketing campaign conducted in a different month have led to more sales? Or is there a new competitor in the market that is undercutting the product price? These are the kinds of questions that management must know to effectively move forward. Causal AI is designed to help organizations figure out what problems they are trying to solve and implement the most effective way to leverage AI technology to that end. In Chapters 3 and 4, we will provide examinations of the elements of causal AI models and how to build such models.

Notes

1. Judea Pearl. *Causality: Models, Reasoning and Inference*, 2nd Edition, Cambridge University Press, 2009.
2. Judea Pearl and Dana Mackenzie. *The Book of Why*, Basic Books, 2018.
3. 2011 A.M. Turning Awards. Judea Pearl, laureate "For fundamental contributions to artificial intelligence through the development of a calculus for probabilistic and causal reasoning." https://amturing.acm.org/award_winners/pearl_2658896.cfm.
4. *On The Mode of Communication of Cholera*, by John Snow, M.D. Wilson and Ogilvy, 1855.
5. Pearl and Mackenzie. *The Book of Why*, p. 27.
6. "The case for Causal AI," by Sema K. Sgaier, Vincent Huang, and Grace Charles. *Stanford Social Innovation Review* Summer 2020.

3

Elements of Causal AI

In the first two chapters of this book, we provided an overview of the journey to causal AI and an overview of terminology, including graphing, models, and the underlying operations of casual AI. In this chapter, we will delve more deeply into understanding the elements of causal AI with a focus on the correlation and causality. We begin this an overview of the conceptual model designed for causal AI and then move into a discussion of directed acyclic graphs (DAGs) and structural causal models (SCMs) and how the combination of these two elements work together to create models. One of the key benefits of a model-based causal AI approach is that it provides a consistent and understandable model that promotes collaboration with all key constituents. As business professionals can iterate quickly across the various scenarios they are considering, they will learn and know what combinations of programs, offers, and sequences of offers will produce the optimal results. Causal-based AI is one of the most likely paths to user-centered empowerment and daily engagement with powerful and useful AI-enabled models.

Conceptual Models

At a conceptual level, correlation-based AI and causal-based AI approaches have the same theoretical roots; both methodologies can produce actionable models based on leveraging statistical and data analysis. These approaches to modeling have input data that is conditioned and transformed for consumption by the models. Both correlation and causality are focused on defining the relationship between variables. The main difference is that with correlation, the goal is to identify how variables are related to each other. In contrast, causality is intended to determine whether one variable causes another variable. A prediction from a correlation-based system will be a forward-looking view of what will happen to the variables of interest. For example, will consumers buy more of a specific product over the next several quarters? A correlation-based AI system does not and will not provide an understanding of why a problem has happened.

A correlation-based approach statistically will provide insights about current reality and project future outcomes. In contrast, a casual AI system begins by modeling the variables and their interactions to provide insight into why an event happened.

Let's look at an example of a vehicle manufacturer and specifically its car production process. Suppose the factory uses an AI system to predict the number of cars that can be produced based on the availability of different car parts.

Correlation vs. Causal Models

In this scenario, we will look at the insights that can be gained via a traditional correlation-based approach to AI versus those that can be gleamed from a causal AI approach.

Correlation-Based AI.   This AI system relies solely on statistical correlations between variables to make predictions. The traditional AI system might take into account historical data on the number of cars produced and the availability of different car parts and use this data to predict the number of cars that can be produced in the future.

However, this system cannot help leadership find the root causes of emerging problems. For example, the AI system may know that if there is a shortage of internally produced door handles, there will be a decrease in car production, but it will be unable to help the team identify the underlying reason why there is a shortage of handles. Company leadership is going to want to know why there is a shortage, not just that production will decrease.

Causal AI.   Causal AI systems are designed to identify the causal relationships between variables and make predictions based on this understanding. For example, a causal AI system might analyze the production process to identify the specific step in the process that is causing the shortage of door handles. The system could then suggest ways to address the underlying issue, such as increasing the supply of a specific material, adjusting the hours for the team that produces the handles, or changing the production process.

By identifying the root cause of the problem, causal AI systems can make more accurate predictions, but more importantly, they can offer more effective solutions. Rather than just identifying the problem, this causal approach to AI gives teams the ability to remediate the issue. The data team can approach company leadership with both the problem and a number of potential solutions.

Understanding the Relationship Between Correlation and Causality

There are many applications where correlation-based AI is the best approach and method for many reasons. Perhaps there is an abundance of historical and ongoing observational data and the current correlation-based AI model performs exceptionally well. Anyone would be hard-pressed to convince the business executives responsible for this operational area to spend the time, money, and effort to replace this correlation-based application with a causal-based application. If these systems provide management with insights, they have the potential to improve business outcomes.

It can also be the case where causal-based AI systems and correlation-based AI systems can work as complements to each other. We have seen applications where simulation and optimization systems can be slow and expensive to operate on large-scale, high-dimensional data in complex environments (e.g., signal processing, optimization of continuous manufacturing or energy production, or global or national econometric models). In these environments, causal-based approaches can be used as preprocessing applications to indicate whether the entire data set should be updated or refreshed, whether the complete simulation/optimization cycle should be undertaken at this time, or whether the data environment or the models are in a state where the extensive effort to run the entire analytical cycle is not justified.

Of course, there are a growing number of use cases where causal-based AI is the most appropriate and optimal approach to take to developing and delivering the most accurate, economical, and powerful models possible.

Part of our interest in writing this book is that we are seeing an inflection point in the development of causal-based AI approaches, methods, techniques, and technologies. Currently, it is still hard for technical experts to understand causal-based approaches and tools quickly and easily, but we see a day in the very near future where early adopters will be leveraging causal-based tools and technologies to develop causal-based models and applications to realize measurable competitive advantage in numerous markets and areas.

Leaders in their respective markets (banking/financial services, technology, consumer packaged goods [CPG], retail, telecommunications, logistics, and so forth) are eager to leverage advances in AI to maintain their leadership in their key operational areas and markets. We believe that understanding and leveraging causal-based AI methods and technologies is an effective way to maintain that advantage. The time is now to begin understanding how you, your analytics team, and your collaborators in your business ventures can be on the leading edge once more through your use of causal-based AI.

Both correlation-based and causal-based approaches are valued and valuable tools that are useful for solving an analytical challenge in a defined use case. There are times when both correlation-based and causal-based approaches will be used in conjunction with each other to provide for performant, scalable, and economical approaches to delivering the most accurate information required for the business requirement at hand.

Causal-based AI has begun to move into the commercial market in collaboration with groundbreaking innovation from the research and academic community. One of the primary objectives of this book is to help technologists and business professionals who are working in corporations to see and understand how causal-based AI can be added to their analytics portfolio and toolkit. A causal AI appraoch increases and refines an organization's ability to discover, analyze, and efficiently and effectively attack new opportunities to establish or increase their strategic and tactical advantage in relation to their competitors.

Process Models

One of the benefits of a causal-based AI approach is that it begins by first creating a business-focused outcome model before integrating data. This first step is to identify a targeted business outcome, for example, sales, customer churn, product quality, or revenue. As with any software development model, once the model is created, there is a process of building analytical models, testing the models, and, finally, using the models in production environments. This high-level approach is descriptive of both families of AI.

While it is possible to create process models that encompass the entirety of a company, it is more practical for organizations to begin by identifying a specific use case or problems that need to be addressed. Focusing on the portion of the company that is of interest is a more productive method to arrive at the specific improvement that is desired. Likewise, there are process models that describe the analytical process from beginning to end. In the subsequent discussions of process models, we are not examining the entirety of the analytical process from the conception of an idea to delivered insights. To simplify and focus our discussion, we are omitting the process steps of business requirements gathering, source data management, and many other aspects and steps included in information management, application design, and related processes.

In the subsequent sections, we will examine the core process models of both analytical approaches to gain a better understanding of the differences in these contrasting, yet complementary, approaches.

Correlation-Based AI Process Model

In traditional, correlation-based AI, the process model is clearly defined, well-refined, widely documented, and understood at a deep level by researchers, academics, experts, technology companies, observers, business professionals, and others. In a correlation-based approach, the amount of data ingested is critical to accuracy. Figure 3.1 illustrates the general process flow employed when building a correlation-based model.

FIGURE 3.1 The core correlation-based AI model begins by identifying raw data from appropriate sources.

As shown in Figure 3.1, the correlation process begins by acquiring raw data; then, through the process of integration, exploration, and analysis, the model defines the features that are most useful for the selected machine learning algorithm. The model that has been created will be tested to ensure that it achieves the expected outcomes. Once this has been established, the model is put into production. In most correlation-based AI projects, the analytics team understands the objectives of their projects. As an example, the analytics team will know that the primary objective of an analytical project or program is to produce a more accurate sales forecast based on a market that is relatively stable. It may be a forecast of sales, a forecast of people visiting a retail location, or a forecast of manufacturing output. The analytical team will be focused on delivering a model or application that reliably and accurately produces a timely forecast number or series of forecasted numbers.

The driving force in the early stages of a correlation-based AI project is to determine the objective function as quickly as possible and narrow the focus of the project and process onto that singular factor. In approaching this process, the team is simplifying their work so that the amount of data required is reduced, the accuracy of the model can be improved, and the probability of success of the project can be increased. The focus is mainly driven by the interest and desire of the analytics team to get to the end of the analytics process effectively and efficiently. Let's contrast that objective with the objective in a causal AI process and discuss how the process model employed in causal-based AI differs from the process model used in correlation-based AI systems. Currently, the broadly held belief is that the more data collected and pushed into the process model, the better the resulting analytical model. As AI has had greater and greater success over the past 10 to 20 years, this view has become more and more commonplace and has come to be almost the de facto view that this is the best and, in some people's minds, the only way, to leverage data in AI applications.

It is not uncommon to see many failures in early-stage AI products. The failure of some AI projects is not due to data scale, high dimensionality, or complexity but rather cultural and organizational issues. A substantial number of books, articles, and research papers have been written to explain why AI projects fail to achieve value realization and to work flexibly and reliably in production environments. In a Harvard Business Review article, Tim Fountaine, Brian McCarthy, and Tamim Saleh argue that "Technology isn't the biggest challenge. Culture is."[1]

Of course, we will have to work with society, organizations, and individuals to increase their basic understanding of these new tools, techniques, and technologies to broaden use, and we will need to work with business professionals, experts, pundits, and commentators to develop an environment where business professionals are interested in leveraging these approaches to further their interests; we will need to explain to the general population where to be wary of these new tools and technologies and where they can expect to gain monetary and personal benefits from the use and deployment of these new tools. All these efforts are part of the long-term societal change that will need to evolve to enable widespread adoption and use of AI technology over the coming decades.

One of the reasons that we see failures in AI projects is because the approaches generally rely on creating models from data. These models are opaque, meaning that it is not possible to see what the algorithms used to create the models actually do. Therefore, these black boxes, as they are known, make it difficult to understand the underlying process. In addition, it is possible this lack of explainability can result in unintended bias. We will provide more details about explainability and bias detection in Chapter 6. In addition, many of these models can also rely on correlation approaches that result in spurious correlations where the cause and effect within the model leads to inaccurate conclusions.

Causal-Based AI Process Model

A significant portion of the power of causal-based AI lies in its focus on why a problem has occurred and the type of interventions (counterfactuals) that can be part of the process, what interventions should be considered, the desired outcomes, and related factors that need to be examined, analyzed, and understood.

Figure 3.2 shows the beginning of the core process model for a causal AI project or program.

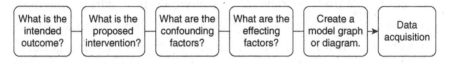

FIGURE 3.2 Causal-based AI model, part 1. A causal AI model models the process from definition of the problem being solved through factoring in counterfactuals and confounders to create a visual graph before data is introduced. Once data is added, the model has to be tested to ensure the outcomes match.

The initial step in the causal AI process begins with modeling the relevant questions, interventions, direct effect factors, indirect confounding factors, unknown or vaguely known environmental factors, and desired outcomes. It will be apparent to anyone who is an experienced analytics professional that this is a completely different approach to building analytical models and applications. In the traditional correlation-based approach, we begin the process by discussing the outcome(s) and the data required, and then we move on to data acquisition, data integration, modeling, and more.

One of the significant benefits of a modeling-first approach is that it provides all members of the team—including analytics professionals, business leaders, and data scientists—with a common language for expressing solutions to complex problems. In the causal-based approach, the initial effort is focused on describing a broader set of influencing factors and players that impact the desired outcomes, possible interventions, and direct and indirect environments. The core causal process ensures that the influences related to the environment and the decisions to be made by the players in the process, as well as the environmental conditions influencing those actions, are considered, described, and included in the model.

Describing both the direct and indirect factors, influencers, and influences leads to a more flexible and robust model. Through this process, the team will be able to generate a broader set of insights into how a market environment or systems environment can be actively managed. This modeling process is an iterative approach designed to achieve a range of desired outcomes given changing, complex internal and external environments.

The driving force and momentum in the early stages of a causal-based AI project is to determine the complete range of influencing factors contributing to the positive or negative movement of the possible outcomes, the range of interventions possible, and the myriad of known and unknown environmental factors at play in the environment and process. The primary focus of the project and process in this early stage is to create the most realistic view or model of the process and environment possible. In the process of modeling processes, the team is expanding the work to be executed so that the amount of data required is complete and multifaceted, the accuracy of the models can be improved, and the probability of success of the project can be increased. It is typical for a team to approach a causal model based as an incremental process. For example, after the basic model is created, different subject-matter experts will add deeper knowledge on specific elements of the causal model. For example, a model that is focused on the cause of a decrease in customer retention will require detailed process information about techniques commonly used in the company to avoid customer churn.

As we will discuss in Chapter 5, the process of modeling requires the participation of a hybrid team. Remember, most analytics teams or data scientists will naturally, by mindset, historical training, and experience, want the focus on data collection, on problem definition, on application, and then on model requirement. They will expect the project to be narrowing in focus once data sources have created the model. Given the traditional approaches to AI development, it is not surprising that there is some discomfort among these data scientists. On the other hand, the business managers and subject-matter experts may be excited by the flexibility and outputs that will provide insights into which interventions may lead to the outcomes they require to meet the mandates required by business executives.

What is different when you compare and contrast correlation-based process models (refer to Figure 3.1) with causal-based AI process models (refer to Figure 3.2)? The stages in the causal based approach are based on understanding the question that the business is grappling with and creating a visual model with the team before ingesting and transforming data. The core process model of causal-based AI approach provides an implicit method for bringing business professionals and analytics professionals together at the beginning of the analytics process.

Collaboration Between Business and Analytics Professionals

The causal AI process begins by modeling the outcomes that the business executives, managers, and subject-matter experts expect to see in the market or operational environment. Business professionals want to understand, examine, and change or vary those outcomes to improve business operations. The goals of causal AI modeling focus on business outcomes. Typically, causal AI is especially important when teams are trying to understand the impact of business decisions or when they are trying to come up with a solution to complex problems. By the nature of that objective, the causal AI process engages the subject-matter experts to think though the range of outcomes that they want to know about, understand, examine, and iterate through. As previously described, the beginning stages and steps of a causal based process are expansive and probabilistic rather than reductive and deterministic.

Over the decades, analytics teams have amassed considerable expertise in predominately correlation-based projects. Therefore, it is typical for the analytics team to want to move through a deterministic and reductive process in order to make the project iterations shorter and easier to manage and to increase the probability of success.

The causal AI process flips the data-first approach on its head and in doing so can be an uncomfortable change for experienced analytics professionals. Not only can it be uncomfortable for the analytics professionals, but it can also be challenging for them. In all likelihood, there need to be staff members leading the causal process, as we discuss in detail in Chapter 5. Subject-matter experts, managers, and executives will not know or understand the new causal process. Business professionals usually rely on the analytics team to guide them through the analytics process. Subject-matter experts and managers will need a leader or leaders to take them through the new process, and the leadership will need to come from the analytics professionals or perhaps outside experts brought in. The core process employed in the causal AI approach drives a more collaborative, iterative, engaged process that results in, or produces, models and applications that are more aligned with the thinking and needs of the business teams. Why is that?

Typically, analytics professionals focus on the model as a technique for evaluating causal relationships. Analytics professionals are striving to build models and applications that provide business professionals with answers to complex questions. Traditionally, analytics professionals have relied on correlation-based processes to analytical efficiency and singular outcomes. The problem increasingly confronting analytics professions is that they are being challenged to understand why a problem exists and what interventions can help businesses change and thrive. Causal-based processes and tools enable us to model the process and environment in a way that provides the ability to analyze, examine, and better understand what will happen if we take an action, a combination of actions, or a series of interventions. Causal-based approaches are more aligned with how business professionals think about how to take action and what will happen over a range of iterative interventions. Causal-based processes lend themselves to producing a range of results and iterating over a set of solutions easier than we have been able to do to date.

Causal AI provides a natural bridge between the two groups: analytics professionals and business professionals. Through the process of graphical modeling, causal AI provides an environment that lends itself to answering a range of questions that can lead to determining the type of interventions that can have an impact on outcomes. This type of modeling requires the inclusion of both internal and external variables as well as factors that may be understood.

From the perspective of an experienced analytics professional, the causal process looks to be more involved, more complicated, and more collaborative in the beginning stages of the analytics process. In fact, it is more complicated in the early stages to create a collaborative environment. There is simply more work involved in modeling the data and interactions based on a deep understanding of the subject matter to determine how to approach complex problems.

The Fundamental Building Blocks of Causal AI Models

Imagine you have a diagram that shows the relationship between a treatment (let's say taking a certain medicine) and an outcome (let's say curing a disease). A backdoor path occurs when there is a chain of connections between the treatment and outcome that does not involve direct causation but instead goes through one or more other variables (let's say age and gender) that may affect both the treatment and outcome.

This means the relationship between the treatment and outcome can be distorted by the presence of these other variables, and it becomes more difficult to determine whether the treatment is causing the outcome or if it is just the presence of these other variables that are causing the effect. Identifying and blocking these backdoor paths is important to accurately determine the causal relationship between the treatment and outcome.

Two of the most important elements of a causal model are directed acyclic graphs and structured causal models. These two techniques are combined to represent and analyze causal relationships between variables. DAGs are used to represent causal relationships between variables in a graphical way, where variables are nodes and directed edges between nodes indicate causal relationships. The acyclic nature of the graph ensures that there are no feedback loops, which simplifies the analysis of causal relationships. SCMs, on the other hand, combine DAGs with additional information, such as structural equations or functional relationships, to provide a more comprehensive representation of causal relationships. These equations describe how the values of variables are determined by the values of their parent variables in the DAG.

The Relations Between DAGs and SCMs

As we mentioned in Chapters 1 and 2, DAGs and SCMs are fundamental to the causal modeling process. DAGs are the structure of the causal AI mode. However, DAGs alone are not sufficient to execute causal analysis. One of the powerful characteristics of a DAG is that it provides a way to demonstrate the relationships between nodes and the strengths of those relationships. So, for example, in the customer churn example, we would create a DAG as a visual representation of all the variables, their relationships, and how they impact the targeted business outcome. Variables are represented as nodes that are connected to each other by directed edges. In the SCM, you would explicitly represent the actual relationship between the variables through a mathematical model. The math would help you determine the strength of the relationships between variables. The underlying mathematical models enable you to simulate the impact of interventions.

Explaining DAGs

In a directed acyclic graph, each of its edges has a direction that defines the flow from one node to another. This directionality is called a *path*, which we discussed in Chapter 1 and cover later in this chapter.

When modeling variables, a team will often begin with a DAG because it creates a visual representation of the relationship between variables. The forward arrows of the edges or connections between variables define the relationships (see Figure 3.3). In a DAG, the edges cannot form a cycle, which means that it is impossible to follow a sequence of directed edges and eventually return to the starting node. Let's say that *A* represents temperature of the atmosphere, while *B* is the consumption of ice cream. There is a direct relationship between *A* and *B*. However, if we have a backward arrow pointing from *B* to *A*, the model would be illogical. The backward loop or arrow would have indicated that eating ice cream will have an impact on the atmospheric temperature. Later in this chapter we will explain the importance of understanding front-door and backdoor criteria.

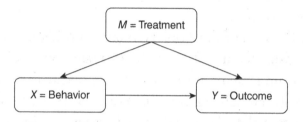

FIGURE 3.3 A sample DAG describes the basic relationships in a model.

While it may seem obvious that a causal AI model must have a well-defined causal direction or path, it is one of the core principles of causal modeling. Therefore, ensuring that the causal relationships are logical and well-defined ensure the ability to analyze the behavior of a system. One of the benefits of DAGs is that they provide a common language to help all members of the hybrid team to intuitively understand the world. Components of a DAG are representations of relationships between variables. DAGs illustrates that the movement of time is directed and does not loop back upon itself, or it is said to be acyclic, or without a recursive cycle. Therefore, the cycle of events can move only forward (i.e., time does not move backwards); as you follow any path in the graph, you cannot return to an earlier node on a path. This relationship reflects our natural world in that causality means events can affect only the future; they never affect the past, and therefore there are no causal loops.

Causal Notation: The Language of DAGs

At this point, we will need to introduce and explain the notation methodology used in causal modeling. Causal notation is a flexible set of tools and techniques used to explain, understand, and plan for the construction, modification, and use of causal models. The notation methodology enables the hybrid teams consisting of analytics professionals, data scientists, and business leaders to describe the causal model and the elements and relationships within the model.

Since the goal of this book is to build a bridge between business professionals and data analytics teams, we will provide a conceptual understanding of how to represent the language of causality without delving into the mathematics of causal AI math. It is important that there is a shared understanding of the concepts and language used in the causal process. Therefore, we do need to explain the unique method for dissecting, describing, and understanding the factors, interventions/treatments, relationships, and outcomes at work in causal-based models. Table 3.1 describes several basic entities in an example causal model. In this situation, Table 3.1 describes the notion that can be used for a better understanding of how to model the desired outcome of a marketing campaign.

The elements outlined in Table 3.1 are a representative set of variables that refer to why a problem has occurred based on understanding the variables defined in the model. However, it is critical that the team understands the specific variables and how they are related to each other. What are the factors that will impact or influence an outcome? You can, and should, include that variable in the model.

As we have been discussing, the causal model can include a wide range of treatments, interventions, known and unknown inputs, confounding factors, and more. A variety of these

Table 3.1   Basic Entities in an Entry-Level Causal Model

Entity	Example
Initial state or behavior (X)	Sales have dropped 30 percent in the previous quarter. Will spending more on a marketing campaign be the right intervention?
Treatment (counterfactuals) (M)	These are counterfactual questions. Will spending twice as much on marketing allow sales to grow? Is it probable that this will lead to more product sales?
Confounders (W)	This shows things like competitive products, competing price offers, past purchases, inventory levels in the household, satisfaction with the product or service, etc. Seeing and considering the new price offer.
Outcomes (Y)	This shows the results of applying counterfactuals and confounders to the most logical result.

elements is possible in real-world situations. These variables should be included in the corresponding model and can be described with various causal notations. The number of each instance of the variables included is unlimited. That is, each model can have as many instances of treatments, outcomes, and other variables as needed to make the model representative of reality.

Operationalizing a DAG with an SCM

An SCM is a powerful framework that represents and analyzes causal relationships between variables in a DAG. The SCM consists of a set of equations that describe variables in the overall causal AI solution. It works directly with the DAG that visually represents the causal structure. Each SCM is associated with a graphical model (DAG) where nodes are variables that are connected via edges that correspond to a causal assumption. A causal assumption is a hypothesis about the context of causal relationships between variables. These causal assumptions are typically based on input from subject-matter experts. This is a fundamental aspect of causal modeling and causal inference.

Causal-based AI via SCM will empower a broader set of data science professionals to build sophisticated models and ensembles of models enabling business managers and analysts to engage with causal-based applications in a way that will allow those professionals to vary the conditions they seek to examine and understand potential outcomes via data and computing based models quickly and easily.

Business professionals will leverage these models and analyses before committing any resources in the real world. Business executives will have a wide-ranging understanding of the external landscape and the internal resources available before making decisions and committing to a course of action.

Once a DAG has been created, an SCM is the mathematical model that formally describes the relationships defined in the DAG. The SCMs provide a technique to mathematically analyze and predict how a system will behave based on mathematical models. SCM will explain how variables in a system are related to each other. It is also possible to use SCMs to simulate the behavior of a system to answer counterfactual questions, such as would revenue increase if we lowered the price of a product offering?

Structural causal modeling is the most commonly used methodology, notation, and language for designing, discussing, and building causal models. We will use SCMs to begin to discuss and describe the more nuanced and advanced elements of causal AI systems. In Chapter 4 we provide an overview of the math behind the models.

Structural causal modeling is an analytical language that provides descriptive tools that enable us to construct and validate causal models. In the next section, we will describe the simple yet expressive notation of data, variables, and relationships between variables. The SCM language and notation will help us to codify, simplify, and understand our ability to describe and discuss causal relationships, models, and our intended use of those models.

The SCM approach makes it possible to simulate many possible interventions simultaneously. Also, SCM allows for the incorporation of expert knowledge to counter the possible limitations of a purely data-driven approach. Experts can, for instance, help to determine which variables should go into the model, they can place conditions on the model to improve its accuracy, and they can help understand results that are counterintuitive.

The Elements of Visual Modeling

One of the strengths of visual modeling is that it provides notation that can help a hybrid team understand the nuances of the models. Visual modeling is a powerful tool in the requirement to build realistic models of the areas that we seek to examine, understand, model, and analyze. It enables us to identify relationships between variables and provides a concrete understanding of how the underlying causal mechanisms govern how that organization operates. As early as the 19th century, there were scientists who began to use causal graphs to infer causal relationships. For example, in 1918, Sewell Wright, considered the father of genetics, used causal graphs to analyze the factors in predicting the birth weight of guinea pigs.[2] Wright modeled his findings with graphs similar to those in Figure 3.4.

Visual models can provide a significant amount of flexibility that helps to explain the complex relationships among variables. One of the benefits of DAG supported by SCM is that it is an efficient and effective analysis of the causal relationships in a variety of fields. Let's walk through an overview of the primary

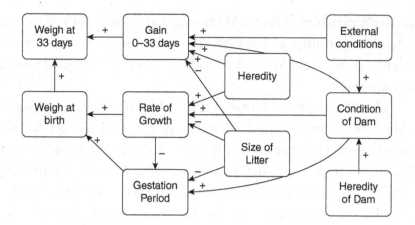

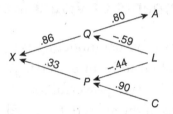

FIGURE 3.4 In Wright's 1921 paper, "Correlation and Causation," he used causal graphs similar to these.

elements of the environment that we will be leveraging when we are building causal models. The key components include the following:

- Nodes
- Variables
- Paths/relationships
- Weights
- Models

Nodes

In graph-based models, nodes are a particular kind of variable that are used to represent entities and their connections. Therefore, nodes are observed variables that are intended to create connection points between other nodes. Each family member is a single node. The model provides an indication of how these nodes relate to each other and have variables assigned to them. The most common ways of describing the relationships between nodes are parents, children, ancestors, descendants, and neighbors. Parents and children refer to direct relationships; descendants and ancestors can be anywhere along the path to or from a node, respectively. To use an analogy, the nodes are the nouns in our models. We name nodes with descriptive names to illustrate the subject of the node such as price, sales, revenue, birth weight, gestation period, size of litter, and so forth.

Variables

In an SCM, different types of variables can be used to represent the system being modeled. One way to classify these variables is to distinguish between endogenous and exogenous variables. Endogenous variables are those that are directly affected by other variables in the system, while exogenous variables are external to the model and are not directly affected by other variables in the system.

Endogenous and Exogenous Variables. Endogenous variables are those that are directly influenced by the model's structure and other variables within the model. For example, in an SCM that models the relationship between education and income, income is an endogenous variable because it is influenced by the level of education.

On the other hand, exogenous variables in causal modeling are the variables with no causal links (arrows) leading to them from other variables in the model. These variables are not directly influenced by the model's structure but rather represent factors outside of the system being modeled that affect the endogenous variables. For example, in the same SCM, the level of intelligence could be an exogenous variable if it is not influenced by education or income but still affects both of these variables.

Understanding the distinction between endogenous and exogenous variables is important for correctly specifying the causal relationships in an SCM. In general, endogenous variables should be modeled as a function of other variables within the model, while exogenous variables can be specified directly as inputs to the model.

Observed and Unobserved Variables. It is important to understand observed and unobserved variables. An observed variable in causal AI is one that is directly measured and included within your model. These observed variables are the nodes within your visual model. In contrast, unobserved variables are elements that are not directly measured or observed in your causal AI model, but they have an impact on the results. In a causal AI model, in order to measure sales, a possible unobserved variable could be brand perception. Brand perception and reputation can have a significant impact on sales but are difficult to measure. Likewise, word-of-mouth can heavily impact sales but is similarly challenging to measure.

Paths/Relationships

Paths are fundamental to both DAGs and SCMs. In an SCM, paths refer to the directed edges between the nodes in the SCM. These paths represent the causal relationships between the variables and are used to compute the causal effects of interventions on the system. When an intervention is made on a variable, the effect on other variables in the system is propagated through the paths in the model, according to the rules specified by the SCM.

A *path* in a visual causal AI model refers to a series of links or relationships between variables. These links connect nodes that have a direct impact on another. As discussed in Chapter 1, paths can be front-door or backdoor paths.

To reiterate, a front-door path indicates a direct causal link between the variables. These front-door paths can also indicate that there are multiple causal links between the variables. Paths in a causal AI model play an important role in determining the strength and direction of the causal relationships between variables and may be used to identify potential mechanisms or mediators that underlie these relationships.

A backdoor path occurs when a treatment variable (the variable you are trying to study or intervene on) and an outcome variable (targeted result) are connected through a variable (a variable that is impacted by the treatment and has a causal relationship with the outcome variable) that is causally related to both the treatment and outcome variables. When a backdoor path occurs, it can cause a bias in the results of the model. For example, let's say we want to know if there is a causal relationship between stress and heart attacks. In a causal AI model, as shown in Figure 3.5, we would represent stress as the treatment preceding variable, heart attacks as the outcome variable, and of course other variables that might influence the relationship between them. Imagine one of these additional variables is smoking, which is related to both stress and heart attacks. In this case, there is a backdoor path between stress and heart attacks through smoking. A person who is under extreme stress might be more likely to have a heart attack. However, stress is not a direct cause

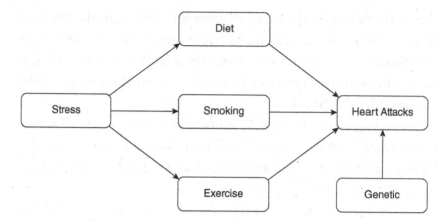

FIGURE 3.5 A sample DAG illustrating the relationship between stress and heart attacks.

of a heart attack. A person under a lot of stress might tend to smoke more and have poor eating habits. This backdoor path can create a spurious association between stress and heart attacks, making it look like avoiding stress will reduce the risk of heart attacks when in fact it does not. Instead, in reality the relationship is simply that people under stress will tend to have other behaviors that will cause them to be more likely to have a heart attack.

Weights

Weights are numerical values that are assigned to the paths (edges) that are connecting the nodes in your model. These weights represent the strength of the causal relationship between nodes in terms of the numerical value associated with the effect that the node has on the subsequent node (see Figure 3.6). It's important to note that weights can be a positive or negative number depending on how one node impacts the other.

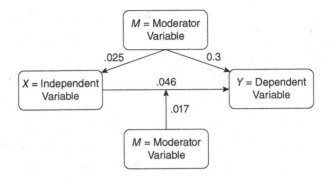

FIGURE 3.6 A DAG with weights illustrated

Weights can be referred to as *edge weights, parameters, hyperparameters,* and other terms. All mean the same thing: the weight of the impact of the effect associated with the path. These weights are instrumental for representing these causal relationships, as the model would use edges with weights that reflect the strength of the causal effect between the variables. Therefore, weights are crucial in the training, tuning, and operations of all models, including correlation-based and casual-based models.

For example, consider a model that is designed to predict the risk of heart disease based on a person's age, gender, blood pressure, exercise level, and cholesterol levels. The model might specify that age has a stronger causal effect on heart disease risk than gender or cholesterol levels and that high blood pressure has a positive causal effect on heart disease risk. Meanwhile, exercise level will likely have a negative effect on heart disease risk. To represent these causal relationships, the model would use edges with weights that reflect the strength of the causal effect between the variables.

Weights in a visual causal AI model are typically estimated using statistical methods, such as regression or machine learning algorithms, which attempt to identify the most likely causal relationships between variables based on the available data. While your DAG shows only visual representations of the relationships between nodes, an SCM that is hydrated with data will show weights that attempt to represent the strength of causal relationships. As the variables are processed and values are passed from the previous node to the subsequent node, the value of the variable is increased or amplified, or decreased or reduced, by multiplying the value by the weight associated with the path.

There are wide-ranging discussions on how to set the initial value of weights across a network or model, how best to modify weights to train models, how weights converge optimally to arrive at a robust model, and many other highly technical and arcane discussions of setting, managing, optimizing, validating, and maintaining weights in models; all of these discussions are outside the scope of this section and book.

Summary

In this chapter, we built a foundation for business professional and analytics professionals to have a common framework and understanding of the elements of the causal-based AI approach to designing, building, and executing causal-based AI projects or programs.

We explained the differences between the two approaches to AI: correlation-based and causal-based. Each approach has its uses for analytics teams but is clearly different and needs to be understood.

We then focused on the two critical elements of modeling: DAGs as the visual modeling approach and SCM as the mathematical underpinnings. SCMs and DAGs are easy to comprehend. They are simple, following the rules of time and direction and reflecting the world we inhabit. At the same time, they are among the most powerful and sophisticated modeling tools at our disposal. When the DAG and SCM approaches are brought together, they provide a powerful approach to causal AI. In Chapter 4, we will delve more deeply into the practical approaches to designing, building, and validating causal AI models.

Notes

1. Tim Fountaine, Brian McCarthy, and Tamim Saleh. "Building the AI-Powered Organization," Harvard Business Review, July–August 2019. https://hbr.org/2019/07/building-the-ai-powered-organization.
2. Sewall Wright, "Correlation and Causation," Journal of Agricultural Research, Volume 20, October 1, 1920 – March 15, 1921.

4

Creating Practical Causal AI Models and Systems

I n this chapter, we will link DAGs to SCMs and how they work in tandem to create a practical and functional causal AI model. Therefore, we will discuss how to turn a causal model based on DAGs and SCMs into a practical and functioning causal AI system. In Chapter 3, we compared the two families of AI: the newly emerging causal-based AI and the more traditional correlation-based AI. We also introduced the foundational concepts of understanding causal AI model building. We talked about basic directed acyclic diagrams (DAGs), and we built a simple model to illustrate the introductory concepts that we are interested in and will be using and building upon throughout the remainder of the book. In this chapter, we will focus on detailing and expanding upon the formal language and methodology used in describing, designing, building, modifying, validating, and leveraging causal models.

Understanding Complex Models

There have been, and are, numerous approaches to naming the elements of causal models, discussing modeling, and communicating causal concepts. One of the impressive aspects of causal models is that the models and elements of causal models can be used to visually describe any model including variables, relationships, processes, and environments that are important for a hybrid team. Any environment, process, or interaction of variables can be described and modeled in a causal-based approach.

If you want to understand the dynamics of air flow into a jet engine and how that relates to fuel consumption and thrust produced, causal modeling can capture and describe the relevant dynamics. If you are interested in understanding consumer behavior and the variations thereof considering the market factors, internal family dynamics, your possible marketing programs, and other relevant competitive factors, causal modeling can be of assistance here as well. Why is this impressive to us?

First, it is impressive due to the flexibility and inclusion that is encompassed in causal language and notation. In most other modeling environments or languages, users and practitioners are required to simplify the complexity of the real world by reducing the number of variables and simplifying the relationships between them to make the models easy to comprehend and reliable enough to proceed. The current state of causal modeling enables us to include as much complexity as needed to make the model representative of the actual events and influences that we see in the actual world.

Second, one of the subtle and powerful facilities of causal modeling is that we can include variables that we cannot empirically observe but that we know exist. We do not need to have observational data to include these variables, and yet we can include them and estimate their impact on the relationships and observed variables in the model. We will discuss how this works in detail later in this chapter.

Third, causal modeling enables us to integrate historical data sets that were collected for similar reasons, but not the same purposes, for and in our current analyses. Causal modeling enables us to treat and condition data so that we can include additional observations and relevant variables while setting aside other elements of the historical data that is not relevant for our work. Causal modeling enables us to collect, condition, and include significant amounts of historical data to increase the accuracy and improve the representative nature of our models.

The transformative nature of causality is that it can take incredibly complex problems and make them accessible and understandable. In the previous chapter, we showed one of the earliest causal models, developed by geneticist Sewall Wright in 1921, that was applied to determine the birth weight of guinea pigs. Increasingly, we are seeing causal AI models being used to understand the effectiveness of marketing campaigns; the effect of price on revenue; the quality; and characteristics of inputs of a manufacturing process to the quality and reliability of the final outputs; the effects of making ethical and moral decisions on the well-being of a population; and many more situations, environments, and processes.

One of the underlying goals of AI, causal or correlation, is to build models of sufficient inclusion, complexity, flexibility, responsiveness, agility, scalability, and accuracy so that we can rely on them to predict and prescribe future events in a timely way. One of our overarching goals is to leverage those models and the results of those models to improve outcomes that are of interest to us.

Analytics professionals, whether they are aware of the fact or not, are striving to build analytical models that are nearly identical to the processes and results based on their perceptions of reality.

One of the important reasons to adopt a causal approach is to gain insights that might not fit into their biases or erroneous assumptions. Our efforts are taking us in the direction of building models that ingest multiple data sources simultaneously and seamlessly invoke numerous models that produce highly accurate and reliable results indistinguishable from what actions and activities in the real world would produce.

The analytics profession is on the cusp of building computing- and data-based analytical models that augment human capacities in real time. We are seeing the first signs that our integrated AI tools, computing systems, and networking connectivity can deliver the foundational capability to enable the realization of this goal. To be clear, the goal is the delivery of machine and augmented intelligence that serves people in a positive manner in their everyday lives.

Let's move from the conceptual to the practical. Let's move to discussing how causal models are actually constructed to achieve the goals we are outlining and exploring. Now that we have a basic understanding of causal notation and the graphs used in constructing causal models, we can move onto examining the causal modeling process.

Causal Modeling Process: Part 1

The causal modeling process is focused on understanding the variables and their direct and indirect interactions and building a model that will enable us to iterate over a set of scenarios to understand why an effect produces a specific result. This is a substantially different process than what we as analytics professionals are accustomed to in correlation-based processes. At a high level, the overall process we discuss in this section and the following one looks like Figure 4.1.

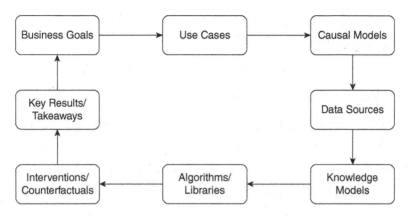

FIGURE 4.1 The process of creating a causal AI model is an iterative process.

Step 1: What Are the Intended Outcomes?

Causal processes and analytics start with an understanding of the problem that the organization needs to address. It is not a process of simply relying on assumptions about the problem and how it relates to coming up with conclusions and solutions. We will discuss the team process in detail in Chapter 5. But first, let's look at the types of questions that need to be addressed before beginning any modeling process. The following will give you an overview of the types of questions that are common in determining the direction of a process. While the overall goal will be to answer what the data's cause and effect from data is, you will want to start with some key questions, such as the following:

- What will happen if a certain course of action is taken or executed?

- What will happen if a certain course of action is not taken or executed?

- What is the process or environment we are interested in analyzing?

- What outcomes are considered: positive, negative, unacceptable, optimal?

- What interventions are we interested in considering?

- What treatments can we feasibly execute?

- What confounding factors might be correlated with both outcomes and treatments?

- What environmental factors do we know exist but cannot accurately measure?

- What related data sets exist that we might be able to combine and leverage?

We will be utilizing various use cases throughout this book. One of the most common problems that companies are trying to solve relates to marketing operations. Therefore, we selected marketing because most of our readers will have exposure to marketing, as any of the following:

- A business professional who has experience in setting up, executing, measuring, and modifying marketing strategies, tactics, and programs

- An analytics professional who has defined an objective function, an outcome, or a range of outcomes; or gathered data and worked with marketing professionals to analyze marketing strategies, campaigns, and programs

- A consumer who has experienced being the target of marketing programs and offers or who has simply observed marketing plans in action on a daily basis

In our marketing use case, let's specify a scenario that we will use for our initial foray into causal process modeling. Our scenario is based on consumer marketing. We will be examining how we might want to vary or iterate on pricing changes to encourage consumers to buy more or less of a certain product in a defined time frame. We selected price as a defining factor in understanding why problems happen in business or industry. Understanding the impact of pricing changes in market share and overall success can have a direct impact on the business.

Let's examine the core process model for causal AI projects and programs in more detail.

Step 2: What Are the Proposed Interventions?

After considering the overall question of desired and intended outcomes, the process moves on to a discussion of the type of interventions or treatments available to change outcomes. The focus in this second step is to begin to move into the details of the intervention techniques based on the objectives of the marketing issues in the context of constraints such as budget or time. These are questions to ask when considering which interventions to include during the causal analysis process:

- Can we introduce a new product?
- Should we buy one or more of our competitors?
- Does bundling the number of products for purchase at one time improve sales quantities over the short term?
- Does bundling products to increase short-term sales inhibit sales growth over the medium to long term?
- Should we advertise and focus on the quality of our product over the competitive options?
- Should we change our pricing strategy to align more closely with our product brand message?

- Should we divest the product line?
- Should we discontinue the product line?
- Should we consider new variations as product line extensions?

These are complex questions, but the power of causal modeling enables us to consider these questions for inclusion in our analytical process after we have gained experience in the process or engaged causal based experts to help us in the process. One of the primary benefits of the casual modeling process is to include subject-matter experts early in the process to ensure that we are aligned and focused on the business challenge at the core of the problem.

Let's extend our marketing use case to include the discussion of questions related to possible pricing interventions or treatments that we might implement.

- What happens to sales when we change the price often?
- What type of pricing interventions would be optimal?
- Should we develop and implement a dynamic pricing model?
- Should price change in relation to how much consumers buy in a defined time period?
- Should price go down if they buy more and up if they buy less?
- Should we develop an individual pricing model for each customer?
- Should we increase prices?
- If so, by how much?
- Is this a one-time increase or a tiered increase over time?
- Should we decrease prices?
- If so, by how much?
- Is this a one-time decrease or a tiered decrease over time?

- Is price a tool to reinforce the position of the product in the market?

- Should the price always be the highest/lowest in the category?

Now that we have decided that price is our intervention, our DAG can be modified as shown in Figure 4.2.

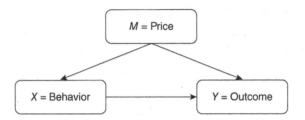

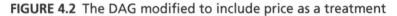

FIGURE 4.2 The DAG modified to include price as a treatment

Step 3: What Are the Confounding Factors?

After considering the overall question of desired and intended interventions, the causal process moves on to the discussion of confounding factors that have an effect on the outcome in a positive or negative manner.

Let's take a moment to clearly define confounding factors or variables. Confounding variables are those that affect the variables in the model in a way that produces a distorted association between the variables being measured (X and Y). They confound the "true" relationship between two variables being examined.[1]

Therefore, the confounder can create a misleading or false relationship between the two variables being examined leading to false results.

Assuming that there is a positive or negative association between two variables, in our model, X and Y, and in that association, both X and Y are affected by a third variable (M) **and** **only** M, the relationship is defined as being unconfounded.

In a confounded association or relationship, there is at least one additional variable, the confounding variable, that changes or distorts the relationship between X and Y beyond, or in addition to, the effect of M. Then the association between X and Y is distorted (some would say spurious), and that distortion is a result of the effect of a confounding variable(s) (W). Hence, the relationship is said to be confounded. Figure 4.3 shows the DAG with a confounding variable added.

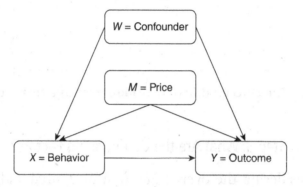

FIGURE 4.3 The DAG modified to include a confounding variable

Confounding variables also can affect two variables that have a causal connection. For example, if X and Y are associated and causally related (for example, if X affects Y), the association between X and Y may reflect not only their causal connection but also the influence of a third variable (W) that affects both of them (X and Y). Thus, the association between X and Y may exaggerate the causal effect of X and Y because the association is inflated by the effect of W on both X and Y. In this case, we could say that the relationship between X and Y is confounded by W, even though it is not a purely distorted relationship.

Let's continue with our marketing example to clarify the concept of confounding variables. In our example, a confounding factor that affects Behavior (X) and Outcome (Y) that does not affect Price (M) could be Competitive Offers (W), Distance to Store (W_1), Amount of Product on hand (W_2), Time to Consume Product (W_3), or various other confounding factors. It is possible for a causal relationship between two variables to be muted or inflated depending on the nature of the confounder. A confounder can make it difficult to tell if one factor is causing another. In the case of marketing, running a marketing campaign to sell winter jackets will have a confounding factor of when the campaign is run. Therefore, running a marketing campaign in the middle of the winter might be too late since customers would have already purchased jackets. Therefore, this factor must be included. However, there will be other confounding variables that should be muted because they cannot be controlled such as an unseasonable warm winter. On the other hand, variables such as seasons may still influence jacket sales, but they cannot typically be adjusted in the marketing campaign. Therefore, it is important for the winter marketing campaign to note typical buying patterns but during analysis adjust for factors that marketers couldn't anticipate.

Understanding and Mapping Relationships

Causal science, mathematics, and practice in the real world are all evolving, and not all analytics professionals, academics, and researchers use these terms in the way that the variables are defined in this scenario. Given the early-stage use of causal processes, approaches, and technologies, the terminology and vernacular are continually changing, and variations exist around the world. No matter the terminology

(continued)

(*continued*)

used, the confounding effects of a third variable are recognized by the majority of people involved in the field.

As we are learning about the causal process and attempting to use the process, tools, and technologies to map relationships and effects that we see in the real world, we are well advised to keep in mind that simple bivariate associations between two variables can be quite unrepresentative of the true causal connection between variables. To be clear, it is rare that we have a business problem or challenge that is impacted and affected by only two variables. We may want to start with two variables to ensure that our model works, but we will in all likelihood need to move to more complex models to deliver practical value to our teams.

Step 4: What Are the Factors Creating the Effects and Changes?

After considering the overall question of confounding factors, the causal process moves on to the discussion, description, and definition of factors that have an effect on the outcome in a positive or negative manner.

Common/Universal Effects in a Causal Model.   The factors creating and causing change in the environment or model are intuitive and easy to understand given they mirror what is occurring in the natural world. The main categories of effects are *total*, *direct*, and *indirect*, which are described in Table 4.1.

Table 4.1   Definition of Common Effects in a Causal Model

Effect	Description
Total causal effect (TCE)	The total effect of all factors in the environment or model that modify the outcome
Direct effect (DE)	An effect typically introduced through an intervention, treatment, or mediating factor that produces a change in the outcome
Indirect effect (IDE)	An effect that is part of the environment that is introduced by another party or is a byproduct of a different process that has an effect on the outcome beyond what has been directly introduced by a planned treatment

Each category of effect is what you would anticipate or expect and is easily defined and reasonably self-explanatory.

Refined Effects in a Causal Model.   As we discussed in Chapter 2, Judea Pearl is one of the leading thinkers, researchers, academics, and advocates for the causal approach and best known for championing the probabilistic approach to artificial intelligence and the development of Bayesian networks. He is also credited with developing a theory of causal and counterfactual inference based on structural models.

Structural models and methods have been an innovation and development that has helped lead to a broader discussion of practical applications of the causal approach. The advancement and leverage of causal methods has been consistent and focused over the past 30 years.

The refined and extended definitions of causal effects in Table 4.2 are derived from Dr. Pearl's 2014 paper "Interpretation and identification of causal mediation."[2]

We just introduced two new terms, *mediator and moderator*, in Table 4.2.

Table 4.2 Refined and Extended Effects in a Causal Model

Effect	Description
Total effect (TE)	Measures the total expected increase of the effect in the outcome as the treatment is implemented. The mediator is allowed to track the change in the treatment as dictated by the defined function.
Controlled direct effect (CDE)	Measures the expected increase in the outcome related to the specific treatment. The mediator is set to a controlled level of applied uniformly over the entire population.
Natural direct effect (NDE)	Measures the expected increase in the outcome as a natural occurrence of the treatment being implemented. The mediator variable is held to the value it would have attained prior to the implementation of the treatment.
Natural indirect effect (NIE)	Measures the expected increase in the outcome resulting from the change of the mediator variable.
Moderated treatment effect (MTE)	Measures the effect of how a treatment differs across subgroups defined by the values of the moderator variable.

A mediator variable is a variable that clarifies the relationship between two other variables. It is a variable that represents the process by which the independent variable influences the dependent variable and sits in a causal relationship between the independent variable (X) and the dependent variable (Y). In other words, a mediator variable indicates the method that enables X to affect Y. A mediator variable helps analysts better understand causal relationships between variables to create more effective treatments or interventions. An example of a mediator variable would be the relationship between exercise and mental health.

A moderator variable, also known as a *moderating variable*, affects the strength or direction of the relationship between two other variables. It is a variable that changes the relationship between the independent and dependent variables. For example, when looking at the relationship between mental health and exercise, a moderator variable could be the age of the people being studied.

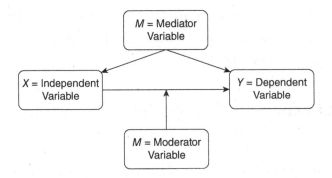

FIGURE 4.4 A mediator variable can unlock the relationship between variables.

Figure 4.4 illustrates how mediator and moderator variables help the analyst better understand cause and effect *relationships*.

Step 5: Creating a Directed Acyclic Graph

In Chapter 3, we discussed the importance of creating a graphical model using directed acyclic graphs. In our discussion, we have been iteratively building DAGs as we've walked through considering the variables and factors involved in causal modeling. We have used DAGs to illustrate our progress, define concepts, and provide a visual depiction of the process. You may choose to build your DAGs in this mode. Many professionals accumulate and define the elements of the model and then, subsequently, build their DAGs. Either approach is acceptable and will result in the DAGs you need to communicate the model that you and your team will be leveraging.

Step 6: Paths and Relationships

In Chapter 3, we introduce the concept of paths. In this chapter, we will provide additional details on how paths and relationships are critical to the implementation of models. Paths, edges, or relationships are how we illustrate the direction of the DAG, connections between nodes, and carry the weighted effect or probability from one node to the next.

Types of Paths   Let's describe and discuss various path types that are used in DAGs.

- **Chain:** A chain is a simple diagram where all nodes are connected with arrows that are all in the forward direction. Figure 4.5 shows an example of a chain.

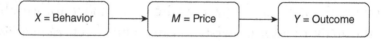

FIGURE 4.5 A DAG illustrating the chain path type

- **Fork:** The majority of DAGs include a fork of some type or multiple forks. A fork can be where multiple arrows fork away from a node, as in Figure 4.6, or where the multiple paths originate from a node and connect to different subsequent nodes.

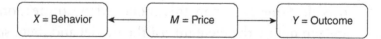

FIGURE 4.6 A DAG illustrating the fork path type

- **Inverted fork:** An inverted fork is where two or more paths converge on a node from two or more different directions.

  - In a path that is, or has, an inverted fork, the node where two or more arrowheads meet is called a *collider*. Colliders are defined in Chapter 1.

- An inverted fork is not an open path; it is blocked by the collider.
- We don't need to account for M to assess for the causal effect of X on Y; the backdoor path is already blocked by M.

Figure 4.7 shows an example of an inverted fork converging on a collider variable via a backdoor path, which will be defined later in this section.

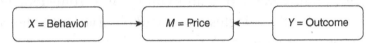

FIGURE 4.7 A DAG illustrating the inverted fork path type

Path Connecting an Unobserved Variable   Unobserved variables play a role in our models, but we do not have direct measurement or observational data for their impact and effect on our current model. Connections to and from unobserved variables (confounders) are indicated with a dotted or dashed arrow (see Figure 4.8). These unobserved variables can have an indirect effect on relationships in the model.

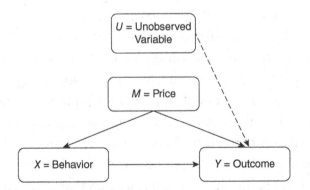

FIGURE 4.8 A DAG with an unobserved variable

Front-Door Paths   Front-door paths are represented by arrows moving to, or directed toward, the outcomes. Another way to say it is that front-door paths are moving away from, or directed away from, the mediators and/or treatments. For example, there would be a direct arrow representing a front-door path between *studying* and *academic achievement*.

All figures in this chapter have front-door paths included and illustrated. You cannot have a DAG without at least one front-door path. Figure 4.5 shows an example of a front-door path, while in Figure 4.8, the inclusion of an unobserved variable could create a backdoor path.

Typically, when we are examining processes and environments that we are interested in modeling and analyzing, it is the front-door paths, or the obvious connections and effects, that we build into our models first. After we have the base model completed or after we have the initial conditions (i.e., nodes, connections, directions, variables) established, noted, and validated, we start to think about, and build the indirect effects, into our models. Indirect effects are referred to as *backdoor paths*.

Backdoor Paths   Backdoor paths are represented by arrows moving to, or directed toward, the mediators and treatments. Another way to say this is that backdoor paths are moving away from, or directed away from, the outcomes. A couple examples of backdoor paths are in Figure 4.8, the path from M to X, and in Figure 4.7, the path from Y to M. As noted in previous chapters, it is likely that backdoor paths will create confounding variables. A confounding variable makes it difficult to demonstrate an accurate relationship between independent and dependent variables. The result will create a spurious relationship between variables that is inaccurate.

Backdoor paths denote the indirect effects nodes/variables can have on each other. Backdoor paths create confounding variables or nodes or confounders. Citing Judea Pearl, Malcolm Barrett writes ". . . confounding is like water in a pipe: it flows freely in open pathways, and we need to block it somewhere along the way. We don't necessarily need to block the water at multiple points along the same back-door path, although we may have to block more than one path."[3]

Typically, we will want to block the backdoor paths when determining accurate causal relationships as these paths confound the effects we are interested in and are attempting to analyze and understand.

We often talk about *confounders*, but we should talk about *confounding*, because it is about the pathway and the effect embodied in the path or relationship more than any particular node along the path.

Modeling for Simplicity to Understand Complexity As we discussed in Chapter 3 and the preceding section, the process of closing backdoor paths are critical elements in ensuring that the resulting models are accurate and causal. Therefore, we need to account for backdoor paths in our analysis. There are many ways to go about conditioning, isolating, reducing, or removing the effects of backdoor paths or the confounding effect(s). Some of the available techniques include placing the variable in a regression model, matching, and inverse and probability weighting, all of which have associated pros and cons. Each approach must include a decision by the business user and data scientist about which variables to focus on, or to deprioritize, in the model.

Some analysts have taken the approach of including all possible confounding effects. This can be considered a shortcut approach because it is easy to put everything into the model, but this approach introduces unnecessary complexity and requires adjusting for colliders and mediators that may not be needed in the model, and this rather indiscriminate approach can introduce bias.

A better, more considerate, and more intelligent approach is to determine minimally sufficient adjustment sets, sets of covariates that, when adjusted for, block all backdoor paths but include no more or no less than the necessary nodes and variables. Of course, there can be many minimally sufficient sets, and if you remove even one variable from a given set, a backdoor path will open. Some DAGs have no backdoor paths to close, so the minimally sufficient adjustment set is empty. If these variables cannot be measured and therefore the backdoors cannot be closed, it may be almost impossible to understand the true causal effect of an independent variable on the dependent variable. To avoid having confounding effects, it is important to carefully identify and measure all important and relevant variables.

One of our goals in modeling is to not build such simple models that they do not represent reality or to build overly complex models that are impossible to manage or validate. As we are iterating through the process of building our models represented by DAGs leveraging the SCM process, we are seeking to build a model of maximum simplicity that contains all the complexity needed to describe and explain the phenomena we seek to examine. As with many undertakings in life in general and analytics specifically, we seek to employ Occam's razor, which postulates that if there are competing explanations, the simpler one is preferred. We seek simplicity to explain and understand complexity.

Step 7: Data Acquisition

Often in the analytics field, the role of data acquisition is downplayed. However, our many years of experience in the business teach us that data and analytics are two sides of the same coin. They are complementary, and both are necessary to drive results and achieve objectives. So, data acquisition is an essential step in the process. When it is done well, it serves as an important enabling step for all the downstream analytics processes.

The good news is that, however, you have collected data in the past, and those are valid sources of data for causal-based processes as well. Even better news is that the data acquisition step that is the first step in the causal process is almost exactly the same as in a correlation-based approach. You and your teams can leverage the data you have previously collected and add new data through data integration and data transformation processes. In addition, it is possible to use synthetic data when there is not enough data to achieve the desired outcome. We discuss the use of synthetic data in Chapter 7.

Why Are We Doing All This New Up-Front Work?

It is apparent that defining and understanding these new terms, factors, and relationships involved and utilized in the causal-based process is a significant change for both business and analytics professionals. Also, we must keep in mind that one of the primary differences between a correlation-based approach and causal-based approach is the role of domain knowledge and subject-matter experts. The correlation-based approach invokes only the probabilities between the variables within data, and the causal-based approach cannot be completely defined by the probabilities in the factual world. Causal AI calls for domain knowledge not only to define the potential or counterfactual causal effects but to specify the causal structure of interest.

(continued)

(*continued*)

As noted earlier, it is useful to keep in mind that the additional steps and effort dedicated early in the causal process leads to greater power, flexibility, empowerment, engagement, and independence of the business professionals later in the analytics journey. Why is that important? It is important for a couple reasons.

First, business professionals want to iterate over their options and possibilities. They are constantly given changing requirements and objectives by their managers, and causal-based applications and tools enable them to answer these questions quickly and easily. This engagement opens their thinking to consider more challenging and interesting scenarios and questions, and it helps them perform better in their roles and jobs by providing them with the agility to consider and answer questions proactively.

Second, analytics professionals want to build new and interesting tools, models, and applications. If they are not limited to answering variations on questions they worked on previously, they can be working in new areas of the business to drive competitive advantage through data and analytics.

Causal-Based Approach: Part 2

The remaining steps in the causal-based process are largely similar, and in many cases identical, to the steps in the correlation-based process (see Figure 4.9). If you are an analytics professional, you can assume that most of the existing techniques you have

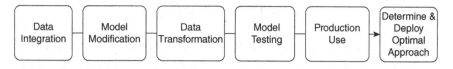

FIGURE 4.9 Causal-based AI model: part 2

used in correlation-based projects and programs will work in causal-based projects and programs.

However, new techniques are available that are useful in the causal-based process. In the following sections, we will focus on those in addition to the tools and techniques that you have learned and utilized in the past.

Step 8: Data Integration

There is an additional opportunity for data collection in the causal process. We will discuss this more in Chapter 7 when we discuss a pipeline for the causal approach and related tools and techniques. The causal approach enables analytical professionals to be able to acquire and leverage data originally collected for a different purpose and treating, conditioning, or transforming that data into a data set that can be aggregated with, and integrated into, other treated data. This data integration and transformation process opens even more possibilities for including and leveraging new data in the causal analytics process.

In correlation-based approaches, we have the opportunity to integrate a substantial amount of transactional data, survey data, governmental data, social science data, commercially available online and offline data, and more into our analytical processes. This does not change with causal-based processes. As noted in the preceding section, we can still leverage that data, acquire new data, and integrate the old and new data together for use in the causal-based process and approach.

Step 9: Model Modification

When constructing our models and the representative DAGs, we must be clear on the relationship of variables to each other. Once the DAG is designed, the data scientists typically use open-source frameworks or libraries to implement the models. These open source libraries, such as DoWhy, are good starting points for building the details of the models. Given the complexity of our final models, we need to test those models to ensure that we are not including relationships or biases that will invalidate or skew our analyses.

We want to note, understand, and control for direct and indirect confounders. If we do not control for these, their existence will bias the model and results, but we also don't want to control for mediators or effects, because controlling those would also taint our results.

There are several critical techniques that are important in ensuring that the models are implemented in a way that achieves the technical and business goals. One of the key approaches is d-separation, which helps the data scientists identify the set of variables that need to be observed to determine the conditional independence relationships between other variables in the model. This approach infers causal relationships between variables, makes predictions based on the model, and identifies variables that are important for understanding the underlying system.

Judea Pearl defines d-separation as "a criterion for deciding, from a given causal graph, whether a set X of variables is independent of another set Y, given a third set Z. The idea is to associate 'dependence' with 'connectedness' (i.e., the existence of a connecting path) and 'independence' with 'unconnected-ness' or 'separation.'"[4] For clarity, the d in the term d-separation stands for *dependance*.

Skylar Kerzner suggests that d-separation can be thought of as the "rules of correctly controlling variables in DAGs."

Uncontrolled variables cause bias and other issues when the "process contains variables that affect each other . . . , variables that are causes themselves but also act as mediators of other causes, and other complex structures."[5]

The d-separation process and technique enable us to ensure that our DAGs and resulting models are as free from bias as possible and will produce the results that we expect and intend.

Step 10: Data Transformation

Once we have acquired and integrated our data and built, validated, and modified our model, it is time to transform our data set to begin testing and tuning our model.

Many, if not all, the common and proven data transformation techniques and processes that we have historically executed in correlation-based projects and programs also are applicable and relevant in causal-based projects and programs. It is great to know that the toolkit of data transformation techniques that we know and leverage on a daily basis is still useful and available to us. As in many aspects of causal-based approaches, we can use many of our existing tools, and we can augment our knowledge base with new tools or expand the use of existing tools to new applications and use cases.

One area of innovation that has been more fully explored and explained via causal-based approaches is the systematic aggregation and transformation of numerous, widely disparate, previously unrelated data sets to arrive at a greater mass of data to analyze and consider as a source of information, knowledge, intelligence, and insight.

Integrating data from multiple heterogeneous sources has become increasingly popular to achieve a large sample size and diverse study population. Recent research and development efforts in causal inference methods have illustrated and proven that we can combine multiple data sets collected by potentially different designs from potentially heterogeneous populations to increase the insights derived from our models. We have seen causal approaches used to combine randomized clinical trial data with external information from observational studies or historical controls and other samples when no single sample or data set has all relevant variables.[6] This novel approach to data transformation has increased the potential to execute analytics on consolidated data sets in a way that has not been widely used before.

We will spend more time examining and delving into data transformation techniques in Chapter 7. For now, we will leave the topic by saying that this is one of the most exciting areas of innovation being brought forth by causal researchers, academics, and early-stage practitioners.

Leveraging Previously Collected Data

One of the incredibly powerful aspects of causal-based AI is the ability to include data from a wide range of previous surveys, observational studies, collections of transactions, and more to enrich the data set we are using in our models.

Of course, data collected for other purposes in previous projects may or may not have all the data elements we want or need to directly align the outside data with our existing data. We may be interested in utilizing numerous data sets, and some of those data sets will prove useful and valuable, and other data sets will look promising but prove to be useless for the models we are building.

Causal-based AI provides the tools to analyze and condition the previously collected data and enables us to select the subset of data that is pertinent and relevant for our current efforts. We can effectively extend our data resources

(continued)

(continued)

as many times as needed to expand our data sets to provide the breadth and depth needed to make our models robust and representative.

In 2016, Judea Pearl and Elias Barenboim proved that a structured and disciplined approach to examining and analyzing data collected for varying purposes reliably produced verified data sets that can be used to augment existing data sets. Pearl and Barenboim asserted,

> The unification of the structural, counterfactual, and graphical approaches to causal analysis gave rise to mathematical tools that have helped to resolve a wide variety of causal inference problems, including the control of confounding, sampling bias, and generalization across populations. . . . [W]e present a general approach to these problems, based on a syntactic transformation of the query of interest into a format derivable from the available information. Tuned to nuances in design, this approach enables us to address a crucial problem in big data applications: the need to combine data sets collected under heterogeneous conditions so as to synthesize consistent estimates of causal effects in a target population. As a by-product of this analysis, we arrived at solutions to two other long-held problems: recovery from sampling selection bias and generalization of randomized clinical trials. These two problems which, taken together, make up the formidable problem called "external validity", have been given a complete formal characterization and can thus be considered "solved."[7]

(continued)

(*continued*)

Pearl and Bareinboim, through their research, developments, and innovations, have extended SCMs with the tools to mathematically prove that externally collected data can be reliably and unerringly analyzed, understood, conditioned, and included in our analysis data sets to extend the data we use in our analyses.

Step 11: Preparing for Deployment in Business

Once models are created and combined with transformed data, it is important that the data science team prepare to move from development to production. In a causal AI solution, model testing, determining production use, and deploying optimal use are critical steps in ensuring the accuracy, reliability, and effectiveness of the solution. In many ways, these steps are the same as correlation-based processes. We may use other technologies and software from new or existing vendors or open-source libraries, but the order of operations, the objectives to be achieved, and the outcomes we are seeking are the same in both approaches.

After creating a model, it is critical to test the model to ensure that the causal relationships between variables are accurate, based on subject-matter expertise. Testing models is essential in assessing the performance, accuracy, and reliability of the model. The data used in creating the model must represent the goals of the model. Once data is selected, data will be prepared and trained based on the model. In addition, it may be necessary to select the right model that most accurately fits with the data and represents the causal relationships between the variables in the data. Different equation models will be used, depending on the relationships between variables. For example, do the results of the model reflect the understanding of subject-matter experts? Is there critical data missing? Are there backdoor paths that can cause bias? Is there noise in the model that is causing confusion? There are a number of techniques and tools available to data scientists. There are books that provide detailed coverage of these tools, and we discuss some important ones in the following "Causal AI Tools for Technical Validation" sidebar and in Chapter 7.

During the testing process, data scientists and other practitioners will often evaluate the performance of multiple models to determine which model best fits the data and accurately captures the causal relationships in the data. Commonly, these practitioners employ a variety of statistical techniques such as cross-validation, information criteria, or hypothesis tests to compare the performance of different models and select the best one. It is critical that testing include the performance and accuracy of the models.

Overall, model testing is critical in causal AI because it helps to ensure that the model accurately captures the causal relationships between variables in the data. By testing and validating the model, researchers and practitioners can identify and correct any issues with the model and ensure that it performs well in predicting causality. This is essential for making accurate predictions or decisions based on causal relationships in the data.

Causal AI Tools for Technical Validation

Technical validation is critical to the success of causal modeling. There are a number of important tools for technical validation. These include mediation analysis, d-separation, and sensitivity analysis. These techniques are commonly used to ensure that the model is accurate,

(continued)

(*continued*)

reliable, and robust, and that it can be used to make meaningful and actionable predictions or decisions. For example, mediation analysis is used to identify and quantify the causal mechanisms underlying the relationship between the treatment variable and the outcome variable and to validate the causal assumptions underlying the model. D-separation is used to identify the independent relationships between variables in a causal model and to identify potential sources of bias or confounding. Sensitivity analysis is used to assess how sensitive the model is to different inputs, assumptions, or parameters, and to improve the model's robustness and reliability.

It is important to ensure that the causal estimates are independent of confounding variables. To achieve this goal, balance diagnostics can be used to determine if the distribution of confounding variables is balanced between the treatment and control groups following the application of propensity score matching, subclassification, or weighting.

There are situations where there simply isn't available data to test a model. Creating a synthetic data set can simulate the relationships between variables, including known causal relationships that can be used to assess the performance of the model. This approach can help to determine whether the model can accurately recover causal relationships and estimate causal effects.

Another important approach to model testing is to deliberately change either the data or assumptions used in the model. These changes will help to evaluate the model's robustness and assess its performance under different

(continued)

conditions. By introducing noise to the data or even removing data points, it will be possible to assess how sensitive the model is to inconsistencies with the data. The same approach can be used to modify important assumptions in the model to see if this will impact predictions or causal relationships. When an analyst introduces changes to either the data or the model assumptions will help determine if the model itself is reliable. In addition, cross-validation or out-of-sample testing can evaluate the predictive performance of the model. This can aid in ensuring that the model does not overfit the data and generalizes well to new data.

Another important approach that can test the effectiveness of a model is to look at how different model approaches will perform. Selecting an alternative algorithm or approach can assist the developer in determining the relative strengths and weaknesses of the causal AI model.

Summary

In this chapter, we provided an overview of the elements needed to create models. One of the strengths of a causal AI approach is the ability to gain a clear understanding of what problems an organization is trying to solve. To be successful, it is critical to understand what techniques are needed to understand how to validate and manage the modeling process. The right data must be integrated into the model so that the result of the analysis is accurate. The underlying models must be built, modified, tested, and validated. We delved further into some of the most important technical concepts that practitioners need to operationalize to create effective causal AI solutions. We explain the necessity of doing the up-front work to prepare for a well-designed causal AI solution.

Causal modeling is difficult to grasp and inaccessible to many in part because nearly every discussion of causal modeling related to causal-based AI begins with a relatively easy to understand description of the upcoming discussion and then immediately dives quickly and deeply into a discussion dominated by algorithms.

One of the key topics of this chapter is to demonstrate that causal AI takes advantage of the immense power of systems and software to collect, structure, process, and iterate over minute details and small but important variations in inputs, intermediate results, and outcomes; all of these are primary elements of causal-based AI. As we will discuss further in Chapter 5, combining the power of AI with human knowledge and understanding is the reason that we are at a turning point for causal AI.

Notes

1. "Confounding Variables," The Inter-university Consortium for Political and Social Research (ICPSR), www.icpsr.umich.edu/web/pages/instructors/setups2012/exercises/notes/confounding-variable.html.
2. Judea Pearl. "Interpretation and Identification of Causal Mediation," *Psychological Methods*, American Psychological Association, 2014, Vol. 19, No. 4, 459–481 1082-989X, Reprint version: https://ftp.cs.ucla.edu/pub/stat_ser/r389-reprint.pdf.
3. Malcolm Barrett, "An Introduction to Directed Acyclic Graphs," An Introduction to Directed Acyclic Graphs (microsoft.com), October 10, 2021.
4. Judea Pearl, "d-Separation without Tears," *Causality*, Second Edition, 2009. Excerpted at http://bayes.cs.ucla.edu/BOOK-2K/d-sep.html.
5. Skylar Kerzner. "A Complete Guide to Causal Inference," Towards Data Science, Feb 21, 2022. https://towardsdatascience.com/a-complete-guide-to-causal-inference-8d5aaca68a47.

6. Xu Shi , Ziyang Pan, and Wang Miao. "Data Integration in Causal Inference," arXiv, October 3, 2021, https://arxiv.org/pdf/2110.01106v1.pdf.

7. Elias Bareinboim and Judea Pearl, "Causal inference and the data-fusion problem," PNAS, Vol. 113, No. 27, March 15, 2016. www.pnas.org/doi/full/10.1073/pnas.1510507113.

5

Creating a Model with a Hybrid Team

In the first part of this book, we defined what we mean by causal AI and the type of services and capabilities that are required to determine the cause and effect of complex business problems. In such cases, the goal of causal AI is to provide a platform that enables it to determine why such problems have occurred and the best approaches for changing outcomes. Causal AI is intended to take the guesswork and emotions out of decision-making. Being successful with a causal AI approach requires a team of professionals across disciplines.

This chapter will provide an overview of the importance of creating a hybrid team to implement a causal AI approach to solving business problems. How can a team understand why a situation has occurred and what to do to make a change? The focus of our discussion will be on what it means to leverage a hybrid team to create a causal AI solution. The process of working with a hybrid team requires a structured approach to defining both the roles of individuals and how they work together on a common goal. The power in the collaborative causal AI approach is that there are not simple handoffs from one team to another but a continual cycle of development.

What does it take to create a model that both is technically sophisticated and reflects the business objectives? In brief, before creating a model, it is important to assemble a group of experts to participate in the project. There will be a core team that will be responsible for managing the entire project. Overall, there can be a large number of members of the extended team of participants. Different team members will participate in different aspects of the project as needed. This team can become a source of expertise and guidance that can help manage future projects. In addition, there will be various professionals who will be needed at various stages of the model creation and deployment. Every member of the expanded team needs to understand the project's goals and objectives. For example, the team needs to include the strategists who are grappling with hard business problems. These strategists may not understand anything about causal AI, but they understand that they need a different solution. To be successful, before beginning the modeling process, it is critical to have a holistic understanding of the business problem by determining the critical knowledge and data needed to populate the model. This chapter will focus on what it means to create a hybrid team of professions who work together to create the model that will answer the cause and effect of business problems.

The Hybrid Team

One of the benefits of causal AI is that it takes a holistic approach to solving problems. Many early AI projects failed because they approached problems solely from a machine learning perspective. In these projects, a data scientist would use data to create the models. Too often these data scientists would work in isolation from the business users and the internal data teams. As a result, the resulting black-box models were unable to produce the solutions to real-world problems. Creating a hybrid team is an effective solution to this problem because it brings together the key constituents who need to collaborate to address complex problems and create business-focused solutions. Therefore, a hybrid team consists of business strategists, subject-matter experts, data experts, and data scientists. When these constituents work in a structured manner, they can focus on a common goal.

Why a Hybrid Team?

Most organizations are incredibly complex both in structure and in offerings. Therefore, it is not possible to assume that a single group can have the knowledge or skills to tackle the solutions to difficult problems. It is not surprising that in a crisis many organizations find that teams and department leaders often resort to finger-pointing to assess blame as to why a problem has impacted revenue or product quality. One of the greatest values of establishing a hybrid team is to create a collaborative framework that gets to the heart of a problem beyond either an observational approach or a narrow understanding of the problem. Therefore, having leadership provide guidance to a team of experts is an important starting point. The hybrid team itself will be experts from a variety of departments with different skills and expertise who collaborate to build a causal AI solution. Team members must have knowledge ranging from data science to an understanding of the subject matter of a domain. Bringing together a team is the best way to create a solution that focuses on why a problem exists and the approaches that will solve important business problems. One of the benefits of establishing a hybrid team is to form the foundation for what can become a center of excellence for causal AI projects. This center of excellence can serve as a way of creating a set of best practices and training as new projects are initiated.

To be successful, causal AI requires an iterative process because the typical business is dynamic and changes over time. Customer requirements change, business processes need to be updated, and the data about the business is updated in real time. Because there are so many elements at play to create a causal AI environment, there needs to be a hybrid team in place.

One of the principles of causal AI is that the team needs to create a model before determining which data sources will help determine why a problem exists and how to address it. The solution goes beyond identifying data. One of the most important characteristics that enables a causal team to successfully collaborate is to have a common language. The team members must have a shared understanding of how a model is designed. What does a model look like? What are the variables that are integrated into the model? What does it mean to conduct a counterfactual analysis of a problem? What is the root cause of the problem based on the strength of causal relationships? Under the causal model are algorithms and inference methods that are understood by the data scientists and developers. While it isn't necessary for the SMEs and traditional data analysts to understand the details, it is critical for the nondata professionals to gain an appreciation of what happens under the covers.

The Benefits of a Hybrid Team

The power of a causal AI model is that it is designed by a cross-functional team. The team that is assembled represents every aspect of the business problem being addressed. For example, there almost always are financial implications and strategy implications to a business problem. For example, the financial team will set a budget for how much will be spent on the specific project. This budget will help the team plan the scope of the project. Likewise, the strategy team has the role of explaining the problem that leadership wants to solve. Perhaps the CEO is concerned that revenue is not growing as fast as anticipated and would like to understand why and what can be done to turn the company's fortunes around. Asking why revenue hasn't increased requires a holistic and full view of every aspect of the business ranging from the effectiveness of the sales team, the quality of the products, and the competitive environment. What data is available to understand where the business is today? Subject-matter experts bring knowledge about the domain and the impediment to growth.

The value of causal AI comes from all team members being able to communicate with a common language and platform. Typically, the organization will be grappling with many complex nuances about their business that cannot be easily understood by a single team. The only way to have groups with different viewpoints and different levels of expertise work together is to have a common language to collaborate. Without this common language there will be too many opportunities for miscommunication. Sometimes different groups might use the same terms to mean something completely different. One of the greatest benefits of a causal graph or model is that it provides a visual representation of the variables that define the business environment. Therefore, it is imperative to bring the hybrid team together before creating a causal model.

Establishing the Hybrid Team as a Center of Excellence

Think of this hybrid team as the foundation for a causal AI center of excellence—a template of best practices that can be replicated in a variety of business units throughout the company. In fact, many sophisticated businesses will establish a management team to lead a cross-functional team to learn how to effectively deploy new technology through a learning process. Once a project is successfully implemented, the leadership team is in a good position to establish a center of excellence for the next projects. In essence, the goal is to "train the trainer" so that as more teams implement causal AI, they are able to bring their learning to subsequent projects. Centers of excellence have proven to be excellent ways for other teams to learn from the mistakes and successes of pioneers.

A proven starting point for defining a hybrid team is to find an executive sponsor for the project. The ideal sponsor is someone who understands the goals and potential of the causal AI project and will run interference when the value of the project is challenged. Once the team finds an executive sponsor, it is time to bring the hybrid team together from across the key disciplines.

As we will discuss later in this chapter, it is important not to create one massive model for the entire company. Each model should be designed to tackle one problem that can be linked to other models. Therefore, the center of excellence will be instrumental in helping each subsequent team build on previous projects and the expertise these teams have accumulated. The most effective way to create a well-designed model is to bring together a team that includes the core constituents.

Designing a causal AI model has some distinct differences from traditional AI models. Therefore, the process of developing a team will be unique. Causal AI is a sophisticated and complex approach to helping a hybrid team within organizations to successfully solve business problems. As we have pointed out in previous chapters in this book, causal AI and causal inference requires both a methodology for creating models that reflect both the business objective and the details of the subject being studied.

It is easy to get caught up in the intricacies of the underlying capabilities such as the semantics, language, and methodologies to create a model. Without this underlying power, causal AI would not work. However, it is imperative to look at the role of the hybrid team in creating an effective model.

How Teams Collaborate

There may be many individuals from different areas of the business that need to be involved in developing and evolving the causal model. While there will be a team leader who orchestrates the process from beginning to end, team members will rotate in when their knowledge is required. It is impractical to assume that all parties will be able to spend countless hours on the project. But it is imperative that they have an overall understanding of the goals and objectives of the project so that when their expertise is needed, they can provide the right information at the right time.

Team Size Matters

It might be tempting to create a massive team to address critical business challenges. It would not be surprising to determine that many individuals will volunteer to be part of this team since it may have high visibility within the company. However, it is important that the team not be too big. There likely will be a core group that is involved with the project from beginning to end. These individuals may become the foundation for a center of excellence that will help jump-start each new initiative. Each role may

(continued)

(*continued*)

have multiple participants depending on the phase of the project. For example, there may be a dozen subject-matter experts who participant as needed. If additional roles are needed, they can be added on an interim basis. To be successful, the core team should meet on a regular basis to ensure continuity of the project. The size of the team will depend on the size of the company and the complexity of the project.

One of the important best practices for getting started with a causal AI project is to begin with a pilot. Therefore, the initial pilot will begin with a small team that designs a very targeted problem to get an understanding of how to define a hypothesis and progress through the stages of defining a working solution. The goal of this small team will be to demonstrate that this causal approach has merit.

But Why?

Organizations have had a lot of success in using statistical correlation to understand problems when you have precise objective data. Correlation is typically successful in situations such as predicting weather over the coming week or analyzing when a machine part might fail to support predictive analytics. In the case of predicting machine part failures, the goal is to identify errors so that a technician can replace a part before it can fail. However, anticipating the failure of a machine part is not the same as understanding why these failures are occurring. It might be more efficient to be able to figure out why parts are continually failing and fit that problem rather than constantly replacing parts. It is also more cost effective to prevent failures.

Unlike traditional correlation-based approaches like preventive maintenance, causal AI relies on understanding the context of solving a problem. Causal AI is different because you are looking to understand why events happen: what the causes and effects are. In complex business conditions, management wants to understand why events happen and what action can be taken to solve problems.

The type of questions that management typically needs to understand can be relatively straightforward. However, there are many business situations where the competitive landscape is changing or when customer requirements have impacted the business. Here are some of the key questions that you might see the management team needs to understand:

- Why are 30 percent of our customers not renewing their contracts?

- Why are impurities suddenly occurring in a critical manufacturing process?

- What is the relationship between the amount of liquor a person drinks and the instances of COVID-19? Is there a relationship or not?

- Why do customers who purchased a product from an online retailer not purchase other related products? And why is the amount of money a customer spends online down by more than 50 percent from six months ago?

- Why did our marketing campaign fail?

Take the example of a failed marketing campaign. In the past, similar campaigns were able to increase awareness of the introduction of a new product. As a result, the campaigns had generated as much as a 20–30 percent increase in revenue. However, the most recent campaign failed to meet the objectives of a

20 percent revenue increase. Why did this happen? The product was well received by the management team. Early customers who tried the product were pleased. The overall market for similar products was growing rapidly. Why did the campaign fail? Was there something wrong with the product? Was the price too high? Were there flaws in the marketing approach? It is not uncommon for those responsible for each aspect of bringing a product to market to point fingers at each other. In contrast, creating a causal AI model based on a team effort can bring a more objective approach to understanding why a problem happened and what type of solution could help to alleviate a problem. It takes more than a single group to figure out why a problem occurred. There need to be team members to represent all aspects of bringing the new product to market to gain an understanding of what the problem is and what approaches will help change the outcome. For example, it is critical to incorporate all of the important variables that explain how the process of selling a new product works. There needs to be enough data to gain a clear and objective understanding of the effects of selling and gaining traction. Addressing the solution to a problem will therefore begin with a hypothesis (i.e., there are competitive products recently introduced to the market or we don't have enough of the right lists of people who are likely to buy the product).

Defining Roles

There are several key roles and responsibilities needed to ensure the success of a causal AI project. However, to be successful, there needs to be a hybrid team leader who has enough knowledge of all those key roles in the team and can help direct them to meet the business goals. Without leadership, the team will not be able to accomplish the goals set by business leadership. There will be a variety of roles that you will want to consider adding to your team. Not every role will be needed depending on the complexity of the problem being addressed, but it is useful to consider them.

Each business is different in terms of the size of the company, the nature of the problems they are trying to solve, and the complexity of the model being created. For example, a huge manufacturing company might have hundreds of subject-matter experts, while a smaller business might have only a dozen experts. Before we list the various roles needed for the hybrid team, it is important to point out that this is not a linear process. All team members work in a coordinated way to define the goals and objectives of the project. One of the values of the causal AI model is that it will create a common language to discuss issues and approaches. The overall team needs to understand that the causal model is not static. As the business competitive landscape changes, the model and the data will have to be adjusted. For example, the cost of commodities could change the nature of the supply chain and could alter how the company does business. Therefore, the team does not disband once the project is completed. Clearly, there will not be the same level of engagement as there would be during the development stage. While there will not be the same level of activity, there is a need to have updates with the team on a regular basis depending on the nature of the solution and the nature of the business hypothesis.

Here are the roles that may be important to include in your hybrid team. Remember that the team members must be able to work in collaboration on an ongoing basis. In general, the following are necessary roles (described in Table 5.1):

- Business strategists and leaders
- Subject-matter experts
- Data scientists, data architects, and data owners

Table 5.1 Key Roles in the Causal AI Team

	Business Strategist/Leader	SME	Business Analyst	Data Scientist/Architect	Data Analyst	Software Developer	IT Expert	Project Manager
Understands	Business goals	Key processes in greater detail	Bridges between goals and specific use cases	Algorithms, libraries, models	Assesses data quality and quantity from appropriate sources	Creates algorithms and models using frameworks and uses DevOps pipeline	Current state of applications environment and helps to guide the team to integrate with existing data and applications	Holistic view of project and the overall goals of the project
Uses Causal AI	Sets key goals Evaluates key results	Defines variables and relationships	Takes recommended actions or decisions	Aligns models and data with causal libraries and selects algorithms	Evaluates and selects appropriate data sources	Creates code to support the goals of the causal AI application	Acts to help causal AI team put results in context with existing IP	Provides best practices guidance throughout the project

- Data analysts and database experts
- Software developers
- Business process analysts
- Information technology experts
- Project manager(s)

Leaders and Business Strategists

For a causal AI project to be successful, there needs to be a sponsor who is high enough in the organization with the clout and influence to ensure that there is funding and support for the goals of the project. Without this level of support, projects often fail. Once there is a sponsor, it will be important to have a business strategist as part of the hybrid team.

The business strategist can help scope the project based on the needs articulated by the management team. This is especially true in emerging technology areas where most of the business leaders do not understand what causal AI is and how it will benefit the company. The business strategist assigned to the team reports to the CEO helping to set overall business strategy and therefore has a deep understanding of the 5-year strategic plan for the business. For example, the plan calls for the company to have six supply chain partners within the coming year. Acting as part of the team, the business strategist will be able to have input into the model so that the team understands what variables are needed to create a model that reflects company goals. Keep in mind that the strategy will not be static. As new competitors enter a market and the business needs to adjust, the model itself will have to be modified to take the changes into account. The business strategist is typically someone who works with the CEO, who sets the overall business strategy and objectives. The business strategist sets the tone for the project and ensures that the solution reflects the goals of the project. It is important that the strategist stays engaged throughout the development process.

The finance leader will typically be assigned by the CFO to be a member of the team. This individual will understand the objectives of the project in terms of the revenue and expenses. The finance team member owns the project budget and can intervene if more funding is needed or if the project is going off in a direction that doesn't meet the project goals.

The CIO will oversee the operation of the technical team and how that team works with the subject-matter experts team. For example, the goal for the coming quarter may be to reduce machine failures by 30 percent to improve customer satisfaction. It is unlikely that the data scientist will automatically know about this goal.

Subject-Matter Experts

One of the reasons that some AI projects fail is because there isn't a connection between the subject area and the modeling that the data scientists undertake. Therefore, the role of the subject-matter expert team is critical because this group is instrumental in defining the scope and design of the causal AI model. Subject-matter experts are critical to the success or failure of a causal AI project. Since the SME team understands the details of the problem being addressed, they are well suited to collaborate with the business strategist to define the scope of the problem. In addition, the team has deep expertise in understanding the underlying data and how it supports the hypothesis. The SME team also knows which outside data sources can be instrumental in the resulting solution. Once testing begins, the team can help validate both the causal relationships and the underlying data and algorithms.

Working with the data scientists, SMEs help to determine what variables are the most critical in creating the causal model. Take the example of a manufacturing company that is experiencing problems with impurities that cause customers to return products. SMEs have knowledge of the key issues about the chemistry of the product production process. These experts understand all the issues related to temperature, humidity, and the characteristics of each chemical that is used to create a product. These SMEs will also have institutional memory of what has gone wrong in the past and how those problems were solved. For example, in a manufacturing company, SMEs understand the intricacies of how products are made and where there are issues that are creating problems.

There typically will not be a single subject-matter expert. Depending on the scope and scale of the project, there may be a leader who directs the subject-matter experts. This leader can then assign the right SMEs to work with the team as it moves through different stages of modeling. The team leader understands the relationship between aspects of the expertise that the business relies on to be successful. It is critical that the SMEs help define the variables and how they relate to each other. Once the model has been created, the SMEs can help validate the model and identify what is missing. For example, SMEs can identify a backdoor path that will cause problems. In addition, the SMEs provide ongoing feedback once data is added to the model. At this point in the process, SMEs can detect when the results are not accurate. The SMEs also help identify the data and the context of that information needed for the model. These professionals have a deep understanding of the data and will be aware of outside data sources that can help ensure that the causal AI model provides the most accurate results. Subject-matter experts will be able to identify bottlenecks in the model development process. This SME team can help design the hypothesis and then help to develop ways to test the hypothesis and validate the causal relationships between variables in the model.

The SME team has a vital role in providing guidance into what data should be collected. Most importantly, SMEs understand the underlying conditions that have caused problems in the first place. Typically, the SMEs can also identify and access specialized data sources and methods that are instrumental in designing a solution. The subject-matter expert is a valuable resource in creating a causal model, bringing their expertise and insights to the modeling process to help ensure that the model is accurate, meaningful, and useful.

Data Experts

While the SMEs understand the details of how the business works from a technical perspective, the data experts own the process of creating the models in collaboration with the rest of the causal team and making sense of the data. The term *data experts* includes the following professionals:

- Data scientists are specialists in interpreting complex data sets to identify patterns, trends, and insights.
- Data engineers build systems that collect, manage, and convert raw data into usable information for data scientists and business analysts to interpret.
- Data architects define policies and procedures for accessing corporate data.
- Data analysts review data to gain business insights from customer data.
- Business analysts work as a bridge between data experts and business leaders.

These experts must make sense of the data that already exists and the relationship between variables. They must be able to understand the flow and architecture of the data. There may be new types of data needed to support a new business strategy or to correct a persistent problem. The data experts bring more visibility to the data and will identify gaps in the data to ensure that once the model is populated with data that it produces the results the business is looking for.

While AI discussions focus on the role of the data scientist, not every company has data scientists on staff. For example, a 200-person company may not be able to afford to hire a data scientist. In some larger businesses, there may be too many data scientists with overlapping responsibilities. Rather than simply hiring a team of data scientists, it is more important to assign specific responsibilities rather than broad roles. Therefore, to be successful, there needs to be a balance between having the right mix of expertise to support business *and* technology goals. In some companies, there may be a high-level database architect or administrator or an overall data owner. This team may be responsible for the integrity of the data and the governance of that data. Is the existing data accurate, and does it reflect the changes in the business? Does the data conform to governmental and business security ethics and rules? Is the data secure? If required, are data privacy issues understood so individual personal data is protected? These data owners collaborate with both subject-matter experts and business leaders to identify new data sources and determine the best ways to leverage existing data to support business goals.

The data experts' role is to use their expertise in statistical analysis, machine learning, and data engineering and business strategy to design and implement causal models that can provide meaningful insights and predictions. These team members are responsible for collecting and cleaning the data, specifying and fitting the causal models, and interpreting and communicating the results to stakeholders. Additionally, they may also be involved in developing and improving the causal inference algorithms used in the project.

To be successful, the data scientists must gain a deep understanding of the problem that the overall hybrid team is tasked with solving. Too often data scientists prefer to focus only on the data that they assume will help build the models. Encouraging collaboration between SMEs and data scientists is not a trivial task.

Software Developers

Depending on the scope of the project and the size of the company, developers will be responsible for taking the algorithms and models that the data scientists design, writing code, and testing the results of the causal models. These developers must have a solid understanding of AI techniques, data structures, algorithms, and programming languages, as well as a deep understanding of the domain or problem area the AI is being applied to.

Software developers do not work in isolation; rather they are active participants in the hybrid team. This collaboration is significant because the development team must understand the goals of the project before it can focus on translating the cause and effect into code. They need to work closely with data scientists and domain experts to ensure that the AI is aligned with the project goals and is making accurate and meaningful causal inferences. Developers also will identify inconsistencies in the model and look to correct bottlenecks in the system. In collaboration with the data scientists and subject-matter experts, developers also are needed to test a hypothesis. Once the initial version of the application is developed and hydrated with data, the results are tested with other team members to see if the results match the expectations for the project. There is a continuous refinement of the application based on feedback from the hybrid team. The model will be improved. Variables may be added to better reflect project goals. Since developers are part of the hybrid team process, they can use their experience to create best practices for future projects.

Business Process Analysts

Business process analysts serve as a cross-functional team within the business. Typically, business process analysts understand how the organization operates and works with the management team and developers. This team helps optimize operations to get rid of bottlenecks that impact the efficiency of the organization. Therefore, the business process analysts already have a cross-functional role and so they are in a good position to bring a collaboration perspective to the causal AI team. They also can help mediate between the subject-matter experts and the data professionals. Business process experts will understand the impact of the new solution on the day-to-day operations of the business. Is the causal AI model aligned with the business's goals as articulated by the management team? How will the new solution impact existing business operations? These analysts are in a good position to have an overview of how other parts of the business can benefit from a causal AI approach. By having business process analysts as part of the team, they will gain insights and understanding of the value of causal AI. In their role as a go-between with management and IT, they can help identify strategic opportunities for a causal approach.

Information Technology Expertise

While the primary focus of causal AI is about modeling and data management, it is critical to manage the underlying technology platform. Therefore, there needs to be a team that understands the internal data services where mission-critical data is managed and secured. Managing internal resources requires that experts understand how to optimize storage and reduce redundancies. These experts have to carefully manage costs that can have a direct impact on the perceived value of the causal AI infrastructure. Information technology experts also provide guidance on where workloads need to be located. With the advent a decade ago of ubiquitous cloud computing services, it is becoming a requirement to use both compute and storage services. IT experts need to recommend which services should be managed internally and which capabilities should be hosted in a cloud service. Organizations need to have experts who understand how to manage a hybrid computing environment so that there is a balance between security and governance and managing costs.

Project Manager(s)

Establishing and managing complex causal AI projects requires project managers who can keep track of all the steps in the process. This is important because as we have shown in this chapter, to be successful, the hybrid team consists of many different professionals from across the company. Project managers will be tasked to understand all of the moving parts of a successful hybrid team. These leaders need to ensure that the team focuses on the business goals of the project and make sure that policies are followed. A key role of project managers is to keep the engine of the causal AI project operating well so that the goals of the project are met on time and within the allocated budget.

Before we turn to the issue involved in defining the problem(s) to be solved and creating models, let's take a high-level look at the process for a hybrid team project.

The Basics Steps for a Hybrid Team Project

Getting off to the right start is critical to the success or failure of the hybrid team. Remember, the goal of a causal AI project is to understand why a problem is happening and then determine how that problem can be addressed. Therefore, the project will be focused on cause, effect, and potential outcomes. The following are some suggested best practices:

- **Start with a strategic kickoff meeting:** The kickoff meeting sets the tone for the project. Therefore, it is critical to have the key stakeholders in this meeting including key members of the strategy team (the CEO if possible). The purpose of this meeting is to ensure that everyone is on the same page. For example, the CEO's goal is to reduce customer churn by 30 percent or to increase sales of new products to existing customers. Based on the business goals, the team leader describes the goals and objectives of the causal AI project. The goals will include the scope of the project as well as the budget limitations.

- **Defining the team goals:** After the kickoff meeting, the team gets to work. While the kickoff meeting presents the overview of the project, the initial team meetings focus on the opportunity and approach.

- **Target a project:** It is a mistake to try to rethink an entire market. Especially when a team is embarking on an early causal AI project, it is best to select one problem and focus on a smaller model that can be well understood by the hybrid team and senior management. The team needs to have a common view of the problem being addressed. Beginning with an exercise of creating a high-level causal model will ensure that the team has a common language to address the problem.

- **Define the hypothesis:** The goal of the causal AI project is to create a set of goals based on knowledge and experience of the business. Therefore, the hypothesis should be agreed upon by both the business and technical teams since it will be the basis for answering why a problem is happening, what the cause of the problem is, and how to approach an issue differently. A hypothesis in a causal AI project is a technique to make assumptions about the relationship between the cause and effect derived from data that is integrated into a causal AI model that has ingested the most appropriate data to address the problem. The hypothesis should be testable so that assumptions can be verified or rejected. The hypothesis shouldn't be overly broad since it needs to be targeted to a set of achievable goals.

- **Incrementally build the project:** In order for the model to reflect both the business and technical requirements, the team needs to take the time to iterate on the model. During development of the project, it may be necessary to add more data that better addresses the problem being solved. If your data isn't accurate for answering causal questions, remember that your analysis will not help your company solve problems. One of the benefits of a causal AI approach is that it allows the team to break down the algorithms into smaller chunks rather than creating one large model that is overly complex.

An Overview of Model Creation

Building complex AI applications requires a great deal of skill on the part of a team of data scientists and a lot of collaborative work by the hybrid team. In Chapter 7, we discuss a causal AI pipeline and walk through all the stages and iterations of the process, including techniques and tools. However, it is useful to consider the general steps in the causal AI process, including one for which the hybrid team is critical: defining and modeling the problem.

1. **Assess the current state of the business issue:** Before you begin the project, it is critical to understand the current problem that the organization is trying to solve. Using the marketing example, sales have been dropping, and you don't understand why. Therefore, you would begin by collecting as much data as possible about the current state of the business. How many customers are part of the business? How fast has the company grown in the past several quarters? Who are the major competitors, and how has the competitive environment changed? Are there products that are selling well? How effective have marketing campaigns been in the past, and what has changed? This assessment will help you identify where to start with your causal AI project. You want to focus on the area of the business that is a top concern for management. If you can understand why results are not as expected, you can have an impact on the future of a business area.

2. **Assemble the team:** Bringing together the right resources to solve a problem is critical to the success of your causal AI project. There will be permanent leaders who are part of the team. These leaders are critical to the success or failure of the process of creating the causal model. The permanent members include representatives who are tasked by the management team to represent the goals of the project—including sponsorship, business objectives, and financial oversight. Depending on the scope of the project, team leaders could be someone from sales or finance. In addition to the permanent team, there will be a group of experts who will be pulled into the project as needed. While these team members may have

a limited role, they must understand the goals and context of the project so when their expertise is needed, the team leaders do not have to first explain the project each time.

3. **Scope the project:** Once the project is scoped based on the key questions that management wants to understand to move forward with the business, the work begins in creating the overall framework. This process begins by having senior management present the business objective for the project. The most effective best practice is to break down the project into small achievable goals. It is a mistake to define the project too broadly. For example, management's overall objective may be to fix the sales process so that more prospects become customers. They also have a goal of upselling existing customers. This may be the most important problem management wants to solve, but creating a single project to tackle this complex issue will result in failure. The task is simply too complex. Another example would be a manufacturing company that wants to solve the problem of product defects in different aspects of the product creation process. There may be many different defects that the company needs to focus on. Trying to address all these problems with product quality at once will mean that it could take years to have anything to show for the effort and cost.

   The management team wants to see fast results that can have an immediate impact on outcomes. Therefore, focusing on an aspect of sales growth, for example, and creating a causal AI solution that can help make a difference in the short term is the best practice. One of the benefits of causal AI is that it enables the team to set an overall ambitious goal for a desired outcome but can create modular solutions that can be linked together over time.

   Beginning to get the work done requires a deep level of understanding or a holistic perspective on the problem. All this knowledge may not be part of an initial solution, but it is the foundation for having a full understanding of the business problem. For example, what is the competitive landscape like today, and how is it likely to change over the next 6–12 months? What is the history of sales over the past 3–5 years? Where has the company had its greatest success, and what has failed? What are customers reporting to the call center? Where are the bottlenecks in processes that are instrumental in supporting customers? In an industrial situation, what are the processes that are causing quality control problems resulting in product defects? Are competing companies having the same problems or have they found solutions? Is there a growing need in the market for the products that the company is manufacturing? If not, why? Are there new innovative technologies on the horizon that will impact the company's ability to compete? Having the resources (either internal or external) to answer these types of questions is the starting point for approaching a problem. It is critical to include the scope of the business issues that the company needs to understand. Having a holistic perspective on the industry and company is the starting point for modeling the problem.

4. **Model the problem:** The next stage begins when the team leadership in collaboration with management determines what the focus of the initial effort will be. The first project may be a pilot that helps to determine why a specific problem identified has happened and how to approach fixing it. The core team will work in collaboration with a combination of representatives of the management team, data scientists, database experts, subject-matter experts, etc. Together the team collaborates on designing the graphical model by selecting the key variables and understanding their causal strengths. This becomes an iterative process of testing, data integration, and analysis.

A common thread that runs throughout the process pertains to the problem the business wants to solve, which is the purpose of causal AI for a business organization.

It Depends on Your Destination

Understanding why a problem occurred is the common question at any organization whether you are talking about a business problem or a software development process. In the case of causal AI, it is the most important starting point. This quote from Lewis Carroll's *Alice in Wonderland* is a perfect explanation of the problem of not setting goals: "Would you tell me, please, which way I ought to go from here? That depends a good deal on where you want to get to," said the Cat.

At the heart of the causal AI approach is the definition of the hypothesis. The hypothesis is intended to set the objective for the problem you are trying to understand and solve. Why did a marketing campaign not increase sales by 20 percent from the previous quarter? The team had assumed that the problem was related to the reach of the campaign and the amount of money spent to market the product. But was this assumption accurate? It is not uncommon for a business to confirm their assumptions by selecting data that confirms their hypothesis, known as *confirmation bias*. You can always find some information that will support a hypothesis—especially if you remove the context for that data. For example, there may have been a study that indicated that in a particular market at a particular time sales increased when the amount of money spent on marketing was increased by 15 percent. This statistic was quoted by countless marketing organizations for years to support their hypothesis that spending more on marketing would improve sales dramatically. One of the benefits of a causality is that it requires the team to take a step back and challenge their assumptions and understanding of the business drivers before arriving at a hypothesis. Understanding what you don't know before you create the hypothesis will lead you to your model and counterfactual testing. The goal of bringing together the hybrid team is to get to the root cause of your problem to determine how to fix that problem.

Understanding the Root Cause of a Problem

Getting to the root cause of a problem requires understanding the relationship between variables. However, simply mapping all the variables is not going to get you to be able to answer why a problem has occurred. For example, there may be a causal relationship between marketing campaign emails sent and the number of bad email addresses; there is not a significant causal relationship between these two variables. Clearly, it would be better if email messages didn't bounce, but it is not the cause of poor revenue results.

How do you begin to understand why situations happen? You need to understand the causal strength of the variables in the models that you create. What are the relationships between variables? There may be a relationship between the amount of money spent on a marketing campaign and revenue. However, the underlying issue that determines revenue may, in fact, be that the product being sold is flawed and product returns are very high. If a team can determine the most important causal strength, then it is more obvious what actions need to be taken to improve the business.

The initial outcome of this modeling process is a causal graph or DAG that indicates all the variables and their relationships to outcomes, as shown in Figure 5.1. Because the model is visual, it provides a way for everyone on the team as well as company management to understand the findings. Figure 5.2 includes the same relationships shown in Figure 5.1 but also includes the weight or causal strength between variables. Causal strength is

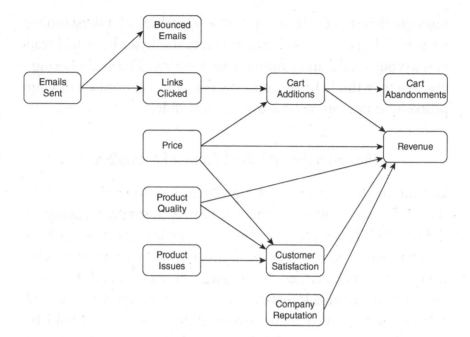

FIGURE 5.1 A basic causal model to determine the cause and effect of a market campaign on revenue growth

indicated by the numbers listed on the lines that connect variables. The closer the causal strength is to 1.0 or better, the more significant the causal strength is. Take, for example, there is a strong causal relationship between product quality and revenue. There is also a strong causal relationship between how a product is priced and revenue. In the example in Figure 5.2 the causal strength between emails sent and bounces has a causal strength of only 0.08. In contrast, the relationship between price and cart addition has a causal strength of 0.68—a strong correlation. In addition, customer satisfaction has a causal strength of 0.63. The higher the number, the more likely that these relationships between variables will provide the team with a direction to figure out why problems occur and where to put their attention. Behind the graphical diagram are complex libraries and data that has calculated the causal strength.

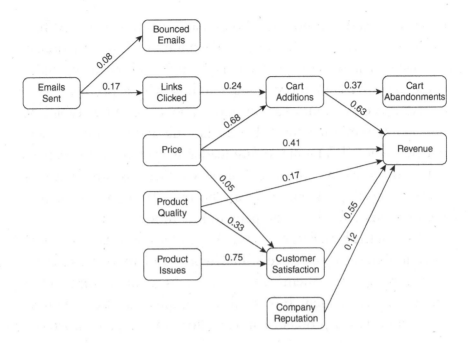

FIGURE 5.2 An indication of the causal strengths of variable relationships in a causal model

Understanding What Happened and Why

In this stage, your hybrid team has designed a model based on the hypothesis for solving the business problem that needs to be solved. At this point, the hybrid team will determine which data is the most appropriate to test the hypothesis. You are not ingesting a massive amount of data at this stage. Rather, you need to ingest just enough data to ensure that you are including the right data sources and that your hypothesis makes sense. Take the example of a mobile phone company that is experiencing a higher than expected churn rate. Typically, the churn rate has been 10 percent, and suddenly the rate has jumped to 30 percent in a single quarter. In the traditional approach, analysis would show results such as how many customers from which regions ended their contracts. The analysis would also indicate the prices that customers paid and how long they had been customers. While this information provides some understanding of the situation, it doesn't explain why the problem happened and how the problem could be solved. Without understanding why a problem happened, it is easy to make assumptions about the cause. Typically, management might assume that the last marketing campaign was poorly executed. The marketing leader as well as each constituent involved in solving the problem will likely assume that it is someone else's problem. After all, no one wants to believe that their actions caused the company to lose money.

One of the benefits of a causal AI approach is to take the politics out of the analysis process. The hybrid team represents a cross section of the constituents who are relevant to understanding the context of the problem. It is not always simple to answer the question about why a problem happens. For example, a competitive analysis team may have important information about changes in the competitive landscape. Is there new data about an overall dip in sales of mobile phones? Are there new vendors in the market that are providing more sophisticated offerings that are more attractive to a category of customers? Are vendors in the market beginning to sell products in a new innovative way that is more attractive to new customers? All this information is critical to modeling a problem. In some cases, there may not be detailed data that can be ingested into a model. The results of a model generated only from that data may be skewed since information about new product offerings will not be considered. More detailed data will be necessary. Sometimes this will involve using synthetic data in the model, discussed in detail in Chapter 7.

The Importance of the Iterative Process

The process of creating and implementing a causal AI model is not a one-step endeavor. Rather, it involves an iterative process involving team members throughout the organization. While the data scientist will create a complicated DAG supported by underlying code, the data scientist will work collaboratively with subject-matter experts to refine the model based on input. Likewise, business leaders will iteratively provide the changing context of business problems that need to be solved. The work of the hybrid team is an iterative process that continues after the model is designed. As we will discuss in Chapter 7, there is a continuous development, testing, and refinement process as the business evolves and changes.

Refer to Chapter 4 for more details on the overall process view. Chapter 7 will be a good source for understanding the details on creating a development pipeline and how data should be managed in this context. In Chapter 8, we will provide a general look at some case studies indicating how an organization can approach building causal AI applications.

Summary

One of the key requirements for a causal AI model is that it reflects the need to understand why a problem has occurred and how to address it. Therefore, the process of building a model requires a team consisting of the key constituents that can collectively get to the heart of why a problem is happening and how to begin to address a solution. One of the key benefits of the causal AI approach is that it begins by identifying and understanding the problem that the model is designed to solve. The modeling process provides a common language so that the team can understand what it means to solve problems based on understanding the root cause of a problem rather than making assumptions about why problems happen. In the subsequent chapters, we will discuss and provide insights into the types of available tools, from modeling to adding the libraries and tools to move from a model to a completed application. We will also provide a critical understanding of what it means to have explainability and bias detection. But before beginning to integrate data and various tools into the model, you have to start with the right team to ensure that you are answering why problems are happening and how to solve them.

6

Explainability, Bias Detection, and AI Responsibility in Causal AI

In this chapter, we will focus on the critical AI issues of being able to explain what a model is doing and detecting problems such as bias. Given the far-reaching and increasing implications of causal AI and AI generally, it is critical that what the systems are doing, and why, is understandable. If models are difficult to understand, they cannot be trusted. In addition to being able to understand what these systems are doing and why, businesses also must be able to demonstrate that the results are unbiased, responsible, and fair. The importance of these issues will only increase as time goes on.

Explainability

Google Trends shows that interest in the term *explainable AI* increased from a popularity index of 0 in February 2011 to the highest level of 100 in February 2020 (and remained at 88 as of March 2023). Therefore, it is no wonder that understanding AI-based models is growing in importance. How do machine learning (ML) models make decisions, and can they be trusted, or are they biased? One of the biggest problems facing businesses is that managers are increasingly relying on AI systems to automate decision-making. Some of the decisions are straightforward, such as the loan applicant's income and whether they have provided proof of ownership. However, many of the decisions that these AI applications are making include complex algorithms and data. The ability to understand how decisions are made and then being able to defend those decisions is critical to the success or failure of AI applications. Figure 6.1 captures the essence of explainability.

Explainability requires an understanding of
data, variables, and algorithms

Data:
Do you have enough
of the right data to
train your model?

Predictions:
What are the
relationships
between
variables?

Algorithms:
How does the
algorithm predict
outcomes?

FIGURE 6.1 Explainability requires an understanding of the data, modeling relationships between variables, and selecting the appropriate algorithms.

Let's start our discussion by further considering the importance of explainable AI and the ramifications when it is lacking.

The Ramifications of the Lack of Explainability

To be successful, the system must be able to demonstrate how the underlying model behaves and how it reaches its conclusions, and failing to do so undermines trust, transparency, and confidence. Explainability is the ability of an artificial intelligence system to provide the ability to understand and interpret insights into its decision-making process. Well-designed AI systems must be able to foster trust, transparency, and user confidence.

The bottom line is that explainability must be able to meet the requirements of the people who are paying the bills for the project to be developed. There can be serious ramifications when a solution impacts the integrity of the business's reputation. One of the biggest obstacles facing organizations creating traditional AI-based applications is that data scientists do not pay enough attention to creating solutions that can be understood by humans. This is one reason why a hybrid team can be so valuable; it brings a wider and deeper range of perspectives to model planning. Once the application is in wide use, it will be too late to go back and build explainability into the model.

What does the ability to explain the actions of an AI solution mean in the real world? Once the application is in use, management will often be faced with demands from governmental bodies to prove the validity of the code and from customers who want to make sure that decisions are not biased. If a business is unable to verify and defend the code it has developed, it will be unable to meet the demands to explain its actions, and it can face loss of trust, regulation violations, fines, additional system development costs, or other financial issues. There have been situations, for example, where companies have been sued when an individual is denied a loan because of a decision made by an AI application. Here are a few additional examples that indicate the depth of the issue:

- Imagine that an individual is rejected from receiving a mortgage. Why was that decision made? Did the individual have a bad credit rating or owe back taxes? Or was the application rejected because of the address of the property being purchased? Did the AI solution discriminate against people who live in a particular neighborhood? Perhaps when the AI application was written, the property was in an area deemed to be dangerous. However, over the past 5 years, the neighborhood was enhanced so that property values increased, but the data in the model has not been updated.

- In another situation, an advanced AI solution used by doctors to analyze the results of image scans identifies a dark spot on a patient's lung. While the AI system did identify the spot, it concluded based on ingested data that there was no cause for alarm. However, in fact, the patient did have the beginnings of a disease, which could have been detected early.

In either case, does the user of that application understand what is happening and how the system arrives at decisions and recommendations? Is the AI application viewed as the decision-maker, or is it a tool to support the professional? The key requirements for a sophisticated AI application are that it be explainable, free of bias, and responsible. Achieving these goals is complicated. However, one of the benefits of causal AI and the reason that there is so much interest in this approach is that these models and underlying approaches are intended to help users create solutions that are explainable and can detect bias in data. These requirements for oversight of applications are a demand not just for management, which is held responsible for defending decisions, but also to meet governmental regulatory requirements.

What Is Explainable AI in Causal AI Models?

The goal of explainable AI is to justify the conclusions and recommendations from models. Explainability is the concept that an ML model and its results can be understood so they make sense to a human. Therefore, explainability broadly requires the ability to understand how the model comes to its conclusions and provides an analysis of the results provided by the ML models. Explainable AI is intended to make systems more transparent, interpretable, and responsible. In other words, how do you verify the decisions and actions of an ML system? The need for explainability is not only an issue for system developers but also a requirement for many government regulators and a business's corporate governance requirements to explain business decisions.

- Is the decision obvious, or are there shades of gray?
- Is all the information current and circumstances accounted for?
- Was the AI system designed to take nuances and human situations into account?
- What was the source of the data, and who selected those sources?
- Is the data clean and well vetted?
- Does the application take into account that if a person has improved their credit rating over a period of time, they should not be rejected?

- What about the situation where an AI system is evaluating the results of a lung scan? Is the spot on the lung cancerous? If so, what type of cancer is it, or is the spot an indication of something else?

Clearly, when using an AI tool as the first line of defense for interpreting a scan, it cannot be the final decision-maker. It is simply not explainable. One of the key reasons that these types of sophisticated applications are problematic is that they are typically built as black boxes based on a variety of techniques including neural networks and support vector machines.

Black Boxes

The primary AI technique employed by data scientists is to develop models from data. These models are powerful and valuable in various situations, particularly when the use case is well-defined. However, one challenge associated with these models is the lack of transparency, which makes it difficult to understand how the model arrives at its results or predictions. The complexity of these AI models makes it difficult to explain their decision-making process. This lack of transparency raises concerns about accountability and bias.

Internal Workings of Black-Box Models   A black box in AI is a type of ML model where the input and output are visible, but the internal operations and decision-making processes are difficult to understand. In fact, the term *black box* refers to the fact that the internal workings of the model are not transparent or perhaps even easily interpretable. However, these applications are incredibly powerful because of the following characteristics:

- They can capture intricate patterns and relationships in large data sets; therefore, they can make highly accurate predictions or classifications. They are often effectively used in computer vision and speech recognition applications.

- These models can learn from vast amounts of data and adapt to changing patterns in the data. Therefore, they are often used to solve complex mathematical problems.

- Black-box models are architected to scale to handle large data sets and high-dimensional feature spaces.

Deep Learning at the Heart of Black Boxes　Typically, a black-box model for causal AI applications begins by ingesting a large data set and then training an algorithm to make predictions and classifications based on learning the patterns and relationships from that data. Because of the model's lack of transparency, however, its outputs can be difficult to understand or explain, and it may not be clear how the model arrived at its conclusions. Many advanced ML techniques such as deep learning are created by adding multiple layers of processing and numerous associated nodes. While a deep learning approach is extremely powerful, there is a limit on being able to detect errors or biases in how the model makes its predictions. Even if one has a list of the input variables, black-box predictive models can be such complicated functions of the variables that no human can understand how the variables are jointly related to each other to reach a final prediction.

Is Code Understandable?　The primary reason why causal AI has generated so much excitement is because the solutions are designed to help organizations understand the cause of an issue,

When It Is Appropriate to Use Black Boxes

Despite these problems with black-box approaches, they are widely used for addressing certain problems. These models are often used for computer vision applications, analyzing genomic data, and credit fraud. However, while there are issues of explainability with black boxes, it is important to recognize the most prevalent models are used by data scientists for developing models. These are some of the most important black-box models:

- Neural networks are ML algorithms that are designed to mimic the function of the biological neural networks in the human brain. Like the brain, these algorithms are composed of layers of interconnected nodes (what you would call neurons in the brain). There are three types of layers: an input layer, an output layer, and hidden layers. Together, these nodes interact with each other to analyze and process complex data to make decisions based on that data. At each of these layers, tasks are executed to perform calculations on the data input. Each layer fits its results to the next layer, and the results are sent to the output layer to offer a decision or conclusion. Neural networks are widely used in natural language processing and computer vision applications where continuous learning from massive amounts of data can provide refined accurate results. Neural networks are widely used to identify patterns in handwriting and facial recognition, predict network errors, and detect credit card fraud.
- Support vector machines are typically used for linear and nonlinear classification and regression problems.

(*continued*)

(*continued*)

They are particularly useful when dealing with highly complex and multidimensional data where there is a need to identify the "hyperplane" or decision boundary separating the different classes in the data space. An important real-world example of SVM usage is bioinformatics used in drug discovery practices. In this example, SVMs are a key technique used to gain an understanding of how a patient will respond to a specific drug to treat an illness. While these techniques are relatively easy for data scientists to use, they are difficult to explain how the ML model arrives at its predictions.

- Random forests and gradient boost machines are both techniques for combining decision trees to make predictions because they can handle large data sets. While they are useful in predicting customer behavior and detecting fraud, it is difficult to understand what the models are doing, like with SVMs.

its effect, and potential solutions. For this reason, it is imperative that these causal solutions be explainable. What does it mean for an AI application to be explainable? As we have shown in Chapters 3 and 4, the graphical causal model and underlying SCM mathematics are designed to be readable and more easily understood by both data scientists, subject-matter experts, and business leaders. There are many tools and libraries that are designed to make creating causal AI applications easier and more approachable. Unlike a neural network, for example, a causal AI solution begins by creating a graphical model that defines the problem being addressed. The model itself visually presents variables, their relationships, and their causal strengths. Because these graphs are highly visual, it is much easier for the team to understand what the model is designed to do. Of course, there are situations where the graph can be incredibly complex and may take some work before truly understanding how conclusions were achieved.

On the other hand, code generated by a neural network cannot be easily interpreted since it is composed of nodes designed in layers, including many that are hidden. Unlike causal AI applications that are intended to explain and understand why events happened, a neural network may be best used for a different type of application. Despite the obvious power of black-box techniques such as neural networks, support vector machines, and random forests, it is almost impossible to explain in business language how the black-box model works without significant and precise training data. The data scientist steeped in these methods understands the approach and has confidence based on previous successful projects. One of the potential risks of this black-box approach is that if the developers anticipate the results that they expect, they may inadvertently select data that will result in the predicted outcome.

For example, creating a natural language processing application is well suited to the complexity of the neural network because this approach is useful for interpreting languages that have complex cadence and structure. Being able to predict weather with a neural network is more reliable because neural networks are adept at processing and analyzing time-series data.

The Value of White-Box Models

Causal models contain a transparent qualitative component that describes all cause-and-effect relationships in the data, so there are no problems of trust. Explanations are always faithful to the model. Causal models don't require another model to approximate them. One of the key advantages of causal AI is that it combines ML techniques with graphical modeling and subject-matter expertise in support of explainability. Being successful with AI requires that the designers and builders of these systems can justify the results of the analytics.

There are several approaches to achieving explainability in causal AI, including the following:

- **Graphical models:** Graphical models such as Bayesian networks and directed acyclic graphs provide a visual representation of the causal relationships between variables, which can help to explain the model's predictions.

- **Counterfactual analysis:** Counterfactual analysis involves examining what would happen if one or more variables were changed, which can help to identify the causal relationships between variables and explain the model's predictions.

- **Model interpretation techniques:** Model interpretation techniques such as feature importance analysis, partial dependence plots, and permutation feature importance can help to explain the model's predictions by identifying the most important variables and their effects on the outcome.

- **Human-readable output:** Finally, presenting the model's output in a human-readable format, such as natural language or visualizations, can help to explain the model's predictions in a way that is understandable to nonexperts. This is often referred to as *intrinsic interpretability*.

Understanding Causal AI Code

What does it mean to have explainability in code? Creating a casual AI model, as we have discussed in earlier chapters, begins with a graphical model that defines variables and functions and how they are related. The model has been created by a team of both data scientists and subject-matter experts. Once the graphical model is complete, it is used as the foundation for the underlying code. One of the important breakthroughs in explainability is the development of Python libraries. The benefit of these libraries is that they result in code that is readable. Once the code has been tested with data, the team will be able to determine if, in fact, the model is producing results that match the goals of the project.

After the design has been created and tested, the data scientists will often use algorithms in the popular Python-based language library known as Do-Calculus to estimate the causal effects of interventions. Do-calculus, a set of rules and methods developed by Judea Pearl, uses a specific technique designed to understand the causal effects from data. The benefit of Do-Calculus is that it enables the system to exclude spurious correlations by eliminating confounding through backdoor criterion. A confounder in this context can result in an AI system making a decision based on a false assumption, which could lead to a biased or unfair outcome. Do-Calculus has given rise to a library called DoWhy, developed by Microsoft and contributed as open-source through GitHub. In 2022, Microsoft and Amazon established a new GitHub organization known as PyWhy, which incorporates DoWhy and other libraries developed by Amazon Research. DoWhy has become one of the most popular Python libraries because of its ability to identify the effects of interventions on outcomes. These libraries can also estimate counterfactuals. One of the most important benefits of these libraries is that they can be useful in understanding the root cause of problems. Understanding the root cause of problems is extremely valuable in understanding issues such as network or supply chain failures.

Techniques for Achieving Explainability

Explainabililty is emerging as one of the most important issues facing IT and business leaders as AI becomes a core business resource. Increasingly, as more applications use the power of AI, more questions are being asked. For example, there was a case where job applicants' video interviews were analyzed by an AI application to determine whether the prospect was trustworthy. An applicant who was turned down after his interview sued the company. How was the company using the AI application able to justify the decision? In this section, we will discuss the complexity involved in explainability.

Achieving explainability requires a variety of approaches and techniques. The approaches will depend on the complexity of the system. No matter what machine learning techniques are being used, the goal is the same: to understand the conclusions of the underlying code. The goal of any technique is to avoid bias and ensure fairness.

Challenges of Complex Causal Models   If you have a DAG that has been well tested and that DAG encodes a system to accurately describe dependencies, relationships, and information flow, you already have explainability. While causal AI can have a profound impact on being able to understand what is happening inside a model, there still may be complexities involved. There can be a number of technical reasons why it is hard to explain a model. Therefore, it may be difficult to understand what is causing complications in the model. For example, there may be *noise variables* that cause problems. A noise variable is a random factor that is not relevant to the focus of the question being addressed. It has the potential to obscure the relationship between the main variables of interest or introduce uncertainty into the analysis.

In some cases, it may be challenging for a team to develop a meaningful DAG. Which variables should be included? There may not be enough data in the model. The model may simply not have been designed to capture some very complex interactions. One of the most obvious problems is the complexity of the model itself. A DAG that consists of 100 variables may be relatively easy to explain. However, if the DAG consists of thousands of variables with a huge number of relationships, it becomes much more difficult to understand. The other key problem with explainability is that the data incorporated into the model may be highly dimensional so that it will be difficult to identify the most important features and how they are related to each other. If the DAG causal structure and the SCM quantitative math that detail the causal relationships are too complex, it will be difficult to interpret the causal relationships.

When there is this much complexity in a model, it is inevitable that the developers will have to make compromises. There are numerous situations when a model is very complex. To ensure that the model is explainable, developers may have to make trade-offs. Therefore, it may be necessary to simplify the model itself. Another approach would require the developer to create a series of smaller models that can be combined at a later time. There is no easy answer when a model is overly complex. Developers have to determine what trade-offs are most appropriate so they can get the job done without sacrificing accuracy. For example, let's say you are trying to determine if you should fire half of your sales force. If that happened, what would be the impact on revenue? The answer may not be simple to determine. You may have a large organization with many internal processes that impact revenue. So that instead of creating a DAG with 200 variables, a complex model may include several thousand variables defining relationships and strengths. In fact, there may be so many variables that are needed to understand the relationship between sales and revenue. One solution may be to break the model into explainable stages so that you can have a better understanding of causal relationships. The reality is that there is no one universal answer to achieving explainability. In the real world, you will have to find compromises to gain as much insight as possible.

Methods for Understanding and Explaining Complex Causal AI Models   The more complex the model is, the greater the need to compromise about how to achieve explainability. Therefore, it is not surprising that it is difficult for the data scientist to explain to the business precisely what is happening inside the model so that decisions can be defended. There are several methods and tools that have been developed to address the problem. There is no single approach that perfectly addresses the issue. It is important to understand that there are methods available to address explainability, and each has strengths and weaknesses.

The most popular model is called SHapley Additive exPlanations (SHAP). Before we discuss the SHAP method, the following is a list of other well-known methods that you might run into that can be used in specialized situations:

- Local Interpretable Model-agnostic Explanations (LIME) focuses on explaining individual predictions.

- Partial Dependence Plots (PDP) shows the relationship between a feature and the predicted outcome.

- Individual Conditional Expectation (ICE) plots visualize the relationship between a feature and the predicted outcome for individual instances.

- Rule-based explanations generate a set of rules that describe the relationship between input features and the model's predictions.

- Counterfactual explanations provide instances where a small change in the input features would result in a different prediction.

The Importance of the SHAP Explainability Method As you can see from the preceding list, there are many methods for helping to understand how a model arrives at its conclusions. Explainable AI doesn't necessarily imply causality. Rather, it explains why predictions were made. When a model is extremely complex, the ability to explain what is happening inside the model is limited. SHAP stands out as one of the most helpful methods. It is a method for interpreting the output of ML models that was developed based on game theory. It is considered more stable than some of the other methods listed. SHAP values are used to determine how much each feature in a model contributes to the final result through the process of measuring the difference in outcomes if a feature is included or removed. This helps the data team better understand the effect that a feature has on explaining outcomes.

By breaking down the prediction into the contributions of individual features, SHAP values offer insights into how the model is making its decisions and which features are most important in determining the outcome for a specific instance. This information can be helpful for understanding the model's behavior, improving its performance, and ensuring fairness and transparency in decision-making processes.

SHAP values are used to explain the output of a model by attributing each feature's contribution to the prediction for a specific instance. SHAP values can help in understanding how different features influence the model's prediction and provide insights into the inner workings of complex models, such as ensemble models, deep learning models, and more. In addition, SHAP can handle counterfactuals so that it is possible to understand the impact of a change in assumptions.

By using SHAP values, one can obtain a more transparent and interpretable understanding of the model's behavior, which can be crucial in applications where interpretability is as important as accuracy. SHAP values can be computed using various libraries in Python, such as the SHAP library (https://github .com/slundberg/shap), which provides tools for explaining the output of popular ML frameworks like scikit-learn, XGBoost, and TensorFlow.

The Shapley value and the Shapley model can be used in causal models to provide explainability and interpretability. Specifically, the Shapley model provides a way to estimate the contribution of each input feature to the causal effect of an intervention, by considering all possible combinations of features and calculating the marginal contribution of each feature to the causal effect.

DARPA's XAI Research Project

According to the U.S. government's Defense Advanced Research Projects Agency (DARPA), "XAI is one of a handful of current DARPA programs expected to enable 'third-wave AI systems,' where machines understand the context and environment in which they operate, and over time build underlying explanatory models that allow them to characterize real world phenomena."[1] This agency's mandate is to develop technologies that could be important for

(continued)

(*continued*)

military uses. Therefore, it is not surprising that DARPA would be extremely interested in explainable AI. Imagine that the military could deploy an AI model that could operate and execute specific instructions and then be able to explain what and why it is undertaking an action in the real world. Therefore, the focus of the program is on both classification and reinforcement learning. The program's goal is to create a ML library that can be used to create a trustworthy autonomous system "to perform a variety of simulated missions" and "modules that could be used to develop future explainable AI systems." Once fully tested and vetted, the toolkit will be made available for commercial applications.

The Pivotal Role of Graphical Processing Units

Clearly, we are experiencing a renaissance in the speed of development in all types of AI applications ranging from deep learning to causal AI. This impressive acceleration is due to technical advances in network performance, cloud services, and the advent of graphical processing units (GPUs). GPUs were first developed in the 1990s as specialized processors intended to handle the processing demands of 3D graphics for other visually intensive applications. GPUs can perform parallel computations efficiently so that they have become an essential tool as the complexity of AI applications has increased. GPUs have a higher memory bandwidth compared to traditional CPUs.

(*continued*)

(continued)

Therefore, GPUs have become an essential tool for improving the performance of causal models that require intensive computations for learning the structure and parameters. GPUs can speed up these calculations, making it feasible to work with larger and more complex models. For example, GPUs can be highly effective in running counterfactual simulations to determine options for determining the cause of a problem. GPUs also speed up the important training process for the increased volume of data needed to accurately predict outcomes from models. In some ways, GPUs are even more important for causal AI than for deep learning as they help accelerate processing the levels of complexity toward understanding why situations occur. For example, if a correlation analysis indicates that in people with cancer, there appears to be a correlation between about 100,000 people in the data who also have diabetes. Is this correlation significant? Is there a causal relationship between cancer and diabetes? Taking advantage of the processing power of GPUs can help determine if the correlation is relevant to treatment.

Detecting Bias and Ensuring Responsible AI

Going hand in hand with explainability is the ability to detect when the results are biased. While the model may be created so that it can be explained, it may not accurately capture the correct outcome and relationships between variables. This bias can happen if the wrong features are included or if the data selected for the model is inaccurate. There could be a situation where the model is trained on too small a data sample that leaves out a demographic or a location that could be important in understanding outcomes. A biased model will result in conclusions that are unfair and even unethical.

Bias in Causal AI Systems

There are many startling examples about how an AI system made mistakes because the wrong data was selected to train the model. For example, imagine a system designed to select applicants to be interviewed for a job. The business wants to ensure that the application selects candidates who would fit well into the company's culture and skills required for the job. The developers used data from the previous 10 years of hiring based on which employees were most successful. While this may sound like a reasonable approach, is there a better method or additional data that might be used for selecting the types of candidates who will be successful employees? It is entirely possible that the results would be biased by the selected data or time period. What type of employees were hired 10 years earlier? If the data was dominated by a particular gender, age, race, etc., it is unlikely to produce a diverse set of candidates. Was the application designed to be biased? Probably not. Rather, the data fed into the model did not reflect the needs of the company and the diversity of applications that would be needed. You must understand the nature of the data that you have and the data that is missing. Missing data also can be a huge source of bias.

Even if the data sources accurately identify job requirements so that the models are trained to identify the skills and aptitude of candidates, other requirements should be included in the training cycle. There are situations where governance should be one of the up-front requirements in building models and ingesting data. Therefore, as with any major development project, it is important to build the requirements for bias detection and fairness into the design. To ensure that the causal model meets the need to reveal the underlying mechanisms, it must be driven by observations rather than simply correlation-based predictions. Governance requires a precise model that is unbiased and clearly understood. Organizations can cause harm to their business if their models do not reflect reality.

Regulating a Causal AI Solution

Increasingly, regulatory organizations will want to understand how your business makes decisions. As AI solutions become more mainstream, it is important to be prepared to explain your causal AI solutions so that they are accurate, fair, and responsible. What are the key factors that you need to consider? The primary goal of a well-designed causal AI system is to answer the driving questions about why events happen and what treatments are available to fix problems. But before you can put one of these powerful solutions into action, you need to be prepared to understand the legal and regulatory requirements to protect sensitive data. The following is a useful checklist to understand what you need to know to be prepared:

- How robust are your internal systems to handle data cleanliness? Is your data accurate? What is the source of the data, and is that data stored?
- Where are the models running? Is there integration with legacy applications?
- How are you using customer/patient data? Have you protected the privacy of sensitive data? Do you have customers' consent? Are privacy regulations applied?

(continued)

(*continued*)

- Are all the ML models and algorithms validated? Are the decisions being made by the models accurate and verified by subject-matter experts?
- Is the data ingested by the model fair and unbiased?
- Do you have a risk management strategy and plan in place to act if there is a bad outcome?

Responsible AI: Trust and Fairness

With all the astonishing developments of AI over the past decade, it is not surprising that our attention will begin to focus on the way in which organization can use this technology responsibly. As we discussed earlier in this chapter, many of the most popular AI models are designed as black boxes that cannot be easily interpreted. One of the reasons for the increased interest in explainable AI is to improve the ability of humans to trust these powerful solutions. The problem is getting increasingly complicated with the advent of large language models (LLMs) like Generative Pre-trained Transformer (ChatGPT) developed by a company called OpenAI. Like many black-box technologies, ChatGPT and other generative AI models use deep learning algorithms to generate text, write computer code, perform textual analysis—among other applications. These generative AI solutions are being developed at a rapid pace from a variety of companies including Google, IBM, and Microsoft (which has licensed ChatGPT from OpenAI). The fear among humans is that we could rely on these generative AI programs to make decisions and take actions without knowing how decisions are made. Because these are emerging technologies, there have been some examples where these programs make up results that are false if they don't have the information to provide a correct answer. No wonder there is an outpouring of interest in responsible AI.

While we can all agree that AI should be responsible, ethical, and fair, it is not an easy problem to solve. To be effective, responsible AI must be addressed at all stages of the development and deployment levels. During data collection, it is critical that both data scientists and subject-matter experts ensure that the data sources are clean, well vetted, and unbiased. If an organization is using a neural network, it will be susceptible to bias if there isn't sufficient attention paid to the quality of the data. Applications such as facial recognition or generative AI are potential sources of bias. A common use of neural networks is for facial or voice recognition. They operate by detecting and learning from patterns and relationships in the data. Based on their analysis, these applications make predictions. For example, if the neural network is trained primarily on images of light-skinned people, a "demographic bias" can emerge. The model may inadvertently misidentify darker-skinned individuals. Likewise, a model may be trained on voices from certain regions and will reject voices from regions with different accents.

The problem with bias and fairness is closely tied to the problems of understanding context and our own expectations. For example, when we see a picture of a brown squirrel, we would describe it simply as a squirrel. However, if we see a red squirrel, we are likely to focus on the color because this is out of context for what we have experienced in our world. Therefore, you could say that we have a bias toward squirrels with a brown color. But if you come from a region where all squirrels are red, you would have a different view. This simplification can be useful because it helps us organize and understand complex information. However, this simplification can also create stereotypes. One of the most popular examples of bias is "When one hears hoofbeats, one thinks horses, not zebras." Correctly implementing bias detection and fairness will reduce the stereotypical generation of output.

When we label something, we are assigning it to a specific group based on certain features or characteristics. This can be helpful in many cases because it allows us to make quick and efficient decisions. However, sometimes the features of a particular label can be confounding or misleading. While the data would include more current hiring data, the results would be skewed and therefore biased.

One very troubling example of bias occurring is in face recognition ML models. When training these models, it has been demonstrated that the algorithms tend to not recognize, or misidentify, female or darker-skinned faces. In another experiment involving systems trained with images that is often cited, an algorithm is trained on pictures of spices. The spice rack from a typical cabinet in a Western country was quickly identified as being spices and seasoning. In contrast, when the algorithm was shown an image of spices from an Asian country, it labeled them as bottles or drinks—no mention of spices. There was clearly a bias. The problem was that the model used was not developed with a diversity of data. ML algorithms, for example, can be trained to recognize patterns and categorize information based on certain attributes. However, if the features that are used to make decisions are biased or incomplete, the decisions made by the machine can also be biased or incomplete.

How Causal AI Addresses Bias Detection

Because DAGs in causal AI are designed to provide transparency, it is much easier for developers and subject-matter experts to collaborate on modeling and understanding the relationships between variables. There are five specific ways that causal AI helps organizations detect bias before it impacts outcomes:

- The ability to focus on outcomes and then produce a model that understands cause and effect relationships can minimize the appearance of bias. Once the variables and their relationships are provided in the graph, data can be added and tested to see if the hypothesis is supported by the data. This approach can more easily detect bias and remove it from the model.

- Unlike traditional AI models that rely on correlations, causal AI is focused on understanding cause-and-effect relationships, which can be critical in minimizing bias. One of the characteristics of a DAG is that it can simulate alternative scenarios by applying counterfactual reasoning. This type of reasoning can determine what the impact of a policy or intervention might be. Will taking one action have a different outcome than anticipated? Identifying these problems early will help create policies and approaches that help avoid bias.

- Causal AI models are explainable. Unlike black-box models, it is much easier to determine what is happening inside the model.

- DAGs are designed to identify confounding variables that typically introduce bias. If a confounding variable is detected, it can be removed before it causes bias when it estimates a causal effect.

- One of the strengths of a DAG is that it is designed with the objective of determining interventions that will avoid the causes of bias. Therefore, casual AI models are designed that fairness is what of the characteristics of a model. Therefore, a well-designed model will include ways to test for robustness of the data and iteratively improve accuracy and remove bias.

Tools for Assessing Fairness and Bias

Assessing fairness and detecting bias in AI systems of all kinds are not simple tasks, but there are some tools and techniques available that are intended to help. The focus on many of these tools and frameworks is to improve fairness, accountability, and transparency.

It is important to be able to test for bias in a solution. Is there a confounding factor that will cause a model to be inaccurate? For example, looking at the causal relationship between heart attacks, age is a confounder. An older individual who has other underlying conditions and has been smoking for many years will be more likely to have a heart attack than a young healthy person who has been smoking for only a few years. Testing for confounders through sensitivity analysis is one way to determine if there is a bias in the model.

While there are no tools that have been designed specifically to address bias detection and fairness, there are several tools that can be helpful in detecting issues. Most of these are well-known open-source tools:

- AI Fairness 360 (AIF360) was developed by IBM and has become an open-source library. It includes a comprehensive set of fairness metrics and algorithms to detect and mitigate bias in data sets and AI models. (See https://github.com/IBM/AIF360.)

- Fairlearn is an open-source Python library that includes a visualization tool that provides fairness metrics and mitigation algorithms. (See https://fairlearn.github.io.)

- What-If Tool (WIT) is another open source tool that Google developed. It incorporates an interactive visual interface for exploring and analyzing ML models that allows users to investigate model performance and fairness. It also performs counterfactual analysis and can compare models. (See https://pair-code.github.io/what-if-tool.)

- SHapley Additive exPlanations (SHAP) is an open-source tool primarily used for explainability, as we saw earlier, but also is able to identify potential biases in the data or in the model. (See https://github.com/slundberg/shap.)

- Local Interpretable Model-agnostic Explanations (LIME) is an open-source Python library that helps detect biases in the model's decision-making process. (See https://github.com/marcotcr/lime.)

- TensorFlow Model Remediation is a TensorFlow library that assists developers with a technique called MinDiff that is designed to reduce unfairness in a model without requiring that the model be changed. (See https://github.com/tensorflow/model-remediation.)

The Human Factor in Bias Detection and Responsible AI

How much can we trust AI to make accurate, well-understood, and trusted conclusions so we can take actions? The original concept of "artificial intelligence" was to imagine a world where a machine would be able to have the intelligence of a person to reason and think. However, although the market for smart machine learning machines has made huge strides, these machines can't think. This is the overriding reason that humans must be in the loop to bring context into decision-making. Having an AI-based solution that can be trusted requires knowledge of experts who understand the problem that is being addressed and the nuances of understanding the data. The powerful human-machine collaboration has the potential to transform our ability to make wise, unbiased, and responsible decisions. After all, humans have the unique ability to understand context even with the access to the smallest amount of information. However, humans do not typically have all of the knowledge and tools to understand why problems happen and how to change outcomes. This partnership between the collaboration of the human in the loop and causal AI is powerful.

Summary

In this chapter, we discussed the fact that causal AI offers significant benefits for achieving explainability, bias detection, and fairness in solutions aimed at helping organizations understand why problems happen and how to solve them. By detecting the underlying cause-effect relationships in data, causal AI enables more transparent and interpretable models so that the end results are better understood and can be trusted. In addition, because causal AI can identify and mitigate biases in the data, the resulting applications will be better able to make better and fairer decisions. While causal AI is designed for explainability and bias detection, there is no perfect solution. If the model is extremely complex or lacks sufficient data, the causal AI solution may not be able to achieve the level of explainability needed.

Causal AI provides many benefits that help organizations better understand how their models reach their conclusions. Unlike black-box models, causal AI provides a graphical modeling approach that increases the opportunity to avoid confusion and errors. These issues are critical to the success or failure of businesses that increasingly have to defend their business decisions that are impacted by governance requirements and the need to be responsible for the outcomes from analysis.

Note

1. Dr. Matt Turek, "Explainable Artificial Intelligence (XAI)." Defense Advanced Research Projects Agency. www.darpa.mil/program/explainable-artificial-intelligence.

7

Tools, Practices, and Techniques to Enable Causal AI

In the previous chapters, we discussed the fundamental concepts and processes to creating a causal AI approach, but there are of course technologies, tools, libraries, and software that support practitioners. This chapter is dedicated to providing a guide to the tools, technologies, and best practices for implementing causal AI solutions.

We will first propose a causal AI pipeline, which aims to identify steps along the way to implementing causal AI within your organization. Keep in mind that the pipeline needs to be thought of as a continuous loop, with multiple detours and subloops. For example, a team may find themselves reworking their initial business question as they begin to gather data. The loop is also continuously renewing. As you begin to operationalize causal AI, your team will iterate models and data inputs and begin to change the scope of the questions you and your team are asking. The goal of the causal AI pipeline is to provide a framework to focus your team's efforts and to create a process that is repeatable and can be implemented for different parts of your business.

As the field of causal AI continues to grow, so too does the number of tools and applications designed to support its various stages. From data identification and model design and development to deployment and continuous learning, this chapter will delve into existing software available for each step of the pipeline. By exploring these tools, you will get a sense of the tools and platforms that enterprise organizations are using. It is important to keep in mind that there are new tools regularly emerging and that this chapter is not meant as a comprehensive guide to every tool. Different teams and organizations will find that it makes more sense from a team skills or budgeting perspective to use one set of tools over another. For example, you may have a team with strong R skills and will want to explore open-source R libraries, while many other organizations will want to invest in Python causal AI libraries. Likewise, the choice of deployments— whether on-premises or the cloud and then which cloud will highly depend on corporate culture, security and governance concerns, and of course, existing licensing agreements.

Understanding the latest developments in causal AI is essential for organizations looking to stay ahead in this rapidly evolving field. As the field evolves, we will likely see more standardization and the incorporation of more industry open-source software. For example, Python is already emerging as an essential language in the development of causal AI tools and technologies. It is important for business and technical leadership teams to encourage your data and analytics teams and causal AI practitioners to experiment with a variety of tools.

Keep in mind that some tools and platforms are designed to abstract the complexities of causal AI and make this approach to data-driven decision-making more accessible to data analysts and wider teams within an organization. By adopting tools and frameworks that make causal AI more accessible, you can accelerate the adoption of this approach within your organizations and create competitive differentiation.

In addition to the causal AI pipeline and tools, we will discuss some specific techniques being used in causal AI, specifically the creation of synthetic data. In addition, although causal AI is an emerging approach, there are already some commercial software vendors offering packaged platforms to enable causal AI.

The Causal AI Pipeline

Throughout this book, we have discussed discrete portions of the causal AI pipeline, such as model development. For example, in Chapter 5, we discussed forming hybrid teams to define an objective. In this section, we propose a causal AI pipeline along with tools, utilities, and packaged software offerings that can help to enable this cycle. This is similar to the "DevOps infinity loop" that many organizations have oriented their DevOps and DevSecOps practices against (see Figure 7.1). You will not successfully orient your organization around causal AI without rethinking your approach to business processes, data, and analytics, and the pipeline is meant to help you think about your current approach and how to begin implementing causal AI.

Like the DevOps infinity loop in Figure 7.1, the causal AI pipeline consists of eight interconnected stages (see Figure 7.2), each with its own set of tools, techniques, and best practices. This structured approach ensures that every aspect of the causal AI process is carefully considered. It's important to keep in mind that although the entire pipeline is meant to be circular and

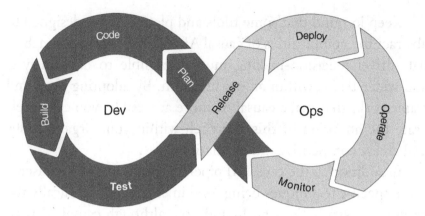

FIGURE 7.1 A typical DevOps infinity loop diagram

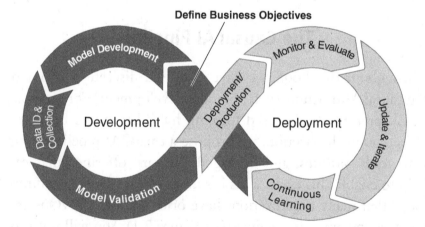

FIGURE 7.2 The iterative causal AI pipeline

iterative, teams may spend weeks focused on testing one or two stages of the entire pipeline. By following the pipeline, practitioners can systematically work through the challenges associated with each stage and ensure that their causal AI models are both robust and reliable.

Your organization may create its own process based on our causal AI pipeline, but creating a structured process that can go from ideation to development to deployment will give your team the ability to take research and data expertise and transform that into business differentiation. Without a well-defined pipeline and the rigor to stick with it, some organizations are destined to get bogged down in the data exploration phases and will never actually benefit from operationalizing causal AI.

1. **Define business objectives:** Identify the main goals and key performance indicators (KPIs) for the business acceleration or transformation needing a causal AI model. This step establishes what the model aims to achieve and the metrics to track its performance.

2. **Model development:** Develop and implement the causal AI model, leveraging causal inference techniques such as graphical models, potential outcomes, or do-calculus. Establish causal relationships among variables and estimate their effects.

3. **Data identification and collection:** Gather relevant data that contains causal relationships and potential confounders. This may involve combining data from different sources, addressing missing values, and ensuring data quality.

4. **Model validation:** Test and validate the model to ensure it is providing accurate causal insights. This step involves checking the robustness of the causal relationships, measuring performance against predefined KPIs, and assessing the model's generalizability.

5. **Deployment/production:** Integrate the validated causal AI model into the existing system or decision-making process. This step includes turning your causal AI model into code and potentially deploying the model in a production environment creating APIs for integration or embedding the model in applications.

6. **Monitor and evaluate**: Continuously track the performance of the deployed model and assess its impact on the system or decision-making process. Collect feedback and monitor real-world outcomes to evaluate the model's effectiveness.

7. **Update and iterate**: Based on the performance evaluation and new data, refine the model or adjust the causal relationships as needed. Update the model to incorporate new insights and re-validate the model before deploying the updated version.

8. **Continuous learning**: Create a culture of learning and improvement, sharing knowledge and best practices for causal AI model development, deployment, and maintenance. Stay updated on the latest advancements in causal inference techniques and methodologies.

Define Business Objectives

Defining a clear business objective is the cornerstone of any successful causal AI project. It is essential to establish a shared understanding of the project's goals among all stakeholders, including business leaders, data scientists, and domain experts. The objectives should be specific, measurable, achievable, relevant, and time-bound (SMART). This ensures that the project has a clear direction and a solid foundation for subsequent stages in the causal AI pipeline.

During this stage, various brainstorming and prioritization techniques can be employed to identify the most critical goals. Techniques such as the MoSCoW method (must-have, should-have, could-have, and won't-have), the Kano model, or decision matrix analysis can help rank and prioritize objectives based on factors such as feasibility, impact, and effort required. These prioritization techniques facilitate the alignment of resources and effort, and they focus on the most important aspects of the project. It doesn't matter what technique your organization selects, but from our experience, it works best when the team rallies around a proven approach.

Collaboration among stakeholders is key in this phase. Business stakeholders bring their understanding of the market, customer needs, and the organization's strategic goals. Data scientists contribute their knowledge of data, algorithms, and modeling techniques. Domain experts offer insights into the specific industry or subject matter. Technology teams bring an understanding of the computing architecture and tools that will work best in the computing environment. By working together, this hybrid team can ensure that the objectives are well-defined and grounded in both business and technical realities.

It is important to involve stakeholders from various departments and levels within the organization to promote a holistic view of the business objectives. For example, members of your privacy, governance, and legal teams need to be involved in your project to think about how the data will be used in your models. This can help identify any potential gaps, conflicts, or synergies between different organizational goals. Involving a diverse group of stakeholders also ensures that the project has buy-in from all relevant parties, which can be crucial for its success.

As we discussed in Chapter 5, the most successful organizations that are implementing causal AI projects have executives connected to the project who can help facilitate cross-team collaboration. These executives help to break down roadblocks and silos that may sidetrack a project. Because causal AI initiatives often span multiple parts of your organization, having senior leadership attached to an initiative helps to eliminate the tendency for teams not to collaborate.

Tools for documentation and communication can play an essential role in defining business objectives. Spreadsheets (e.g.,

Google Sheets, Microsoft Excel) can help organize and visualize the objectives and KPIs. Project management tools (e.g., Trello, Asana) can facilitate collaboration and task management among team members. These tools help create a shared understanding of the project goals and ensure that everyone is working toward the same vision.

Establishing clear key performance indicators (KPIs) is vital during this stage of the pipeline. KPIs are quantifiable measures that help track the performance of the causal AI model and assess its impact on the organization's goals. By identifying relevant KPIs, the team can set targets and benchmarks for the model, ensuring that it delivers tangible value to the business.

As the project progresses, it is essential to revisit and reassess the business objectives regularly. This helps ensure that the project remains aligned with the organization's strategic goals and allows for any necessary adjustments or refinements based on new insights, changing market conditions, or feedback from stakeholders (see Figure 7.3).

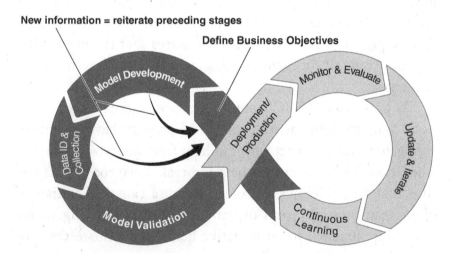

FIGURE 7.3 The cycle isn't just a continuous loop; instead, there are epicycles within the larger framework as your team encounters new data and challenges.

As we've discussed throughout the book, this definitional stage is a critical first step in the causal AI pipeline. By setting clear, measurable, and relevant goals, and by fostering collaboration among stakeholders, organizations can build a solid foundation for their causal AI projects. This foundation enables the team to work cohesively throughout the subsequent stages of the pipeline, ultimately delivering impactful results that drive business success.

Keep in mind that the first causal AI project will not be your last. Creating a repeatable and systematic framework will help other organizations within your business gain value from causal projects. At the same time, as your team begins to learn from their first deployment, you will quickly see the value of causal AI to tackle other adjacent challenges.

Model Development

Model development is the core of the causal AI pipeline, where data scientists, domain experts, and your hybrid team work together to design and implement the causal AI model. This stage involves selecting appropriate causal inference techniques using visual models. The goal is to create a model that accurately captures the underlying causal structure of the data and provides meaningful insights into the business objectives.

To begin the model development process, your team must first understand the problem domain and the relationships between variables. Note that this is different from the way data science has approached challenges in the past. In previous generations, data scientists were focused on finding a needle in a haystack and didn't care whether they understood what a needle or a haystack actual was. As we discussed previously, your data team must truly understand the business problem. So, for example, in a chemical manufacturing use case, the data team will need to work closely with chemical engineers as well as the employees who run the manufacturing processes. Domain experts will provide valuable insights into the subject matter, helping the data scientists identify potential confounders and important variables.

Once the causal relationships are identified, data scientists must select the most suitable causal inference techniques for the problem. To create your DAG or SCM, you can use a number of different tools. Two popular open-source offerings are DAGitty and ggdag. DAGitty is a popular browser-based environment written in R and designed to help teams visually create a DAG. Likewise, ggdag is an R package based on DAGitty but offers additional capabilities. Potential outcomes frameworks can begin to be determined. Do-Calculus, based on Judea Pearl's Causal Calculus, allows for the estimation of causal effects by intervening on variables in the causal graph. To make Do-Calculus more accessible, an open-source Python library was created, called DoWhy. The DoWhy library has been downloaded more than a million times.

The next iteration of DoWhy is called PyWhy. The PyWhy open-source library emerged when Microsoft and Amazon combined their research efforts around causal AI. This is an active and diverse community that is building tools and techniques to make causal AI accessible to Python developers. Although there will be other emerging libraries that may gain significant traction based on specific horizontal or vertical use cases, PyWhy is currently the library and community that most teams are rallying around.

A variety of other open-source libraries and tools can be used to create causal AI models. In addition to PyWhy, other Python-based libraries such as CausalML, EconML, Causality, and Pyro offer a range of causal inference techniques and algorithms. For those who are trained in R, software packages such as CausalImpact, CausalQueries, and bnlearn can be used to build and analyze causal models. The choice of tools and libraries depends on the team's expertise and the specific requirements of the project. It's important to keep in mind that these libraries aren't mutually exclusive.

It is also important to continually document the development of your model, including the assumptions you are making, the causal relationships that are identified, and the different techniques you are using. This documentation enables teams to work asynchronously across time zones and helps to track the model development over time. In addition, when the model is presented to various team members and leadership groups, the documentation can provide fast answers when you're inevitably asked, "Why did you assume X doesn't impact Y?"

With a well-developed model in hand, the team can then proceed to the next stage of the pipeline: data identification and collection. By taking a model-first approach, your data team can focus on capturing the right kinds of data rather than simply trying to gather as much data as possible that may or may not provide actionable insight.

Data Identification and Collection

Data identification and collection are crucial steps in the causal AI pipeline, as the quality, relevance, and timeliness of your data will directly impact the accuracy and reliability of the causal model; low-quality data can result in meaningless models. During this phase, the focus is on gathering data that contains causal relationships, potential confounders, and relevant variables that can help you to populate your visual causal model with data. This process may involve combining data from multiple sources, addressing missing data, and ensuring data quality. In many cases, you will need to look outside of your organization to find potential data.

This is one of the pipeline steps where having executive buy-in is important. The executive doesn't need to attend every meeting, but it is important that it is clear that the various teams that are involved in the project know that company leadership supports the causal AI efforts. Different teams within your organization are generally not motivated to share data. In addition, they are often reluctant to share data because they don't know what will be done with it or if it will be changed in a way that removes context. Senior leadership can remove blockers to accelerate the sharing of data and create a centralized mechanism for collaboration.

Data engineers and data scientists play a significant role in this stage of the pipeline. They must collaborate to identify the necessary data sources, establish data pipelines, and preprocess the data to make it suitable for modeling. Domain experts may also contribute valuable insights about the industry-specific data sources, as well as provide guidance on the relevance and importance of certain variables in the context of your visual model and original objective.

Web scraping libraries and APIs are essential tools for collecting data from various sources, especially when dealing with online data. Open-source Python libraries like BeautifulSoup, Scrapy, and Selenium can help with web scraping. A wide variety of APIs can give you direct access to structured data from various platforms and services. These APIs can be used to access internal systems or third-party data sources, many of which are available for purchase. Data from multiple sources can be combined and enriched to create a comprehensive data set that captures the relevant causal relationships. For example, if you find that your internal data is not broad enough, you can supplement it with external data. For example, there are large demographic data sets easily available. Or if you are working to improve your IT operations using causal AI, you can get IT operations data, both freely available and for a fee. Some resources include Amazon Web Service's (AWS) Data Exchange, Google Dataset Search, and Kaggle. Kaggle is a community-led endeavor to help machine learning and data science teams, while services like AWS offer a huge number of third-party data for free and for pay.

Data storage solutions play an important role in organizing and managing the collected data. Depending on the data's structure, volume, and complexity, different storage options can be utilized, such as SQL databases (e.g., PostgreSQL, MySQL), NoSQL databases (e.g., MongoDB, Cassandra), or data warehouses (e.g., Amazon Redshift, Google BigQuery). These storage solutions allow for efficient querying, retrieval, and analysis of the data, which is crucial for model development. Depending on your approach to causal AI, you may find that it makes sense to consolidate all your data in a data lake or other large repository. An alternative approach is to leave data where it currently resides and connect your causal model to your data through APIs.

As we mentioned, data quality is an integral part of the data collection stage. Inaccurate, inconsistent, or incomplete data can lead to misleading or unreliable causal models. Although causal AI doesn't require massive amounts of data, you do need to have a wide variety of sample data so that your model captures a variety of potential scenarios. Data quality tools like OpenRefine (open source) and Trifacta can help you wrangle, cleanse, and standardize messy data sets.

Data Privacy, Governance, and Security   Data privacy and security considerations should not be overlooked during the data collection stage. The same data privacy, security, and governance concerns that are involved with other data projects are in play. Some organizations attach an attorney, data governance expert, or data privacy professional to their hybrid team to make sure that a project doesn't violate corporate, industry, and regional data regulations.

Sensitive data must be handled with care, and appropriate measures should be taken to protect personal data and comply with relevant regulations, such as the General Data Protection Regulation (GDPR) or the California Consumer Privacy Act (CCPA). Techniques like anonymization, masking, or differential privacy can be used to safeguard the privacy of the data while keeping it relevant enough for modeling. Similarly, you need to maintain the same security safeguards you keep around your data no matter where it resides. It is important to work with your internal data security team to understand the security implications of your causal AI project. However, the security team should not have veto power over your project; instead, they should help you safely access data. This is why involving somebody from the security team as early as possible is a best practice, rather than trying to get their blessing right before you try to deploy a model.

Synthetic Data   We will discuss synthetic data in more detail later in this chapter, but in some cases, it may be necessary to generate synthetic data when the available data is insufficient, biased, or restricted due to privacy concerns. Synthetic data generation techniques, such as variational autoencoders (VAEs) or generative adversarial networks (GANs), can create realistic data samples that maintain the underlying causal structure and relationships of the original data. This synthetic data can augment the available data set, enabling more robust and reliable causal modeling. The challenge with synthetic data is that you need to have the natural and original patterns and randomness built in so that it replicates the real world, but you also need to maintain causal relationships.

Model Validation

Model validation is needed to ensure that once your model is populated and trained with data, it can provide accurate causal insight. Your hybrid team should include subject-matter experts to evaluate the model's performance, robustness, and generalizability, meaning that the model must be able to accurately identify causal relationships as it is fed new data. By testing the model against key performance indicators (KPIs), you will assess the model's ability to provide meaningful business insights in various scenarios. This testing will help provide your team with confidence in the model's effectiveness before it is deployed.

To begin the validation process, data scientists must define the performance metrics and evaluation criteria. No model is perfect, and you will need to determine what amounts of variation are acceptable in your use case. These metrics will be closely aligned with the business objectives and KPIs established in the defined business objectives stage of the pipeline. Examples of performance metrics may include the effect size of a variable, prediction accuracy, or the ability to identify causal relationships when confounders are introduced.

The choice of evaluation methods depends on the specific causal inference techniques used in the model development stage. For instance, graphical models can be evaluated by comparing the inferred causal structure to a "ground truth" (see Chapter 2) or by assessing the model's ability to predict interventions accurately. You may also use other techniques such as sensitivity analysis and robustness checks among others. Data scientists can insert irrelevant additional confounders to test whether the model is robust enough to not deviate too much when these are included.

It is essential to validate the model using multiple sets of data samples that reflect the complexity and variability of the real-world scenarios. It is nearly guaranteed that once you put your model into production, the incoming data will be more varied and unpredictable than you originally thought. As with other AI and machine learning models, your data science team may divide the available data into training, validation, and test sets, or apply techniques like k-fold cross validation to obtain a reliable idea of how your model will perform.

Another type of testing that your team will likely perform is *sensitivity analysis*. Sensitivity analysis is akin to stress testing for a model, where we change some of the factors to see how well the model holds up. It's like testing a bridge by putting different weights on it to see whether it remains stable. It is a valuable technique for assessing the robustness of the causal relationships identified by the model. Sensitivity analysis can give you a sense of the reliability of the model's predictions. This information can help the team identify potential issues or limitations in the model. If your team identifies the need for improvements, you may need to go back and find more diverse sets of data or relook at the visual model that your team assembled.

The model validation process needs to also consider the generalizability of the model. What this means is that the model needs to perform well on new, novel data. Generalizability is a critical element; creating models and anticipating the outcome on known data sets is easy. Techniques like out-of-sample testing, holdout validation, or external validation are all meant to test generalizability. The way these validation methods work is to hold back some of your data and test the model on data it has never seen. If a model performs well under these tests, you can be more confident that it will perform as expected in real-world applications.

During this model validation stage, it is crucial to maintain close collaboration between data scientists and domain experts. Data scientists will be performing the actual testing; however, domain experts can provide feedback on the model's performance and the insights it is providing in the context of business operations. For example, during testing, domain experts can help a data team understand if the model is no longer relevant. The data science team can then go back and make alterations to the model.

It is important to keep in mind that the model validation process may use simulated data. You may want to use synthetic data when testing a model because you don't have enough real-world data or your data is biased or not diverse. For example, suppose you are working on a causal model to predict student success in terms of academic performance and graduation rates at a university. However, the available data set primarily includes information from a specific department or academic program, lacking diversity across disciplines, socioeconomic backgrounds, and student support services. To address this limitation and ensure the generalizability of the causal model, synthetic data can be utilized for testing. By generating synthetic student profiles that encompass a variety of disciplines, socioeconomic backgrounds, and engagement with support services like tutoring or counseling, you can evaluate the model's effectiveness in predicting success across different student populations. Synthetic data allows you to simulate a broader range of student experiences, helping identify patterns and interventions that can enhance student success on a university-wide basis.

Deployment/Production

The deployment/production stage is where your validated causal AI model is integrated into the existing system or decision-making process. This stage is essential for transforming the insights generated by the model into actionable intelligence that can drive business value. Successful deployment requires careful planning, seamless integration, and ongoing monitoring and maintenance to ensure the model continues to perform as expected under real-world use.

Before deploying the causal AI model, the team must determine the most appropriate deployment strategy based on the specific requirements of the organization and the use case. This may involve deploying the model on-premises, using cloud-based infrastructure, or embedding the model directly into applications. The choice of deployment strategy will depend on factors such as cost, performance, scalability, security requirements, and existing business processes.

To integrate your causal AI model into existing systems, your team must develop APIs or other interfaces that allow for seamless communication between the model and the target application. This may involve creating RESTful APIs, GraphQL APIs, or other integrations that are suited for your application. Proper documentation of the APIs and their usage is critical so that data scientists, domain experts, and software engineers can collaborate.

It's important to keep in mind that your deployed model is software code, and as such, you need to plan for its compute requirements. You may want to optimize the model for faster performance by parallelizing computations or using specialized hardware such as GPUs or tensor processing units (TPUs). GPUs enable the decomposition of complex problems into thousands or millions of separate tasks and work them concurrently, while TPUs were designed specifically for neural network loads and have the ability to work quicker than GPUs while also using fewer resources. A cloud deployment can be a good option because you can get quick access to specialized hardware—and pay for it on an as-needed basis. By carefully considering the computational demands of the model, the team can ensure that the deployed solution is efficient, scalable, and responsive to the needs of the organization.

It is crucial to establish clear communication channels and workflows between the data scientists, domain experts, and software engineers during this stage. You will want to adopt a DevOps approach, where teams work together rather than tossing code over the wall to a different internal group. Regular standup meetings, documentation, and executive buy-in from someone who helps to facilitate collaboration will help create a cohesive team.

Monitor and Evaluate

Monitoring and evaluating is an important stage of the causal AI process and involves continuously tracking the performance of the deployed model and assessing its impact on the system or decision-making process. You can think of this stage as continually validating your model. This stage is crucial for ensuring that the causal AI model remains effective and continues to provide valuable insights. By collecting feedback, monitoring real-world outcomes, and evaluating the model's effectiveness, the team can identify areas for improvement and continually improve the model.

To successfully monitor and evaluate the deployed causal AI model, the team should revisit the KPIs that were established in the first phase of the pipeline. Those metrics should be designed to assess the model's performance across a number of factors such as accuracy, effect size, or the ability to identify causal relationships in the presence of confounders. Keep in mind, these are the same types of KPIs you will look at when validating your model. Note that, as you deploy the causal model, you may need to adjust your KPIs to account for variations due to the model encountering real data.

The monitoring process should involve collecting data on the model's performance in real-time or near-real-time, allowing the team to quickly identify and address any potential issues or anomalies. This data can be collected using the monitoring and logging system established during the deployment stage, as well as through feedback from end users and stakeholders. Regularly reviewing this data can help the team ensure that the model is performing optimally and providing the expected benefits to the organization.

In addition to monitoring the performance of the deployed causal AI model, the team should track the real-world outcomes from the decisions that were influenced by your model. This may involve collecting data on key business metrics, such as revenue growth, customer attrition, cost savings, or customer satisfaction, and comparing these outcomes to the predictions generated by the model. This tracking will help give you insights into your model's effectiveness and identify areas to focus on for continued improvement.

As with other stages, regular communication and collaboration between data scientists, domain experts, and other stakeholders is essential. By sharing experiences and feedback, the team can foster a culture of continuous learning and improvement, ensuring that the causal AI model remains relevant and effective as the organization and its data evolve.

As part of the evaluation process, the team should from time to time reassess the assumptions and causal relationships contained within the underlying model. This may involve revisiting the DAG or SCM used in the model development stage and refining the PyWhy equations or other underlying equations you are using. By regularly reevaluating the model's foundations, the team can ensure that it remains grounded in the latest scientific knowledge and best practices. As the field of causal AI matures, we will see improvements in the underlying calculations, as well as new and emerging libraries that may give you better results.

The evaluation process may also involve comparing the performance of the deployed causal AI model to alternative models or approaches. This could include benchmarking the model against traditional statistical methods, machine learning algorithms, or predictive models. This "model versus model" competition helps you to refine your initial assumptions and can help to identify model drift as your business and the world around your application continues to change.

It is essential to maintain a feedback loop between the evaluation process and the model development and deployment stages of the causal AI pipeline. The insights gained through this monitoring and evaluation stage will provide guidance for you to refine your model and its deployment strategy. Your team should create a cycle of continuous improvement that focuses on keeping your causal AI as relevant and as helpful as possible.

During the monitor and evaluate stage, you should also consider the ethical implications and potential biases of the deployed causal AI model (see Chapter 6). This may involve evaluating the fairness of the model's predictions across different demographic groups, assessing the transparency and explainability of the model's insights, and examining potential unintended consequences. Because your model is likely seeing new, never before seen data patterns, you need to continuously track potential ethical concerns.

Update and Iterate

Refining, updating, and improving your causal AI model is centered around leveraging the insights and feedback gathered during the monitor and evaluate stage to continuously improve and refine the causal AI model. This process can involve updating the model's causal structure, adjusting various parameters or assumptions, or incorporating new data sources to ensure that the model remains accurate and relevant as your business requirements and the world around you changes. By fostering a culture of continuous learning and improvement, the team can maximize the value and impact of their causal AI practice.

The first step in the update and iterate stage is to identify areas for improvement based on the feedback and insights collected during the monitor and evaluate stage. This should involve pinpointing weaknesses in the model's performance, addressing biases or ethical concerns, or updating the model to reflect changes in the organization's objectives or data sources. By focusing on these areas for improvement, the team can prioritize their efforts and ensure that the model remains aligned with the organization's needs. Keep in mind that making sure your causal AI model remains relevant and highly effective is important not only for business results but also for building trust on a causal approach to solving business problems.

Once the areas for improvement have been identified, the team can revisit the model development stage of the causal AI pipeline to update and refine the model. By regularly updating the model's foundations, you can ensure that your model maintains relevance and useful insights.

In addition to refining the model's causal structure, the team may also need to update its parameters, such as the weights used in the learning process. This can be achieved through techniques such as gradient descent, Bayesian optimization, or evolutionary algorithms—all meant to fine-tune your model's results. This fine-tuning of the model can help to improve performance after your model begins to encounter real-world data.

Within this stage of the causal AI pipeline, you may also incorporate new data sources or features into the model. This can help address data limitations or biases, improve the model's generalizability, or enable the model to capture new causal relationships that were not previously considered. It's important to keep in mind that no model can capture every single causal data source; therefore, you will always have unobserved variables.

What's important is to incorporate these variables if they begin to have a strong causal impact on your target objective. Continually expanding and updating the model's data sources ensures that the model remains relevant and effective.

As part of the refinement process, the team should also consider exploring alternative causal inference techniques. This could involve experimenting with different graphical models or experimenting with machine learning algorithms to identify the most effective and efficient approach for capturing the causal relationships in the data.

Keep in mind that this is a pipeline, so once the model has been updated and refined, it is essential to repeat the model validation stage to ensure that the updated model performs well and meets the organization's predefined performance metrics and KPIs. You will redo the validation steps originally performed while potentially challenging your updated model with new data that has been observed in your real-world deployment.

After validating the updated model, the team will go through the deployment stage to integrate the revised model back into the organization's system or decision-making process. This may involve updating the APIs or interfaces used to communicate with the model and adjusting the deployment environment to accommodate any changes in the model's computational requirements. You may also need to retrain end users on the model updates and new capabilities. As you can see, documentation is critical for this iterative process to run smoothly.

As with the previous stages of the causal AI pipeline, this update and iterate stage requires close collaboration between data scientists, domain experts, and other stakeholders. It is important for the data team to understand feedback from end users on the applicability of the model, as well as incorporate domain experts as the model begins to encounter real-world data. Regularly meeting to review the performance of the causal

AI application against predetermined KPIs will be important to help ensure that the model is performing as expected.

This stage of the causal AI pipeline is what will help make your causal application a business differentiator for your organization. Your initial model is never going to be the best and most accurate representation of causal relationships in the real world. This ongoing refinement process is essential for improving the effectiveness and relevance of the causal AI model in a rapidly changing data landscape and ensuring that it continues to provide valuable insights that inform critical decisions and drive business value. In addition, as you refine the model and the original business objective, you will likely identify new business problems that are ripe for causal AI. As these new business problems are identified, you can replicate your existing causal model and use that as a starting point.

Continuous Learning

The causal AI pipeline is largely focused on creating a framework to continuously improve your model, validate it, and redeploy more accurate, robust, and generalized models. But there is also a larger theme at play; for most organizations, the journey into causality won't end with a single causal AI-driven application. Instead, business and data teams will begin to implement new causal applications and augment existing decision-making processes. By creating a culture of continuous learning and improvement, your organization can maximize the value and impact of taking a causal approach to AI.

Creating a center of excellence (CoE) within the organization is a helpful practice for promoting continuous learning and improvement and in spreading the knowledge about the potential impact of causality within different groups of your organization. A CoE is a dedicated group of experts and professionals who are responsible for driving the adoption and implementation of best practices in causal AI. Your CoE may certainly include members of the first hybrid team that successfully deployed a causal AI project. This group of experts will be data scientists and analysts, as well as domain experts and business leaders. Oftentimes an executive will sponsor the CoE and help to promote the group's visibility within an organization. The CoE members will help to provide guidance, support, and training to other teams as they develop, deploy, and refine causal AI models. Establishing a CoE can accelerate the adoption of causal AI within the organization and help ensure that all teams are working toward the same goals and objectives. In addition, as the CoE matures and there are more use cases for causality, best practices, lessons learned, and pitfalls to avoid can be formalized.

Identifying and nurturing internal employee champions is another critical aspect of fostering continuous learning and improvement. Employee champions are individuals who possess a deep understanding of causal AI and are passionate about driving its adoption within the organization. These champions can act as catalysts for promoting the use of causal AI across various teams and departments and advocating for the adoption of best practices. These champions typically attend industry meetings, talk to various vendors and researchers on a regular basis, and are aware of emerging research and new offerings that are becoming available.

Internal champions also play an important role in enabling knowledge sharing and collaboration between teams. By organizing workshops, training sessions, and informal learning lunches and events, employee champions can help to share what they are seeing in the industry across various teams. In many cases, business teams don't know the questions to ask or the problems that causal AI can address. These internal champions can help provide these teams with the knowledge to begin making informed decisions.

This continuous learning aspect of the causal AI pipeline may be overlooked by some organizations, but it is critical if you want causality to begin to truly drive differentiation in your business. By embracing a culture of learning from each other and formalizing learning into a knowledge center, teams will create lasting value rather than one-off causal applications. This may involve creating documentation, tutorials, and workshops that explain how causal AI works, its benefits, and how it can be used in a variety of use cases. Establishing a center of excellence, nurturing internal employee champions, and fostering inter-team learning are essential aspects of this process, helping to create a cohesive and effective approach to causal AI.

The Importance of Synthetic Data

In the context of causal AI, the quality and availability of data play a crucial role in the development, validation, and deployment of robust models. Synthetic data, which is artificially generated data that mimics the characteristics of real-world data, can be an important resource for addressing data limitations, enhancing privacy, and improving model performance. In this section, we explore its importance, benefits, and potential applications, as well as the techniques used to generate it.

Why Create Synthetic Data?

Data is everywhere and being created at breakneck speeds, so you may have an obvious question: why would you need to create simulated data? The bottom line is that real-world data can be dirty, unorganized, and inaccurate. It is difficult to control for real-world situations, and privacy and regulatory restrictions make it challenging to use real data for training and validating some models.

Overcoming Data Limitations   One of the primary reasons to create synthetic data is to address the limitations often encountered with real-world data sets. These limitations can include insufficient sample sizes, missing values, or unobserved variables, which makes it challenging or nearly impossible to create accurate and robust causal AI models. Synthetic data can help overcome these challenges by generating additional data points that closely mimic the properties of real data, allowing researchers to enhance their data sets and improve the performance of their models.

Enhancing Data Privacy and Security   Synthetic data can be a valuable tool for preserving privacy and ensuring compliance with data protection regulations such as the General Data Protection Regulation (GDPR) and the Health Insurance Portability and Accountability Act (HIPAA). By generating data that mimics the characteristics of real-world data without revealing the identities of individual data subjects, synthetic data allows organizations to share and analyze data without risking privacy breaches. In these scenarios, simulated data removes a massive barrier to creating and training models that use protected personal data. Furthermore, many masking techniques may remove so much data that the data loses relevancy and no longer contains enough context to perform analysis. Tools like the open-source Python library SDV (Synthetic Data Vault) or the commercial offering Synthesized.io can help in creating privacy-preserving synthetic data sets.

Model Validation and Testing   Synthetic data can be particularly useful for validating and testing causal AI models, as it enables teams to generate data sets with known causal relationships and ground truth. By testing and validating models on synthetic data, teams can evaluate the accuracy and robustness of their causal model, as well as identify areas that need refinement. Tools like the open-source Python library PySyft library helps to decouple private data from model training.

Expanding the Range of Possible Scenarios   Synthetic data can also be employed to explore a broader range of scenarios than might be possible with real-world data alone. By generating data that represents a variety of different conditions, researchers can assess the performance of their causal AI models under diverse circumstances and identify potential weaknesses or areas for improvement. This will help your model increase its robustness and generalization when it is deployed. The open-source tool Faker is a tool that can be used to create large, diverse synthetic data sets.

Reducing the Cost of Data Collection   Collecting real-world data can be expensive and time-consuming, particularly in cases where data must be gathered through surveys, experiments, or other labor-intensive methods. For example, there are some healthcare scenarios where the data collection takes years to acquire and many hours of interviews with experiment participants. Synthetic data provides an alternative, more cost-effective means of generating data for causal AI models. By leveraging existing data sources and supplementing it with additional synthetic data points, organizations can reduce the cost and effort associated with data collection. It is important to note that synthetic data creates opportunities to validate the accuracy and efficiency of your models. It should never be used to publish findings or results.

Improving Data Imbalance In many real-world data sets, scenarios or outcomes may be underrepresented, leading to imbalanced data. This imbalance can cause biases in the causal AI models, leading to poor performance and biased conclusions. For example, if you are creating an employee attrition model, you may not have a diverse enough set of employees (education backgrounds, distance from office, income, etc.) to create an accurate model. Synthetic data generation techniques can help address this issue by creating additional data points for under-represented groups, categories, or outcomes, leading to a more balanced data set and improved model performance.

Encouraging Collaboration and Openness Synthetic data can facilitate collaboration between organizations, teams, and third-party consultants and contractors by providing a means of sharing data without violating privacy regulations or revealing proprietary information. This may be legally required or corporate policy and is a good way of enabling collaboration while keeping data safe and secure.

Streamlining Data Preprocessing Real-world data often requires extensive preprocessing because it is messy and not uniform. Data teams often spend huge amounts of time performing data cleansing, inputting missing values, deduping, and ensuring consistent data labeling. Synthetic data can help streamline this process by generating clean, well-structured data that is ready for analysis. This can save time and effort and allow teams to focus on model development and validation rather than data prep.

Supporting Counterfactual Analysis Synthetic data is helpful when teams explore conducting counterfactual analysis, which involves estimating the potential impact from different interventions. By creating synthetic data that represents a range of possible counterfactual scenarios, you can begin to estimate the effects of various interventions.

Fostering Innovation and Experimentation   Synthetic data can play an important role in promoting innovation and experimentation in the field of causal AI. By providing teams with an easily accessible and customizable source of data, synthetic data enables them to test new ideas, methodologies, and algorithms more quickly and efficiently without getting bogged down with data collection, cleansing, and the privacy and security concerns. This use of synthetic data can help your teams explore new approaches and techniques.

Creating Synthetic Data

Now you understand the role of synthetic data and why it's important in our world where data is seemingly everywhere. The question is how you go about creating synthetic data. There is some complexity, because your simulated data needs to be random enough to reflect the real world, even having occasional outliers, but it also can't be so random that there are no causal relationships. Of course, you also need to put restraints on the randomness. For example, if you are creating synthetic data for climate predictions in New York City, you know that the temperature will never be 190 degrees or negative 70 and that windspeeds will not be 600 miles per hour. In this section we will discuss some of the ways that organizations go about creating synthetic data.

Generative Models   Generative models are a popular approach for creating synthetic data. As the models learn the underlying patterns and distributions of real-world data it will generate new data points based on those patterns. These models can be implemented using a variety of machine learning libraries such as TensorFlow, PyTorch, or scikit-learn.

Agent-Based Modeling   Agent-based modeling is a simulation-based approach to generating synthetic data that involves creating individual "agents" that interact with each other and their environment according to predefined rules. These interactions generate data that can mimic the behavior of real-world systems, making it useful for creating synthetic data sets in complex domains such as social networks, traffic systems, or financial markets. Tools like the open-source Python library Mesa or the commercial offering AnyLogic can be used to create agent-based models for generating synthetic data.

Data Augmentation   Data augmentation techniques involve applying transformations to existing data to create new, synthetic data points. Data augmentation is typically used when you, of course, have some data but you want to add diversity to your training data to reduce biases and increase generalization. This can include techniques such as oversampling, undersampling, or the synthetic minority over-sampling technique (SMOTE) for addressing class imbalance, as well as methods such as data perturbation, rotation, or scaling for creating variations of existing data points. Many machine learning libraries, including scikit-learn, TensorFlow, and PyTorch, provide built-in support for data augmentation techniques.

Data Synthesis Tools and Platforms

Several tools and platforms have been developed specifically for generating synthetic data, ranging from open-source libraries to commercial offerings. Some popular open-source options include SDV, a Python library for generating synthetic relational and time-series data; and Faker, a Python library for creating fake data such as names, addresses, and dates. Commercial offerings such as Synthesized.io, Tonic.ai, and DataRobot provide more synthetic data generation solutions, including data privacy preservation features and integration with various data sources and storage systems. While some offerings are focused on creating synthetic data, others offer it as a feature within a broader data platform.

Conditional Synthetic Data Generation   In some cases, it may be desirable to generate synthetic data that satisfies specific conditions or constraints. You would use this technique when you have existing data and want to create more data with similar characteristics. This can be achieved using techniques such as rejection sampling, importance sampling, or Markov Chain Monte Carlo (MCMC) methods, which generate data points that conform to specified criteria. These methods can be implemented using statistical computing libraries such as NumPy, SciPy, or PyMC3.

Synthetic Data from Text   Generating synthetic data from text sources, such as natural language or structured documents, can involve techniques such as text generation, text summarization, or data extraction. Open-source natural language processing libraries such as the Hugging Face Transformers, GPT-2, GPT-3, GPT-4, or BERT can be used for generating synthetic text data, while tools such as the Python library Beautiful Soup or the commercial offering Diffbot can be used for data extraction and synthesis from structured documents.

The Limitations of Synthetic Data

Although using synthetic data is a powerful way to test causal AI systems, they of course cannot fully capture the real world. Ensuring that synthetic data accurately represents the original data can be a significant challenge. Synthetic data generation techniques may not capture all the nuances and complex relationships contained within the original data, leading to inaccuracies or biases in the generated data. Tools such as pandas, seaborn, or scikit-learn can be used to compare the distributions and statistical properties of synthetic data with the original data to assess their representativeness.

The quality of synthetic data is often dependent on the quality of the original data used to generate it. If the original data contains errors, biases, or missing values, these issues may be replicated across your simulated data set. There are a variety of tools, including pandas or the Python library, to help identify data quality issues in the original data set before generating synthetic data.

Keep in mind, you do not want to overfit your models using synthetic data. Model overfitting occurs when a model performs exceptionally well on the training data but does not have enough generalization to perform well when confronting new, unseen data. While synthetic data can augment existing data sets and help to create variances that aren't seen in your existing data, overfitting can occur if your synthetic data is too similar to your original data. Techniques such as cross validation and regularization, implemented with tools like scikit-learn, can help mitigate overfitting risks.

While synthetic data can help mitigate privacy risks, it is not a cure-all. There is still a possibility of inadvertently disclosing sensitive information or re-identifying individuals in the synthetic data, especially when it closely mimics the original data. Privacy-preserving techniques such as differential privacy or k-anonymity, implemented with tools like PySyft or DataRobot, can help address these concerns,.but they must be carefully applied and validated to ensure privacy is maintained. If you rely solely on automation without carefully checking your simulated data, you may inadvertently replicate protected information.

Generating synthetic data for certain domains, such as healthcare, finance, and the social sciences, can be a challenge because the data is complex and sensitive. There are specialized tools and techniques, such as domain-specific data generation tools or privacy-preserving methods, that may be required to generate synthetic data that accurately reflects the unique characteristics of the domain. For example, in healthcare, tools such as Synthea, Simulacrum, or MedGAN can be utilized for generating synthetic healthcare data. Similarly, in finance, tools such as Faker, RandomDataGenerator, or PyDBGen can be employed to generate synthetic financial data.

Current State of Tools and Software in Causal AI

As the field of causal AI continues to evolve, the availability of powerful tools and software will play an important role as the field of causal AI matures. In this section, we discuss the important role that open source plays in the development of causal AI along with the work that commercial software vendors are doing to help democratize causal AI and deploy it within businesses.

The Role of Open Source in Causal AI

As you have seen throughout this chapter, open-source software plays a large role in the field of causal AI. In addition, it is why the pace of development in the field is moving at an impressive speed. Open-source software provides researchers and practitioners with accessible tools, libraries, and frameworks that enable experimentation without large financial commitments or the need to standardize on a specific vendor offering. In addition, because of the flexibility of open-source offerings, teams can customize the tools and adapt them to their specific needs.

Given the rapid adoption levels of causal AI, tools, technologies, and practices, it is fair to characterize the market as a moving target. However, because many of the software tools and libraries being created today in causal AI are written in Python, choosing to adopt it can offer a hedge against the moving target. There are several reasons why Python has emerged as the language of choice for causal AI. First, it is a well-known coding language that is easy for new users to learn and become proficient. In addition, when it comes to working with data, there are excellent libraries for data manipulation and analysis. Finally, because Python is open source, it is freely available, can be distributed by anyone, and has a rich ecosystem of integrations.

In addition to seeing Python as the dominant language, you've probably also noticed that the software packages we've mentioned are largely focused on specific functions. For example, some focus on a specific type of synthetic data, others offer algorithms for manipulating and transforming data, while still others have causal models. In many cases, organizations that are performing causal AI are piecing together a half dozen or more tools to perform their analysis. Of course, building projects by using many underlying tools is fine for experts who understand the tools and technology, but it does not scale. As larger, more diverse data teams want to begin using causal AI, it will be more and more difficult to build models using many underlying tools. This landscape of lots of open source and many functional tools should be expected in an emerging technology field.

The rapid adoption and revolution of causal AI is propelling the emergence of new, open-source projects. This continual innovation has created a rich landscape of resources that allows researchers and developers to experiment, adapt, and optimize their tools and methodologies.

The following are three active and popular open-source projects that have made significant contributions to causal AI. In Appendix A we offer a variety of tools and open-source projects that may be helpful for your data and analytics teams to become familiar with:

- **PyWhy**: An intuitive Python library for causal inference, PyWhy provides a unified interface for model specification, identification, estimation, and robustness checks. It combines various causal inference methods under a single umbrella, making it a versatile tool for researchers and practitioners.

- **CausalML**: CausalML is a Python package that leverages machine learning algorithms to derive causal inferences. It provides a suite of uplift modeling and causal inference methods using machine learning algorithms based on recent research.

- **Dagitty**: This is open-source software that allows for graphical modeling and analysis of causal diagrams (i.e., DAGs). It's particularly useful for identifying minimal sufficient adjustment sets for estimating causal effects.

In addition to these open-source offerings, some existing data and analytics platforms will likely begin investing in causal AI. It would not be surprising to see commercial software vendors extend their data and ML platforms to begin to integrate causal AI. In addition, we are seeing startups that are specifically focused on causal AI emerge. In the next section, we will discuss two of these early vendors, but you can expect the market to evolve as new entrants enter and the existing vendors potentially shift their focus or focus on specific vertical or horizontal use cases.

Commercial Causal AI Software

Two prominent commercial software vendors are fully focused on developing and delivering causal AI solutions for clients: CausaLens and Geminos Software. Both companies are taking a well-proven path of basing their software on open-source offerings and then extending their capabilities, offering enterprise level support, and offering new functionality and usability. These commercial offerings can in some cases incorporate the entire causal AI pipeline, making it easier for teams to begin seeing value from taking a causal approach to AI.

We are in the early days for these commercial companies, and it would not be surprising to see the focuses of these companies evolve as their clients' needs change and the market for causal AI begins to mature. This section isn't meant to give an in-depth review of the offerings but instead a high-level view of what is being offered in the commercial software market.

CausaLens CausaLens is a London-based software vendor that provides software and consulting services to support the development of causal-based AI models and applications. The company received a venture capital investment in January 2022. CausaLens' initial focus was on the financial services space, but the company is broadening its focus to other industries as well.

The CausaLens team has put a significant amount of focus on building software that enables the building of complete applications to address specific customer business challenges. CausaLens has prebuilt applications for wealth management, market mix modeling, pricing and promotion optimization, customer churn, portfolio optimization, credit risk management, real estate investment optimization, and fraud prevention.

According to CausaLens, the company has a strong academic background and has created its own development lab to manage their relationships with universities and co-develop software and applications.

CausaLens' philosophy of developing software to drive the evolution of the causal AI market is based on the following three principles:

- Causal discovery is critical to the success of causal models and applications. The best discovery processes are a combination of human focus augmented by software and automation. CausaLens offers a combination of causal discovery algorithms developed by CausaLens joined with options from the wider open-source community. CausaLens' approach enables subject-matter experts to inject domain expertise to enhance causal discovery.

- Building models from the discovered causal drivers into an explainable, scalable, accurate model can be challenging. CausaLens provides software for building causal models based on decision trees.

- Leveraging outcomes and outputs from models needs to be converted to practical, actionable recommendations. CausaLens' software assists with validating models, ensuring model accuracy, and moving outputs to related business processes and other software environments to enable action and recommendations to be leveraged in everyday operations.

Geminos Software Geminos Software is a software vendor with offices in California and the UK providing a software platform to enable clients to develop, collaborate, and deploy causal AI models. In addition, the company offers consulting services to help accelerate customers' projects. The Geminos Causal AI platform is called Geminos Causeway. The company's initial projects are in the areas of industrial processes, defense and intelligence, agriculture, predictive maintenance, and IT operations.

Enabling teams to make better business decisions is at the core of Geminos Software's philosophy. The Geminos team describes how a focus on causal modeling can lead businesses forward in the digital transformation and can provide differentiation versus organizations that are focused on correlation-based AI and ML.

Geminos Software explicitly says that they are taking a Pearl-based approach to causal AI by leveraging Judea Pearl's methodologies.

Geminos Software's position is that causal modeling within the Causeway platform is the starting point for understanding how a business operates. The company takes a model-first approach. Geminos' approach relies on collaborative teams and domain experts as humans in the loop.

Geminos' platform is built on a battle-tested open-technology technology stack including Node-RED and TypeDB, PyWhy, and other open-source technologies. The company used these underpinnings so that the platform can connect with customers' existing data sources.

Summary

In this chapter, we proposed a causal AI pipeline that enables a structured approach to developing, validating, deploying, and continually improving your causal AI projects. The pipeline is meant to help you begin to understand how to see value from causal AI by moving past model development and into deployment. In addition, we expect businesses to have multiple causal AI projects, and by following a standard methodology, teams will be able to begin to create best practices and learn from one another.

At this point, there is a clear leader in the market for developing causal-based models and applications, and that leader is PyWhy. Having Microsoft and AWS join forces to put their combined efforts behind developing and supporting PyWhy has given the market a singular project to put their weight behind. That is a good thing at this time in the evolution of the market. Fragmentation of effort slows the market and causes division of focus and effort. Other companies will join the market, and development efforts will evolve, but for now having one leading code base is a positive state for the market.

Within each step of the pipeline, there are a variety of software tools to help your team as well as packaged commercial offerings that incorporate the entire causal AI pipeline. Expect the tools to change rapidly evolve as causal AI gains traction. We are still in the early days of seeing causal AI emerge from academia and enter the business world. As this change takes place, we will see tools, libraries, and software that are more focused on usability and commercial business problems as opposed to academic research. Of course, academic research will still use causal techniques, and their contributions to causal AI will continue to be extremely important, but emerging tools should lower the bar of entry for teams that want to begin using causal AI.

CHAPTER

8

Causal AI in Action

At this juncture in our journey to analyze and understand causal AI, we have examined the elemental/foundational concepts underlying the approach, the hybrid teams that are needed to understand the core issues and execute causal AI projects, the tools and technologies that have been developed, the relationship of causal AI to traditional AI, and the potential for causal AI to drive the evolution of the field of AI to include not only an understanding of what is most likely to happen next but also why it will happen.

In this chapter, we will examine, describe, and discuss causal AI from an applied perspective. How do you navigate the process of designing, developing, and deploying a causal AI-based application? One of our primary objectives of this chapter is to bring to life the process of building and applying causal AI to a real-world scenario. We will provide six use cases in this chapter. The first use case is an overall example of how the management team takes a holistic view of enterprise marketing. This use case will be based on a typical enterprise organization's marketing operations or a routine scenario faced by marketing professionals on a regular basis. We will discuss a hypothetical marketing situation, walk through the process of leveraging causal AI to examine and propose approaches to analyze the marketing environment, and consider how it can suggest changes to the marketing mix focused on pricing and product portfolio management to achieve the desired marketing outcomes in an efficient and effective manner. The value of this use case is to provide an overview of the issues and constraints of being able to successfully market products within a hypothetical business to consumer business. The subsequent five use cases focus on creating causal AI solutions within vertical markets.

Enterprise Marketing in a Business-to-Consumer Scenario

We will refer to the company as Driving Demand Company (DDCo). Let's set the stage for our hypothetical company.

At DDCo, this is the scenario in which the chief marketing officer (CMO) and her team operates.

Driving Demand Company is:

- An emerging, design-driven, private-equity-backed, company offering luxury household goods including couches, chairs, pillows, rugs, paint, lamps, fair novelties, candles, statues, dressers, tables, chest of drawers, art, design services, white-glove delivery service, and more.

- The pricing strategy is to always be in the top 10 percent in each category that they operate in.

- The inventory strategy is to move every piece of inventory out of the supply chain before the middle of the subsequent season in which the product was offered if the item or category is no longer being stocked. If the item or category continues in the product portfolio for the next season or for the foreseeable future, then the inventory cost of items needs to be less than 2 percent of all inventory carrying costs.

- The promotional strategy or discounting strategy is that any item that has not achieved three inventory turns in a single season is marked down by iterations of 10 percent until the inventory turn objective is met.

- The communication mix is the DDCo website, printed catalog, email, banner advertising and ads on HGTV, retailers, and their own custom content and TV shows.

- Their competition is all top-tier lifestyle retailers, including Serena & Lily and J. McLaughlin, and can include lifestyle brands such as Coach, Filson, Yeti, and other specialty brands.

- Cost and price are considerations, but only as it matters to not devalue the brand. Pricing needs to remain high and be in the top 10 percent of all comparable offerings.

- The product mix is complex and varied. All products need to be perceived of the highest quality from the perspectives of materials and workmanship in the category, and all products need to be cohesive from a design perspective.

- Products are offered in and shipped in the continental United States only. No international shipments or offers are available, but DDCo has observed a small amount of international diverting by third-party firms.

- Being owned by a private equity firm, the marketing budget is closely monitored, and any additional spending requires approval by the board of directors. The CEO and COO cannot approve incremental additional spending.

- Creative control and decisions are vested in the CEO. Her decisions are final.

- All orders are taken via the web presence, which includes the company site. Order traffic is directed to the company website where all orders are executed.

- Every effort is made to ensure that customers do not connect with DDCo staff for customer service inquiries, returns, complaints, exchanges, or any other company interaction. Automation and AI are leveraged extensively to keep costs down.

- All operations and staff members are in the United States.

- Products are sourced on a global basis, but all inbound shipments terminate in the U.S.-based distribution center and are shipped to customers from that location.

- The CMO has a team of 10 marketing staff members. The marketing team is augmented by a creative agency, an online marketing consultancy, and a handful of freelancers specializing in luxury goods marketing.

While building our causal AI model, we will consider DDCo's operations, budget, locations, consumers, challenges, capacity, constraints, pricing, desired and planned objectives, competition, current and planned marketing mix, and any other relevant factors that we should take into account to monitor and manage the marketing mix as we are building our causal AI application.

DDCo Marketing Causal Model: Annual Pricing Review and Update Cycle

Each year the CEO, CMO, and their marketing team meet to review and discuss the topic of price. The team examines and analyzes the price of all individual products and the portfolio as a whole. The macro-economic environment of the United States is a prime consideration in the discussion. The current economic conditions, the short-term outlook, and consumer sentiment have an impact on the types of products and their related prices that are considered as new additions to the portfolio as well as the new seasonal products that will be considered as additions to the portfolio.

The directed acyclic graph (DAG) in Figure 8.1 is a representation of the primary factors that the DDCo team takes into consideration. Of course, there are other factors that come into play and can be considered, but the DAG illustrates the factors that have a major effect on which products are selected and their relevant price points.

DAGs are one of the primary tools used in visualizing and understanding causal relationships. It is important to start with a business process or challenge that the business team understands well and can explain in detail to the analytics team. The analytics team needs to constrain the number of factors in the early stages of building and using a causal AI model or models to be able to ensure model accuracy and relevance. As with many things in life, the simpler the model, the better, especially when a team or company is starting its journey to leverage causal or traditional AI.

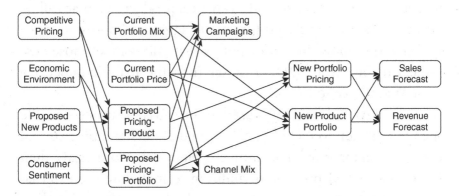

FIGURE 8.1 DAG for the DDCo annual pricing review and update cycle

In traditional AI, experienced data science professionals often chain together multiple simple models in an analytical pipeline. Causal AI can leverage this same approach. By building smaller models with fewer elements, both causal and traditional-based AI pipelines and models are more easily maintained and are easier to understand and explain.

Some people might even say that the DAG in Figure 8.1 is too complex for a starting point. That opinion can be debated, but in reality, the DAG in Figure 8.1 is quite a simple model, limited to one section of the overall marketing process. DAGs can be very complex with numerous elements and multifaceted relationships. For our purposes in this book, this model strikes a good balance between being too simple or overly complex.

Incorporating Internal and External Factors in the Model and DAG.   In the pricing review and update cycle, the DDCo executives and managers are primarily interested in understanding the current and short-term economic atmosphere and the mindset of the target audience. As DDCo is an emerging company subject to oversight by the private equity firm that has invested in the company, it is critically important for DDCo to manage the relevant costs and to create a product mix that will be attractive to the target customers at aggregate portfolio price points and at individual price points that will compel those customers to buy from DDCo rather than the many competitive options available to them.

Casual AI and the DAGs used in the causal AI process enable the DDCo team to include, analyze, and understand the external economic climate in their annual cycle much more easily than the traditional AI process. In addition to including the external factors, the DDCo team can explain the factors that drive their decisions as to *why* they are changing the price of a product, dropping or adding a product, or skewing the overall pricing mix in one direction or the other.

After quantifying and considering the external factors of the economic climate and consumer spending, the team's attention turns to the portion of the model that brings in internal considerations of the current product portfolio, portfolio price in aggregate, the change in the product portfolio, and the new aggregate price when a select set of new core and seasonal products are added into a hypothetical product mix.

Easily Enabling Iterating.   One of the key strengths and primary attractions of the causal approach and causal models and modeling that is being visualized and exposed to the marketing team via the DAG in Figure 8.1 is the ability for the marketing team to iterate through scenarios and to see the results of those alternate scenarios or counterfactuals in a model.

Let's be clear about the power provided in the causal process. Typically, the end users cannot iteratively drive a predictive model on their own; it is too complicated a process. But with causal tools and techniques, the technology team and the analytics team can set up the data infrastructure, the causal models, and the appropriate user interface whereby the marketing team can formulate their varying hypotheses; debate the most probable, the most interesting, and the most profitable; and run the causal model as many times as they want. They can even run the model while all the team members sit in a room together. As the new results are produced, the team can follow any line of debate or discussion that they deem fruitful.

Perhaps an example can help to provide a bit of clarity: a subset of team members may believe that economic growth will be robust, competitive pricing will increase by double digits, and large items should dominate the additions to the core product portfolio. And, in the same pricing review cycle, another subset of team members believes the complete opposite. No problem. Both scenarios can be run through the model in different iterations, and the results can be compared to determine which environment is most probable. The marketing team can iteratively run through this process as many times as they want, with just the marketing team and maybe even with a subset of the marketing team.

This end-user-driven, nimble process enables the experimentation and results that end users have been requesting for the entire time that I have been in analytics. By contrast, in traditional AI, this lack of user-driven data and scenario-based iteration has been one of the primary friction points slowing and limiting adoption.

End-User-Driven Exploration.   As we discussed earlier in the book, users want to explore their options, and in business the options are numerous, and most, if not all, elements interact with each other. When you change price, it affects the optimal marketing mix. When you change the marketing mix, it affects the channel mix, and on and on. This knock-on effect continues with each change. No company can execute an unlimited number of changes in the real world. It is not possible, and many of the changes would produce a negative result, not what any team intends or desires.

As an example, to illustrate the power of the causal model and value to the marketing team, the DDCo team has the ability to vary and iterate through a set of products and price combinations that skew the portfolio toward large purchases in times of economic growth and consumer confidence. Also, and perhaps in the same review cycle, the DDCo marketing team might disagree on whether the U.S. and global economy is going to grow, remain at the same level of purchasing activity, or contract. A causal model and approach enables the DDCo team to review how the portfolio might perform in times of economic slowing and consumer concern by modeling the product mix in an orientation that skews toward smaller, lower-price purchases. Iterating through the model with a number of relevant but highly varied scenarios can provide insights and guidance as to how the team should modify the product mix and price to achieve their overall goals.

To provide a more detailed view of the previous example, most teams would like to understand each variable in the model in isolation and in conjunction with the other variables in the marketing mix and in the causal model. The team could agree that they want to vary the economic indicators in the model (e.g., GDP growth, consumer price index, probability of an interest rate hike by the U.S. Federal Reserve), and they would agree on the increments of movement in each model iteration. Let's say that each iteration of GDP growth is by a 10th of a percent, each iteration of CPI is by half a percent, and the probability of a rate hike is measured by increments of 100th of a percent. By agreeing on the increments, then the team can debate which combinations of these factors and all the other factors that they want to vary and in the defined increments that they will vary each factor. This can be done manually, or the team can set up a programmatic approach whereby all the possible combinations are run to determine the best possible outcome. This automated approach is where the market leaders are operating today. All possible variations (e.g., billions to trillions of combinations) of all possible factors are modeled and run through the causal model, and all the outcomes are compared to find the optimal course of action. An incredibly powerful approach and tool.

Bench Testing.   Causal AI and tools such as DAGs are exceedingly valuable to business users, as those executives and managers can begin to run through a wide range of possible scenarios and simulations without actually testing those scenarios in the market. The executives, as individuals or as a group, can see the external indicators under consideration and model their possible reactions and product/price mix before taking any concrete action, expending any resources, or spending any money.

Once the product mix and desired price levels have been modeled and the team agrees that they have selected the best product/price option, the team can move onto iterating through the possible marketing programs and channel mix.

Of course, the channel mix is a significant decision, as are the following considerations: which products are appropriate for TV spots, which products should be online only, and which products should be purchased in volumes substantial enough to fill the stocking requirements of the brick-and-mortar stores across the United States. These are decisions that require significant iterations to optimize the ultimate selection. Causal AI is uniquely suited to this task and can help the DDCo team model and arrive at a channel mix that then enables the even more complicated and multifaceted question of which marketing programs are optimal for the upcoming season.

Now that the DDCo team has the new marketing programs and the channel mix modeled and agreed to, based on the projected economic conditions and expected consumer sentiment, it is time to examine the new product portfolio and associated prices determined by the model. Again, one of the strengths of the causal approach is that if the DDCo team does not feel confident in the new product mix or price point, they can vary the inputs and execute the model again.

The final output of the model is the forecasted sales and revenue estimates. In many cases, sales and revenue *are* the primary goal of the modeling exercise. And while these numbers are important elements of managing the business, in this exercise, they are also used as checks on the causal model.

DDCo maintains its traditional AI forecast of sales and revenue and, additionally, executes a bottom-up sales and revenue forecasting system that collects and includes input from retailers, online sales environments, and sales from related categories and competitors. Sales and revenue forecasts are collected from all these internal and external systems and sources and are cross-checked and compared.

In the DDCo environment, the end result of the causal model is another data point in the sales and revenue forecasting process, and the other sales and forecasting numbers and sources are a reality check on the results of the causal model.

While the causal model produces sales and revenue forecasts, those numbers are validation points and additional data. The real value of the causal model and approach is the empowerment of the business teams to model their differing views of relevant external and internal factors in a way that enables a deep exploration of the possibilities that they might want to implement without needing to rely on the technical or analytical teams to gather additional data and run the models for the business users each time a new scenario is envisioned by the business users.

Analyzing and changing price at a portfolio level is a strategic decision that requires deep analysis and clear thinking. Our experience has shown that price is the element of the marketing mix that executives are the most reticent to change.

In times of economic expansion, no one wants to change prices for fear of slowing down the momentum of sales and the business in general. In times of economic slowing or contraction, executives do not want to change price for fear that the change will further slow or contract sales or revenue, but it has been proven that analyzing and understanding price is one of the most powerful tools available to management. The development and implementation of causal models is a valuable asset for management teams that have the courage to dig into and understand the true market dynamics that can be unleashed by understanding and optimizing prices of products and the overall portfolio. Strategic and routine pricing reviews are valuable and can be a true competitive advantage for a company, but developing and implementing a dynamic pricing environment is a game changer for not only the company that is bold enough to take this leap but can change the performance of an entire industry if done well.

One of the significant contributions of causal AI to the world is to be able to decompose a sophisticated and multifaceted challenge or process down to the elemental components and then enable business managers and executives to iterate through the process to examine all the possible options. This is a game changing capability. Once a business user, manager, or executive has access to this kind of modeling capabilities, they will never do business without this or something even better ever again.

Let's move to discuss how DDCo might want to extend the initial model into a new process and model that brings more internal and external factors into the product planning cycle.

DDCo Marketing Causal Model: Semiannual Product Planning Cycle

In the previous section we examined the DDCo annual price review and update cycle and the causal model and DAG representing that process. On a semiannual basis, the DDCo team examines the product mix and determines what new products to add and which products to discontinue. Price is examined in this process, but it is a secondary factor in the process we will examine now.

In the semiannual product planning cycle, the CMO, the CEO, and the marketing team review the following:

- Evaluting the current overall product mix to anticipate customer needs.

- Reviewing core product portfolio for relevance.

- New or returning products to be added to the core product portfolio are proposed, considered, and added.

- Seasonal products are proposed, considered, and a few are added to the current line-up.

- Slow selling products are marked to be discontinued in the upcoming season.

- The overall portfolio product price is reviewed.

- The economic environment and consumer sentiment are assessed to determine whether pricing or product portfolio changes are required.

- Prices are adjusted on individual products based on their sales performance, alignment with current trends, and fit or alignment in the portfolio.

The DAG in Figure 8.2 illustrates the semiannual product review cycle at DDCo.

The DDCo team utilized the DAG shown earlier in Figure 8.1 in the pricing process as a basis for the new DAG supporting this more detailed product planning process.

Always Consider Model Reuse. DAGs are important tools in visualizing and understanding causal relationships. One of the useful aspects of DAGs is that they can be modified, extended, and leveraged in subtle ways. You do not need to develop or redevelop each model from scratch. You can use a related

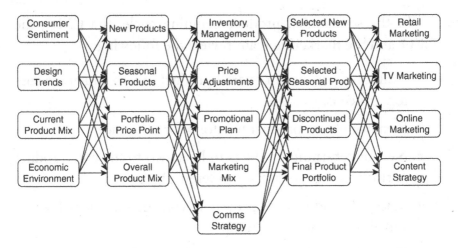

FIGURE 8.2 DAG for the DDCo semi-annual product review cycle

existing model that proved valuable and useful in a previous process and extend or modify it to meet the needs of a completely new process, or you can tweak the existing model to work in understanding a new, yet related process.

One of the valuable aspects of causal modeling is that the modeling process and the resultant model mimic the human thought process and the process followed in the real world. We have many models and processes that we use for a specific limited process. In the preceding section, we examined the price of individual products and the portfolio in general. The process described and illustrated in Figure 8.1 is a subset of the annual product portfolio review; hence, it is natural to use that smaller process to accomplish the larger process.

It may seem obvious once it is overtly stated but is important to be explicit. If you have a causal model that works, the next step in building the portfolio of causal models for an organization is to look for places where that model can be extended to serve a larger process without redeveloping part of the new model that you have already built.

Give and Take in Building a New Model.   As you can see in Figure 8.2, in the new model, in the first layer (which is represented by the leftmost column), we retain Consumer Sentiment and Economic Environment from our previous model and add in two new elements or nodes, Design Trends and Current Product Mix. Given that the focus of this new model is on the product assortment and composition of the product portfolio, we need to bring in the primary elements of the marketing mix to make those product-related decisions, while retaining the elements of the previous model that are relevant for understanding the need or options for adding and removing products from the seasonal mix and core product portfolio.

We retain about 40 percent of the nodes from Figure 8.1 as we build the new model for the semiannual product review cycle. In both DAGs in this use case, the nodes of the models are almost all fully connected. However, it is important to note that in Figure 8.2 there is one node that is not fully connected, and that is Discontinued Products. Discontinued products affect only the downstream nodes of Online Marketing and Content Strategy.

Typical Model and Process Operation: Iterating.   As we described for the annual pricing review process, the DDCo team iterates through the model varying the internal and external factors that play a part in the marketing mix affecting the product assortment. The process represented in Figure 8.2 is similar in that the DDCo team varies the inputs representing the internal and external factors that result in outputs from the annual product review process. Those outputs are the recommendations for developing the marketing mix elements represented by the nodes of Retail Marketing, TV Marketing, Online Marketing, and Content Strategy.

These four nodes and the content produced by those nodes are the optimal recommendations for the marketing mix elements. Those recommendations and model output represent the starting point for subsequent processes that the DDCo team will undertake. We will not be extending the current use case to include these subsequent processes given that we could write an entire book on causal modeling in an enterprise marketing use case context.

Keeping the Process/Model Scope Manageable and Understandable. In discussing the current use case, we want to point out that these example processes are bounded to keep the DAGs and models simple to represent and to understand. All models and their resulting DAGs can be very complicated if the complete, end-to-end process is modeled and represented.

Where you place boundaries around a process is your choice. You can select to start and end a process at any point, but it is best to start and end a model and a process where you and your team have the deepest understanding and clarity of how the process has historically and actually worked, the direct and indirect relationships and all the relevant factors that have an impact in the process, and, of course, where you and your team have the cleanest and most well-understood data.

The DAGs and models in this use case are a good starting point of a realistic example of part of an enterprise-class process that you could undertake, develop, and use in a real-world process in a manageable manner.

We are at a point where sophisticated organizations and enterprises are experimenting with AI environments that include generative AI, causal AI, and traditional AI. It is clear that AI has arrived and is available in many forms.

Leveraging LLMs in Model Building

Not all output from an LLM should be used verbatim, but the output is useful and a good starting point for the next portion of nearly any process.

An application for LLMs that is relevant for causal AI is to ask an LLM to discover and provide a list of all the direct, indirect, confounding, conflicting, and relevant nodes/elements that should be considered where building a DAG that represents a specified process.

There is no longer a need to start with a blank page when beginning a causal modeling process. Anyone can start by leveraging generative AI to build a list of relevant nodes of all types. And, if you want to take this example a step further, you can ask an LLM to build your first draft of a relevant DAG as well.

Moving from Strategy to Building and Implementing Causal AI Solutions

In the marketing use case, we have delved into a high-level strategic perspective of how leadership can embrace and utilize causal AI. We explored the decision-making processes involved in annual pricing reviews, semiannual product planning cycles, and the power of causal models represented by directed acyclic graphs (DAGs). These insights have provided a foundation for understanding the impact of causal AI on overall business strategy.

However, to clearly understand the full potential of causal AI, we will now shift our focus to tactical use cases. In the upcoming sections, we will dive into the practical implementation of causal

AI within specific applications and business processes. We will explore how hybrid teams can move from defining problem statements to constructing DAGs that accurately represent the complex relationships within a given system. Moreover, we will demonstrate the transformative effects of implementing causal AI models, enabling teams to make data-driven decisions and optimize their operational efficiency.

By bridging the gap between strategic vision and practical application, we aim to provide a comprehensive understanding of how causal AI can be integrated into the fabric of an organization. From leaders shaping high-level strategies to teams implementing causal AI models at a tactical level, the true potential of causal AI emerges when both perspectives harmoniously work together.

In this section, we will present five use cases, where teams understood the value of causal AI and created applications or modified existing decision-making processes with causal AI. The use cases are as follows:

- **Agriculture:** Enhancing crop yield
- **Commercial real estate:** Valuing warehouse space
- **Video streaming:** Enhancing content recommendations
- **Healthcare:** Reducing infant mortality
- **Retail:** Providing executives actionable information

Agriculture: Enhancing Crop Yield

In the agricultural industry, optimizing crop yield is a critical objective for farmers. With the advent of advanced technologies, such as causal AI, there is an opportunity to revolutionize traditional farming practices and unlock the potential for substantial improvements in productivity. This use case explores how a farmer's cooperative that includes more than 1,000 farms is helping its member farms take advantage of advanced technology.

The cooperative's goal is to help small to medium-sized family-run farms stay competitive against massive, industrial-scale farming operations. By pooling their resources, the cooperative is able to put emerging research and technology in the hands of its member farmers. This causal AI project is specifically focused on increasing crop yield. By harnessing the power of causal AI, the cooperative can gain valuable insights into the intricate cause-and-effect relationships that govern crop growth and make informed decisions to maximize productivity. Through the construction of a DAG and the examination of key causal variables, farmers can enhance their understanding of the factors influencing crop yield and implement data-driven strategies for sustainable and efficient agricultural practices.

Farming has always been subject to numerous, often unpredictable factors that impact crop growth and yield. From soil conditions and climate variability to irrigation practices and pest management, farmers navigate a complex web of variables when making decisions about their agricultural practices. Traditionally, these decisions have relied on correlation-based approaches, which often fail to capture the true causal factors driving crop productivity. The emergence of causal AI presents a transformative opportunity for the agricultural sector. By moving beyond correlations and focusing on causal relationships, farmers can uncover the underlying mechanisms that directly influence crop yield. This allows for precise interventions and targeted resource allocation, leading to optimized farming practices and increased crop productivity. The integration of causal AI into agriculture holds tremendous potential for sustainable food production, economic growth, and environmental stewardship. Through this use case, we will explore the practical implementation of causal AI to enhance crop yield and revolutionize agricultural decision-making.

Key Causal Variables.   When constructing a causal AI model to increase crop yield in agriculture, it is essential to identify and include key causal variables that directly or indirectly influence crop productivity. The cooperative used the latest research along with expertise from its members to identify key causal variables. These variables serve as the nodes in the DAG and provide a comprehensive understanding of the factors at play. The following are the causal variables that will be included in the causal model:

- **Soil nutrients:** The presence and levels of essential nutrients, such as nitrogen, phosphorus, and potassium, impact plant growth and overall crop health.

- **Water quality:** Ensuring that the water has the proper nutrients can be critical to improving crop yield. In addition, sufficient and well-timed irrigation is crucial for providing plants with the necessary water resources for optimal growth.

- **Temperature:** Crop growth is influenced by temperature variations, including optimal ranges for germination, photosynthesis, and flowering.

- **Light exposure:** Adequate sunlight is essential for photosynthesis, which is the primary process through which plants convert light energy into chemical energy.

- **Pest and disease pressure:** Managing pest infestations and diseases is critical to protect crops from damage and yield loss.

- **Crop variety:** The selection of appropriate crop varieties can significantly impact yield potential, disease resistance, and adaptability to specific environmental conditions.

- **Fertilizer application:** The type, timing, and amount of fertilizer applied influence plant nutrition and can enhance crop growth.

- **Weed competition:** Managing weed populations is crucial to reduce competition for resources, ensuring that crops can access essential nutrients and sunlight.

- **Pollination:** Pollinator presence and activity, such as bees, significantly impact fruit set and yield in many crops.

- **Crop rotation:** Implementing crop rotation practices helps break pest and disease cycles, enhances soil health, and improves overall yield.

- **Irrigation management:** Proper management of irrigation schedules, including timing and water application methods, is vital for efficient water use and crop health.

- **Soil pH:** Soil pH affects nutrient availability, microbial activity, and overall soil health, thereby influencing crop growth and yield.

- **Genetic traits:** Plant genetics play a role in determining yield potential, disease resistance, tolerance to environmental stresses, and overall crop performance.

- **Pruning and training:** Proper pruning and training techniques can enhance light penetration, airflow, and overall plant vigor, leading to improved yield.

- **Harvest timing:** The timing of crop harvest can impact yield and quality, ensuring that crops are harvested at optimal maturity for maximum productivity.

These key causal variables provide a foundation for constructing a comprehensive causal AI model to optimize crop yield in agriculture. By considering the interplay and relationships among these variables, farmers can gain valuable insights into the factors influencing crop productivity and implement targeted strategies for maximizing yield.

Creating the DAG.   Constructing the DAG is a crucial step in developing a causal AI model for increasing crop yield. The DAG represents the causal relationships between the key variables identified in the previous section and provides a visual representation of how these variables influence each other.

For all the examples in this chapter, the team has to go through the process of creating a DAG. The overall DAG creation process will be similar in each case. Therefore, we will not repeat the step for creating the DAG for the subsequent use cases.

One of the main challenges faced by the team was the complexity and interconnectedness of agricultural systems. Agricultural environments are dynamic and multifaceted, involving numerous interacting factors that influence crop growth and yield. Capturing the intricate cause-and-effect relationships among these variables and representing them accurately in the DAG required a deep understanding of the domain and collaboration between domain experts, data scientists, and agronomists. Balancing the level of granularity in the DAG while keeping it comprehensible was a challenge, as too much complexity could make the model difficult to interpret and apply in practice.

Another challenge was the availability and quality of data. Developing a reliable and robust causal AI model relies on high-quality data that accurately represents the relationships between the variables. However, in agriculture, data collection can be challenging due to various factors such as variability in field conditions, variations in crop management practices, and limited historical data. The team had to carefully select and integrate data sources, considering factors such as data completeness, accuracy, and representativeness of different agricultural contexts. Addressing missing data, data inconsistencies, and data quality issues required meticulous data preprocessing and validation efforts.

Furthermore, the team faced the challenge of dealing with confounding variables and identifying causal relationships among variables amid correlations. In agriculture, multiple variables often exhibit correlations due to shared influences or confounding factors, making it crucial to disentangle the causal relationships from spurious associations. Overcoming confounding required a combination of domain expertise, statistical analysis, and causal inference techniques to identify true causal links and avoid misleading conclusions.

Despite these challenges, the team's collaborative efforts, domain knowledge, and expertise in causal modeling allowed them to overcome the hurdles and create a robust DAG that accurately represented the causal relationships among key variables. The DAG served as a foundation for developing the causal AI model, guiding subsequent steps in leveraging the power of causal AI to increase crop yield in agriculture.

Moving from the DAG to Implementing the Causal AI Model. The farmer's cooperative implemented the causal AI solution, ensuring that its member farms can leverage the benefits of new technology and compete more effectively with large-scale industrial farms. With a focus on simplicity and accessibility, the cooperative has developed a user-friendly application that abstracts the complexities of the underlying causal AI model, allowing individual farmers to easily access and utilize the solution without requiring extensive technical knowledge. The individual farmers of course are focused on running their businesses rather than diving deep into causal AI.

The application that is available as a web application and mobile/tablet friendly version is built on top of the causal AI model and provides a seamless interface between the farmers and the causal AI model, enabling them to interact with the system effortlessly. Through the intuitive application, farmers gain access to personalized insights, recommendations, and decision support based on the outputs of the causal AI model. The application presents the information in a clear and actionable manner, empowering farmers to make informed decisions about their farming practices. Farmers can input specific information about their farm to customize the application for the conditions on their property. For example, farmers can input their soil types, crop mix, and topography of their fields and get specific, actionable suggestions about actions to take.

Through a combination of natural language processing and visualization tools, the cooperative has successfully abstracted the complexities of the causal AI model. Farmers can easily understand the model's outputs through narratives and visual representations, enabling them to understand the underlying causal relationships and make well-informed decisions. The user interface of the application is designed to facilitate easy exploration of different scenarios, allowing farmers to simulate the potential impacts of different interventions or changes in their farming strategies.

One critical feature of the causal AI-based application is that farmers can interrogate the recommendations. This means the farmers don't have to blindly follow the recommendations; instead, they are able to see the reasoning behind the suggestions. For example, the application might choose a planting date based on a variety of causal factors. While a machine learning (ML)–based application will simply tell the farmer to plant on Day X, the causal application can explain *why* the farmer should plant on that day. This level of explainability and transparency helps to build trust in the software solution.

To ensure the accuracy and relevance of the causal AI model, the cooperative has trained it using historical data collected from the member farms. The model takes into account each farmer's particular key causal variables. By leveraging advanced ML techniques and the insights derived from the DAG, the model accurately captures the complex interplay of causal factors and generates precise recommendations tailored to each farmer's specific circumstances.

The cooperative has also prioritized scalability and adaptability in the implementation process. They have developed a robust infrastructure capable of handling data from multiple member farms and seamlessly integrating with various data sources, including IoT sensors, satellite imagery, and weather forecasts. This ensures that the model can effectively process and analyze a vast amount of data, providing timely and accurate insights to farmers.

To support the farmers in effectively utilizing the causal AI application, the cooperative provides ongoing training and assistance. They conduct regular training sessions, workshops, and webinars to familiarize the farmers with the features and functionalities of the application. The cooperative also offers personalized support to address any concerns or challenges faced by the farmers, ensuring a smooth and seamless experience throughout their interaction with the causal AI solution.

With the implemented causal AI solution, the member farms of the cooperative have witnessed significant improvements in their farming practices. By leveraging the power of technology and data-driven insights, farmers are able to optimize their operations, make informed decisions, and increase their competitiveness in the market. The cooperative's commitment to implementing a user-friendly and accessible solution has empowered individual farmers to embrace new technology without being overly complex, resulting in a causal AI application that has enhanced productivity, profitability, and sustainability for their farms. The benefit to the causal AI approach is that farmers will have a tool to help them determine the optimal approach to gain better outcomes and revenue.

To view a DAG that is publicly available and focused on increasing crop yield, visit https://github.com/Agri-Hub/AAAI23-Eval-AgriRecommendations. As you will see, this DAG is supported by a paper and data so that you can create the DAG and create a causal AI model on your own.

Commercial Real Estate: Valuing Warehouse Space

In the competitive landscape of commercial real estate, accurate valuation of properties is crucial for making informed investment decisions. Large international commercial real estate investment firms are constantly seeking opportunities to maximize returns and gain a competitive edge. This use case explores how a large commercial real estate investment firm is leveraging causal AI to value warehouse space. The firm's acquisition team, equipped with strong analytical skills but limited knowledge of ML, AI, and causal AI, require an application underpinned by causal AI to analyze properties and provide transparent recommendations on pricing and the best and highest use for warehouse spaces. The key benefit of the causal AI approach, compared to traditional ML, is its transparency, allowing the team to understand the underlying factors influencing valuations without delving into complex mathematical models.

The acquisition team faces the challenge of identifying potentially underpriced warehouse spaces in the market. Traditional valuation methods rely on historical data and correlation-based approaches, which may overlook the true causal factors driving property prices. The team recognizes the need for a more advanced and accurate solution that considers the complex web of variables influencing warehouse valuations. The final solution for the acquisition team needs to be complex enough to give the team an in-depth understanding of how the causal AI solution is generating its recommendations without going into the complexities of the causal algorithms.

Key Causal Variables.   The firm collaborates with a variety of experts in the fields of economics and real estate to identify the relevant factors influencing warehouse valuations. The following are some of the key causal variables considered in the model:

- **Location:** The geographical location of the warehouse, including proximity to transportation hubs, major roads, and customer markets, impacts its desirability and market value.

- **Size and configuration:** The total square footage, layout, and configuration of the warehouse space influence its functionality, scalability, and potential uses, affecting its value.

- **Access to amenities:** The availability of amenities such as loading docks, parking, and security systems can enhance the attractiveness and value of a warehouse.

- **Infrastructure and utilities:** The quality and reliability of infrastructure and utilities, including power supply, water, and Internet connectivity, are crucial considerations for warehouse tenants, impacting the value of the space.

- **Zoning and regulations:** Local zoning regulations and land-use policies affect the permissibility of certain activities and potential restrictions, influencing the value and potential uses of the warehouse.

- **Market demand and trends:** The current market demand for warehouse space, along with emerging trends in the industry, can impact the pricing and competitiveness of properties.

- **Rental and lease rates:** The prevailing rental and lease rates in the market, including factors such as lease terms, incentives, and tenant profiles, directly influence the valuation of warehouse properties.

- **Economic factors:** Macroeconomic indicators, such as GDP growth, employment rates, and interest rates, play a significant role in shaping the demand and pricing dynamics of commercial real estate, including warehouse space.

- **Industry and tenant profiles:** The specific industry requirements and tenant profiles, such as e-commerce, manufacturing, or logistics companies, can influence the demand and value of warehouse properties.

- **Market competitiveness:** The level of competition within the local market, including the availability of similar warehouse spaces and the presence of competing properties, affects the pricing and negotiation dynamics.

By incorporating these key causal variables into the causal AI model, the firm gains a comprehensive understanding of the factors influencing warehouse valuations. This enables the acquisition team to accurately identify potentially underpriced properties and make strategic investment decisions.

Implementing the Causal AI Model. The firm develops a user-friendly application that hides the underlying causal AI model, making it easily accessible to the acquisition team. The application, available as a web and mobile-friendly version, provides a seamless interface between the team and the causal AI model. Through this intuitive application, the team can input property data and receive personalized insights, recommendations, and decision support based on the outputs of the causal AI model.

Unlike some causal applications that fully abstract the complexities of the underlying model, the application the firm's IT and data science team built for the acquisition team can provide detailed data on why the model is providing a specific valuation for a warehouse property. For example, if a property is potentially undervalued, the acquisition team can do a deep dive into the data that is driving the model's suggestion. In essence, in this use case, the team takes an approach that human intelligence plus machine intelligence is far greater than on its own. The acquisition team has a deep understanding of commercial real estate, but the causal AI model is able to analyze massive amounts of data quickly.

With the implemented causal AI solution, the firm's acquisition team gains a competitive advantage in the commercial real estate market. The transparency and explainability of the causal AI model provide the team with deeper insights into warehouse valuations, enabling them to identify undervalued properties.

The commercial real estate firm has transitioned from traditional correlation-based property valuation methods to a causal AI model, which has led to significant operational changes. This model leverages a diverse set of causal variables, providing more precise valuations. The firm developed a user-friendly application that created a transparent interface between the acquisition team and the AI model. The blend of human expertise with machine intelligence allows the team to identify undervalued properties and optimize investment strategies. Adopting causal AI has enhanced the firm's competitive position in the highly competitive commercial real estate market.

Video Streaming: Enhancing Content Recommendations

In the rapidly evolving landscape of online video streaming, personalized content recommendations play a pivotal role in providing an engaging user experience. A worldwide streaming video service is harnessing the power of causal AI to rethink its content recommendation system. The service's data science team, composed of experts from various disciplines such as biology, psychology, economics, and statistics, has made significant contributions to advancing causal effects research in recent years. By integrating causal AI into its recommendation engine, the service aims to deliver more accurate and transparent content suggestions to its global user base.

The challenge faced by the streaming video service is to enhance the effectiveness of its recommendation algorithms by efficiently estimating causal effects. Traditional approaches that rely on correlation-based methods fail to capture the true causal relationships between user preferences and content recommendations. While correlations can provide some level of association between user preferences and recommended content, they often fail to uncover the underlying reasons behind user preferences. This limitation poses a significant challenge for the streaming service as it aims to deliver highly personalized and relevant content recommendations to its users.

For example, let's consider a scenario where two users, User A and User B, have a high correlation in their viewing habits.

Based on this correlation, a traditional correlation-based recommendation system might suggest similar content to both users. However, upon closer examination, it is revealed that user A's preference for a specific genre is due to their passion for a particular actor, while user B's preference is driven by their interest in a specific director. The correlation-based system fails to capture these individual causal factors behind the users' preferences, resulting in inaccurate content recommendations. As a result, user A might receive content recommendations that align with their passion for the actor but miss out on content from other genres they enjoy, while user B might receive content recommendations solely based on the director, disregarding their broader interests. This example highlights the limitations of correlation-based recommendations in capturing the nuanced causal relationships between user preferences and content recommendations.

Key Causal Variables.   To build a robust causal AI model for content recommendations, the data science team works across the business to identify key causal variables. The following are some of the variables that will be included in the causal model:

- **Viewing history:** The user's past viewing habits and preferences serve as strong indicators of their content preferences.

- **Genre preferences:** User preferences for specific genres, such as action, comedy, or drama, influence their content recommendations.

- **Similar user interactions:** Analyzing the behavior and preferences of users with similar viewing patterns helps identify content that may be of interest to a particular user.

- **Content attributes:** Features such as language, duration, release year, and cast members contribute to content relevance and user engagement.

- **Viewing context:** Factors such as time of day, day of the week, and location may impact a user's content preferences and viewing patterns.

- **Social influence:** The influence of social connections, such as friends or family members, on content recommendations and user preferences.

- **User feedback:** User ratings, reviews, and feedback provide valuable signals for understanding content satisfaction and tailoring recommendations.

- **External factors:** External events, such as holidays or global trends, may influence user preferences and content relevance.

By incorporating these key causal variables into the causal AI model, the streaming video service gains a deeper understanding of the factors driving user preferences and content relevance. This enables the service to provide more accurate and personalized recommendations to its vast user base, resulting in improved user satisfaction and engagement.

Implementing the Causal AI Model. To integrate causal AI into their recommendation engine, the streaming video service undertakes the task of converting the causal model, based on the identified causal variables and the constructed DAG, into code that can integrate with the company's existing infrastructure. This approach allows the company to leverage the power of causal AI without the need to rewrite or change their entire recommendation engine. Instead, the existing ML algorithm used for content recommendations will be replaced with the causal algorithm.

The data science team collaborates closely with the engineering team to ensure a smooth integration process. They work together to translate the causal model's logic, derived from the DAG, into code that can be executed within the recommendation engine's framework. The team leverages their expertise in software engineering, algorithms, and data processing to implement the causal algorithm efficiently and optimize its performance. Of course, processing speed is important, and the team uses graphics processing units (GPUs) to provide near real-time recommendations.

During the integration process, the team ensures that the causal algorithm integrates with the recommendation engine's existing data pipelines and interfaces. The algorithm takes into account the relevant causal variables and their relationships, allowing it to generate precise content recommendations based on the underlying causal effects. The implementation process also includes thorough testing and validation to ensure the accuracy and reliability of the causal AI model within the recommendation engine.

Once integrated, the causal AI model becomes an integral part of the recommendation engine's workflow. The implementation of the causal AI model brings significant improvements to the company's content recommendation system. The integration of causal AI enhances the precision and relevance of content recommendations, leading to increased user satisfaction, engagement, and ultimately higher customer retention. By leveraging the power of causal AI, the streaming video service establishes itself as a leader in delivering highly personalized and engaging content experiences to its global user base.

To improve the ability to respond to changing customer requirements for video streaming, a causal AI approach helps management gain a deeper understanding of the causal relationships behind user preferences, such as history and social influence.

With a carefully curated causal model, the service is able to replace a traditional ML algorithm with a causal model without having to rebuild the underlying recommendation engine. This approach improves the relevance of content suggestions and increases customer retention.

Healthcare: Reducing Infant Mortality

Infant mortality remains an important concern in many parts of the world, including emerging countries struggling with limited access to quality healthcare. These regions face unique challenges, such as cultural preferences for home births and insufficient healthcare infrastructure, contributing to alarmingly high infant mortality rates. Recognizing the urgent need to address this issue, a nongovernmental organization (NGO) has partnered with local health officials to implement innovative approaches using advanced technology. The NGO aims to leverage the power of causal AI to develop a mobile application empowering local health workers to provide evidence-based recommendations and bridge the gap between traditional practices and modern healthcare.

The emerging country at the center of this use case struggles with cultural norms favoring home births over deliveries in healthcare facilities. This cultural preference, coupled with limited access to quality healthcare, poses significant challenges to reducing infant mortality rates. The NGO's research along with peer-reviewed academic research has identified a causal link between births in healthcare facilities and a reduction in infant mortalities. A major challenge the NGO faces is how to get this information to pregnant women—especially those in remote areas. There are a variety of volunteer groups and local health workers that are focused on providing medical information and evidence-based approaches to healthcare throughout remote villages. However, trust remains a major challenge along with relatively low literacy rates.

The goal of the NGO's work is to create a healthcare ecosystem that bridges the gap between cultural traditions and modern medical practices, ideally leading to a significant reduction in infant mortality rates.

Key Causal Variables.   The NGO is, of course, not the only group researching infant mortality. There is a large body of research from academia as well as on-the-ground research that has been done in other countries. One of the complexities that the team ran into when identifying causal variables is that they need to make sure the variables and the relationships between the nodes are reflective not only of the country but the specific region where they are working. The NGO's research team needs to work hand in hand with local groups that understand the intricacies of the local culture. Even though the NGO has been working in the country for a number of years, the delicate, private, and religious nature of the reasons why people make birthing decisions can be difficult for outsiders to understand. The hybrid team that the NGO assembled to come up with the causal variables and identify their relationships, including a diverse set of people such as religious leaders, healthcare experts, and a number of young married women who had recently delivered children in the last several years.

The following are the key causal variables that the team included in their model:

- **Birth setting:** The location and type of birth setting, such as home births or healthcare facilities, have a direct impact on infant mortality rates.

- **Prenatal care:** Access to and utilization of prenatal care services play a crucial role in identifying and managing potential risks during pregnancy.

- **Maternal health:** The overall health and well-being of expectant mothers influence the health outcomes of both mother and child.

- **Neonatal care:** Quality and availability of care for newborns, including essential interventions and medical support, contribute to reducing infant mortality.

- **Vaccination:** The timely administration of vaccines helps protect infants from life-threatening diseases.

- **Nutrition:** Adequate maternal and infant nutrition is essential for healthy growth and development.

- **Socioeconomic status:** Economic factors, including income level and access to resources, can impact healthcare accessibility and quality.

- **Education:** The level of education of mothers and caregivers can influence health-related knowledge and practices.

- **Sanitation and hygiene:** Access to clean water and sanitation facilities is critical for preventing infections and reducing infant mortality.

- **Family support:** The presence of a supportive family network can positively impact maternal and child health outcomes.

- **Health worker training:** The training and skills of healthcare professionals directly affect the quality of care provided to mothers and infants.

- **Health infrastructure:** The availability and adequacy of healthcare facilities and services are crucial for timely interventions and emergency care.

- **Health policies:** Government policies and initiatives aimed at improving maternal and child health can have a significant impact on reducing infant mortality rates.

- **Cultural practices:** Understanding and incorporating cultural beliefs and practices is essential for effective healthcare delivery.

- **Community engagement:** Active involvement and participation of communities in healthcare initiatives can enhance awareness and utilization of healthcare services.

Implementing the Causal AI Model. The most important part of the NGOs project is getting the results of the causal AI model into the field so that they can positively impact healthcare outcomes. To implement the causal AI model, the NGO's team of experts builds a mobile application that serves as a powerful tool for local volunteers and health workers that directly interact with pregnant women and their families. The application, developed based on the underlying causal AI model, aims to empower health workers with evidence-based information and personalized recommendations while considering cultural and economic factors. The application was built using open-source software designed to work on Android devices with lower compute and memory requirements. In addition, the application is able to provide some insights when it is disconnected from the Web. These design features of the application make it scalable and practical to get insights into the field.

The mobile application abstracts the complexities of the causal AI model, ensuring that health workers and patients can benefit from its capabilities without requiring any understanding of causal AI or ML. The focus is on providing practical, personalized, and actionable information to reduce infant mortality rates. The application enables health workers to gather relevant data about pregnant women and generate evidence-based recommendations tailored to the specific cultural and economic context. By considering the identified causal variables, the app generates customized recommendations and provides explanations for each recommendation.

One of the biggest benefits of the application is that volunteers and healthcare workers can sit down with pregnant women, women who are planning on trying to have a baby, and their extended families that they tend to live with to have informed discussions. Instead of the healthcare provider simply declaring that a certain course of action is the right approach, the worker can explain to the family how they reached the determination by customizing the application for that woman. The application doesn't go into the details of the actual DAG, but via natural language processing it presents clear reasoning and explanations on why it is presenting a course of care—and how that suggestion can positively impact the health outcome for both the expected mother and the baby.

Finally, as the NGO continues its research, the team can also present findings to governmental officials on how changes to economic, gender, and educational policies can reduce overall infant mortality rates. As the team further pushes for governmental action, they can use causal AI to prove that reducing infant mortality can overall increase the country's GDP, reduce civil unrest, increase imports, and improve the country's outlook overall. Of course, this final finding is a lofty task, but it begins by creating a causal AI-based application individuals in disconnected villages can interact with.

Being able to respond to an increase in infant mortality rates in emerging countries, an NGO has utilized causal AI to implement a mobile application that can help local healthcare teams. The application means that local health workers have access to a tool that helps them better understand what actions to take in their field. The causal AI approach helps the healthcare team execute a plan based on the cultural and economic issues to support pregnant women and their families. The combination of causal AI and local knowledge bridges the gap between traditional practices and modern healthcare to reduce infant mortality.

Retail: Providing Executives Actionable Information

In the highly competitive retail industry, the need for intelligent and informed decision-making is paramount. Effective product positioning—encompassing merchandising, pricing, and marketing strategies—is a critical driver of success. A national retail company needs to constantly innovate and adapt their product positioning approaches in response to the changing dynamics of the market, consumer preferences, and competitive forces.

This use case presents an example of a national retail company seeking to rethink the way it positions products. The company's merchandising, pricing, and marketing teams are embarking on a collaborative project, drawing from the success of previous causal AI projects within their IT operations group. They aim to harness the power of causal AI to gain deeper insights into the interplay of variables influencing product positioning and optimize their strategies accordingly.

The ultimate objective is to have a comprehensive dashboard that business decision-makers can utilize to understand the key causal factors impacting their business. This dashboard will act as a decision support system, showing the possible impact of different decisions and highlighting the levers that decision-makers can pull to drive change.

In contrast to traditional ML approaches, the causal AI model aims to provide actionable insights that can directly inform decision-making. For example, if the price of a product drops, the model can provide insights into how much they would need to augment marketing and sales efforts to compensate for the drop in price. This is a level of granularity and causality often missing from correlation-based ML models.

Key Causal Variables   To implement a causal AI model for product positioning, the joint team has identified the following causal variables:

- **Product price:** The pricing strategy of the product significantly influences consumer purchasing decisions.
- **Product quality:** The perceived and actual quality of a product impacts its market acceptance.
- **Marketing budget:** The amount allocated to marketing activities can directly influence product awareness and sales.
- **Marketing channels:** The choice of marketing channels (online, TV, print, etc.) affects the product's visibility and reach.
- **Competitor pricing:** Competitors' pricing strategies can influence the relative attractiveness of the product.
- **Product availability:** The availability of the product in physical and online stores affects its accessibility to consumers.
- **Customer preferences:** Changing customer preferences and tastes can sway the success of a product.
- **Seasonal factors:** Seasonal trends and events can cause fluctuations in product demand.
- **Product reviews:** Online reviews and ratings influence customer purchasing decisions.
- **Product features:** The set of features that the product offers influences its attractiveness to consumers.

- **Brand reputation:** The reputation and trust associated with the brand can impact product sales.

- **Economic conditions:** Macro-economic factors such as disposable income and consumer confidence influence buying behavior.

- **Product life cycle stage:** The stage of the product in its life cycle (introduction, growth, maturity, decline) affects sales.

- **Product packaging:** The attractiveness and functionality of product packaging can sway purchasing decisions.

- **Discounts and promotions:** Sales promotions and discounts can boost short-term product demand.

- **Distribution channels:** The efficiency and reach of the distribution channels affect product availability and sales.

- **Consumer trends:** Current trends in consumer behavior can impact the popularity and demand for a product.

- **Product positioning:** The perceived value and positioning of the product in the market influence its success.

- **Sales force effectiveness:** The skill and effectiveness of the sales team can impact product sales.

- **Regulatory environment:** Changes in regulations or compliance requirements can affect product availability or features.

Implementing the Causal Model.   The result of the project needs to be an interface that leadership teams can interact with. The team used the company's preferred data visualization tool (i.e., Tableau, Microsoft Power BI) to transform the causal AI model into an intuitive, user-friendly dashboard. This creation empowers the business leadership team with the ability to navigate the complex relationships between various pricing, marketing factors, and merchandising.

The dashboard's interactive nature gives the leadership team an unprecedented level of control over their decision-making process. They can manipulate different variables, or "levers," to observe and understand their impacts in real-time, thus enabling them to take strategic, proactive actions instead of reactive ones. For example, before the team increases prices, they need to understand and simulate the impact of that new pricing and how they can medicate a hit on revenue by, for example, changing merchandising and increasing marketing to sell more volume.

In addition, this causal AI–driven dashboard is designed to allow root-cause analysis. This function helps the team identify the underlying reasons behind specific outcomes. If a particular strategy did not achieve the expected result, the team can dig deep into the causal relationships to uncover the fundamental cause. Conversely, if a strategy has led to a significant success, the root-cause analysis can reveal what actions drove this favorable outcome, allowing them to replicate the strategy.

Furthermore, the business-facing dashboard also has the ability to highlight and scrutinize outliers. These are instances that deviate significantly from the norm. Outlier analysis allows the team to understand these rare occurrences and yield valuable insights. The team can analyze outliers to determine whether they are anomalies to be avoided or successful exceptions to be emulated. For example, if a particular merchandising endeavor led to a spike in sales, the team can dig into what caused the outlier and how it can be replicated in the future.

Through this causal AI-enabled dashboard, the business leadership team gains a robust analytical tool that facilitates an in-depth understanding of its product positioning strategies. This potent blend of causal AI and data visualization gives the team the data-driven insights and the power to direct its operations more effectively.

In the competitive retail landscape, the benefit of causal AI helps organizations optimize their strategy. The value of causal AI is that it can provide actionable insights into issues such as property pricing, marketing channels, and customer preferences. By being able to provide an interactive dashboard, management can manipulate variables to better understand the impact of different approaches to the market. The solution can indicate the root cause of a market issue and thus uncover what is behind specific outcomes and indicate outliers that they need to better understand. This integration of causal AI and data visualization enables management to create strategies that improve revenue and overall business outcomes.

Summary

In this chapter, we detailed six use cases to demonstrate different approaches to understanding and using causal models. We first provided insights into a strategy view of bringing a team together to understand the nuances and complexities involved in a corporate marketing organization to create a causal model. In the next five use cases, we focused on how critical issues within several vertical markets can be addressed through a causal modeling approach. While our first use case was very broad, taking into account the overarching strategy of solving go-to market issues, the subsequent use cases apply a narrower lens to look at specific aspects of the organization with a causal AI approach.

In examining the causal modeling approach, we were able to illustrate how causal modelling empowers the business users to clearly articulate their needs to their colleagues in technology and analytics teams to enable the hybrid team to build the required data integrations, the data acquisition processes and tools, and the causal models that we have seen explained in the various DAGs in the chapter.

One of the primary value streams delivered to business managers and executives, and to the organization as a whole, is the ability of the business teams to freely iterate across many scenarios and to follow their ideas and intuitions in pursuit of the optimal mix of process, product, and operational elements to enable optimal performance.

In an environment in which traditional AI models and modeling are being used, the iteration cycle requires the technology and analytics teams to closely support the business teams when the business teams want to investigate a new scenario, and while this can, and does, work, it is much slower than the iterative cycle that is empowered in the causal approach.

We are all aware that change is the only constant in the world today and that the rate of change continues to accelerate. With the advent and proliferation of generative AI and LLMs, that acceleration, for those willing to embrace it, has just gone to a new level. But, also in this new level of acceleration is a benefit that inures to those that want to engage with and leverage causal AI.

One of the most difficult and insurmountable hurdles (until now) of engaging with causal AI was the discovery of the relevant elements that are involved in even simple business processes such as those that we have seen in the two use cases outlined in this chapter. Generative AI and LLMs with their no-barrier-to-entry interface driven by a conversational paradigm has made the discovery of relevant causal elements in any process accessible to everyone.

We have undertaken a journey of describing, outlining, and explaining what causal AI is and how it fits into the world of scalable organizations. We have walked through how to understand causal AI and related tools and technologies and how to apply causal AI to use cases that we can all understand and connect with.

Now it is time to turn our attention to the future of AI and the role that causal AI plays in that new and exciting chapter of AI, business, and our world. Let's move on to our final chapter and talk about the future of AI.

9

The Future of Causal AI

In this chapter, we will discuss the future of causal AI. We will ground our discussion in what has developed in the field up to today and lay out where we see the field growing and going in the coming years.

Where We Stand Today

As we discussed earlier in the book, the field of causal AI is emerging before our eyes. Causal AI is being developed and moving out of academia into the commercial world. It is rare and unusual for a new field to be born in front of our eyes, and we are living at a certain period in the evolution of causal AI.

Up until the present day, causal inference and the solutions that we refer to as causal AI are increasingly being embraced by technical innovators and leading data scientists. In the last several years, more businesses are beginning to understand that causal AI could be a valuable, important, and strategic technology.

Executives, business managers, technologists, and data science professionals are all beginning to understand the value and potential of being able to model and analyze the true and actual underlying cause-and-effect relationships of nearly any and every process that they seek to manipulate and manage in a proactive manner. Can managers and executives really change outcomes if we understand why those outcomes are taking place? Can business professionals model several scenarios well in advance of decision-making to determine the optimal course of action during the relevant planning cycles? This is one of the promises of causal AI, and as we move closer and closer to viable commercial causal AI products, this promise is becoming a reality for early-stage innovators today.

One of the primary reasons that we decided to write this book was to provide you, our readers, with the fundamental understanding of what causal AI is and how best to use the technology, techniques, and tools in a business context.

Causal AI is a reflection of the reality of how humans think, analyze, and make decisions about their options about how to invest, manage, and where to direct the resources under their control to address organizational requirements. Causal AI is the embodiment of how the real world works.

Causal AI is a departure from the idea that we can create purely data-driven AI systems that are devoid of the interventions of humans. For example, in the early 2000s, there were academic practitioners and data scientists who believed that it was possible for an AI system to have the ability and capacity to think and reason like humans. While there are many practical applications for traditional AI, those applications do not fundamentally help us solve the problems related to why things happen. Much of the attention, as we have discussed in earlier chapters, is thanks to the groundbreaking thinking and work of Judea Pearl. Dr. Pearl has encouraged business managers, executives, and data scientists to begin to think about using AI to explain the cause and effect of important problems through his innovations in causal AI.

Foundations of Causal AI

Causality is one of the most powerful and fundamental paradigms that we know and leverage in our daily lives, and it is one of the most sophisticated fields of AI. The majority of the enduring ideas that evolve to the point of being built into physical manifestations of technology such as hardware or software are reproductions of how we as humans think and act. This type and style of development has been seen in multiple fields: business, psychology, sociology, and most prominently computer science, specifically in the area of AI. We have also seen a measurable positive impact in industries including consumer healthcare, manufacturing, pharmaceuticals, and agriculture.

Causality is an elemental force or phenomena in our daily world, and seeing it becoming a real and operational part of our technology and AI ecosystem is a monumental achievement that cannot be overstated.

In the process of creating causal AI, conceptual models needed to be documented, codified, refined, and standardized. There were new ways of thinking about how causality actually works, how one force, directly and indirectly, affects another force or element, and how elements and forces confound each and conflict with each other. An extension of calculus had to be invented, vetted, refined, documented, explained, and taught to an entire generation of computer scientists and mathematicians. All of this, and much more, needed to be examined and reduced to first principles. This complete corpus of work had to, and has been, completed, and most of it has been completed in the past 50 years.

The Causal AI Journey

We are witnessing the evolution of the field of causal AI and are now at a point where the pioneers of the field are beginning to be recognized for their brilliance rather than being dismissed as chasing a pipe dream. And causal AI is being experimented with by a wider and wider group of academics, technologists, analytics professionals, and thought leaders in the business realm. All of this effort has laid the foundations of the causal AI subfield. We are starting to see the emergence of the causal AI industry. Let's discuss what we see taking shape as a new set of commercial companies and the supporting ecosystem.

Causal AI Today

The global ecosystem that produces software has evolved. Today, most of the leading-edge software development begins as open-source software. Thirty years ago, before the creation of open-source software, the majority of software was created by entrepreneurs as part of their small, innovative startups. Think of Oracle or SAP; if anyone had suggested to Larry Ellison or Hasso Plattner that they provide easy and broad access to their source code, the two early-stage inventors would have said that the idea was the complete opposite of the guiding force for their companies. Providing access to source code was what early innovators tried very hard to prevent and was one of the core principles of building a defensible competitive strategy for a software company.

From our review of the current state of the causal AI industry, most, if not all, of the software available has its roots in open source. Those open-source projects that started in garage-based ideas, government- and corporate-funded incubators, university research labs, and corporate innovation labs have become the basis of the causal AI industry that we see today.

A handful of early-stage companies have been founded to extend the development effort with integrations between discrete open-source libraries, proprietary wrappers, new libraries, layers to improve core functionality, refinements to the user interface and user experience, enterprise-class support, and more.

Today, causal AI has many of the elements required to become a global force in the AI industry. However, it is not a quick solution to complex problems. Unlike some technological innovations, causal AI requires a collaboration between humans and machines. Data scientists, analytics professionals, business leaders, and subject-matter experts must be able to collaborate on solutions. Currently, causal AI is not a widespread competency or capability for AI, analytics, technical, or business professionals. When we talk with AI professionals, it is clear that only a fraction of the population in any organization and in the AI field in general knows what causal AI is, and even fewer have a deep understanding of the causal AI field.

We can use any of the well-known market maturity models from any of the established technology analysts or we can create our own, but the market dynamics described are all the same. First, a technology is created. In the next phase, the innovators create alternative offerings and compete for market dominance or leadership. PyWhy is the clear leader, with Microsoft and Amazon joining forces. There are other tools and technologies that will be created and will challenge PyWhy for leadership, but it will be hard for those efforts to pass PyWhy.

It is not necessary for any challenger to supplant PyWhy as the market leader. The majority of markets support three market leaders/participants. The clear market and functionality leader, in the case of causal AI, is PyWhy. Next is the market innovator, the firm, project, or effort that keeps pushing the boundaries of innovation and driving their efforts and, by association, the market forward. Finally, there are the fast followers. The fast follower is the company or project that provides a low-cost or entry-level function in contrast to the market leader, which is typically the offering with the highest or premium pricing. This market dynamic is well established and has played out repeatedly in the global market, and it will play out in the causal AI market as well. It will be interesting to see who becomes the market innovator and fast follower in the causal AI market; we will be watching with great interest.

What's Next for Causal AI

In the remainder of this chapter, we will examine the top trends and predictions for the future of causal AI. Businesses are starting to understand that causal AI offers a unique opportunity to begin to truly transform the way their businesses operate. Business leaders can effectively understand why problems are occurring and what they can do when they discover outliers that are causing problems for customers.

The software that is the basis of the causal AI market needs to evolve, it is too hard to use, it has functional gaps, and it is not robust enough for reliable enterprise-class use today. While that may sound harsh, it is true, but not problematic. All software starts out like this, and the software that is successful transitions through the subsequent hurdles and stages to become global technological and economic assets.

In building new and innovative software, it is common to build the same software three times or more. The first iteration proves that the idea will work. The second attempt refines the approach and implementation, and the third round of work standardizes, hardens, and builds software that is reliable, robust, and scalable.

That is not to say that all software stagnates after the third round of innovation. Successful software continues to evolve, expand, and gain more functionality. The takeaway from the three-cycle innovation model is that the software needs to be proven, refined, and hardened. If those primary objectives can be achieved in the initial three projects, then there is a chance that the software can be refined and expanded further. The first three efforts provide a solid foundation for the future growth and use of the software by companies, governments, universities, not-for-profit organizations, and more.

The causal AI software market is in the process of moving past the three-cycle model. Libraries such as DAGitty and systems such as PyWhy and others are proven and are the basis of continued experimentation and expansion. Early-stage innovators are experimenting with the current offerings and finding use cases where the software can be applied and drive business results.

We have seen the market maturity model in software play out in enterprise resource planning (ERP), customer resource management (CRM), business intelligence (BI), and many more software markets. Causal AI is unique in its functionality—it needs to be, or it wouldn't be a distinct market or offering—but the maturity model that has applied to all of these previous software systems will apply to causal AI as well.

We think it is valuable and beneficial for business leaders to understand the landscape of causal AI. But where do we go from here? As we have noted, the causal AI market is young and evolving. Most of the technology that we have described is quite complex, and the language for explaining the intricacies is the domain of the data scientists. But as the market matures, we are beginning to witness the abstraction of complexity so that organizations from complex businesses and healthcare can put this powerful causal AI approach to work.

We have organized the next section of this chapter into the top trends that will impact the future of causal AI.

Integrating Causal AI and Traditional AI

Today, AI is not a single discipline but rather a wide field of discrete tools, technologies, and approaches. Each area of AI has developed a wide array of tools and technology that are used to solve specific discrete tasks. This is because of the states of evolution in each area and the fact that the practitioners in each area are not focused on integrating the tools and technologies yet. There is too much development, growth, and application of each subfield for a significant number of practitioners to turn their attention to integration, but this is just an artifact of the current state of play.

We have seen early experimentation with integrating causal AI approaches with traditional AI, and the results have been encouraging. For years, we have seen researchers chaining together generative AI models to programmatically create output from one model that is input to another model. Simulation systems are routinely used to generate hundreds, thousands, millions, or even billions of scenarios that are then ingested into optimization systems. We see the same in predictive systems feeding prescriptive models and applications. One promising use of this approach is to leverage AI tools already used in healthcare to make it easier to identify the root cause of an illness. Traditional AI tools are very good at predicting the likelihood that a patient will develop a condition. However, traditional approaches are not good at understanding why a patient will become sick and what approaches may help to determine the best treatment option.

For example, a healthcare provider could use causal AI to analyze a patient's medical history, lifestyle, and environmental factors to identify the root cause of their high blood pressure.

The Imperative for Managing Data

While there is never a lack of data, AI and causal AI solutions are hampered by the inadequacy of data preparation and data management. Ensuring data quality is one of the most important problems facing organizations trying to use all forms of AI to solve complex problems. Therefore, data must be cleansed so that it is accurate, reliable, and well understood. What are the sources of the data? Is there enough data available to produce accurate results? Without enough of the right data, the causal AI model will not produce accurate results, even if the data is properly cleansed. Have the data sources been vetted so that models and algorithms can be trained? There are emerging tools that are being used to provide an end-to-end view of data pipelines so that the data and the supporting infrastructure to manage that data is optimized for accuracy and security. The data used to support AI systems must also meet policies to meet both corporate and governmental compliance requirements and goals. While problems of data management are not new, causal AI requirements elevate the requirements for proper data management and governance to a more critical level.

Ensembles of Data

When we reach this point in the evolution of the model's life cycle, an ensemble of data is the way to go to reach for further performance gains on all axes of interest. By ensembles of data, we are talking about bringing together many sources of data.

Those sources can and in some cases are very large, as large as some of the training data sets used in LLMs, but in the majority of cases the data sets will be smaller and more diverse.

Ensembles of data are a path forward to deliver robust, reliable, accountable, fair, explainable, and trusted results, and it also continues our long-established path of building computer-based AI systems that mimic how people make decisions and process a wide array of informational inputs.

So, the future of all AI models is to ultimately arrive at a point of using a wide range of (relatively) smaller data sets to describe the many elements of a situation that we want our models to consider and leverage in their training, in their fine-tuning, and in how they produce and deliver results to us.

This approach is a requirement for causal AI because it reflects how people think. It is rare for people to make decisions based on one piece of data. The simplest of decisions typically involve more than one data element. Think of what happens when you wake up in the morning. You push away the covers on your bed, and you immediately sense if it is cold or hot; you look out the window to see if it is snowing or raining or if the day greets you with sunshine. You sense in your body if you are hungry or need to use the restroom.

The ability to combine a variety of datasets from different sources will be instrumental in allowing causal AI to gain a more comprehensive understanding of the world and the process that a model seeks to understand and analyze. Too often early versions of causal AI models do not encompass enough data to provide a deep understanding of the cause and effect of business problems. Being able to have more data will improve the ability of causal models to provide a more accurate understanding of the system being analyzed and therefore result in better predictions and more accurate causal models. Ensembles of data can result in more sophisticated input data sets that will help to reduce the risk of overfitting and improve the reliability and accuracy of the model.

Generative AI Is Emerging as a Game Changer for Causal AI

Currently, we are seeing and experiencing the rapid acceleration of the capabilities of generative AI. Television programs, front-page news, and the technology-focused media are replete with stories of the opportunities and risks associated with this approach to collecting, analyzing, and presenting data to almost anyone who has access to a computer and the Internet.

Generative AI, beyond the breakthroughs associated with large language models (LLMs) or foundational models (FMs), has popularized and made entirely new populations aware of and comfortable with conversational interfaces. Conversational interfaces enable a new way to engage with AI and to interrogate the massive amount of information synthesized into LLMs in a fast and easy method.

Generative AI has provided an accessible path to encoding a significant portion of the information available on the internet in one model. This massive encoding coupled with the conversational interface has made it possible to apply AI to any question that can be conceived.

It is exciting to see AI leaders talking about the fact that LLMs are not the end goal, far from it. LLMs are only the first stage of generative AI. LLMs prove that generative AI works, and works in the real world, at a global scale, not just theoretically in a tightly controlled laboratory setting. The current stage and evolution of LLMs and generative AI is just the starting point of this technology. We will see greater adoption and an explosion of use cases where LLMs are applied to significant positive effect.

For clarity in this discussion, we need to separate the name and descriptor *large language model*, which describes the size of the underlying neural network from the data that is used to train the LLM. LLMs are much larger in size than the language models (LMs) that went before them.

The leading developers of LLMs are careful not to divulge how many nodes are their latest creations, but we do know that the data being used is much larger than the data that was leveraged to train the previous generation of LMs. BERT, a widely used language model, has a training set that is approximately 110 million parameters. The newest LLMs leverage 175 trillion parameters in the training process.

The future of generative AI and LLMs in causal AI will include techniques to enable a better understanding of complex systems and their causal relationships. This will be important when the causal models are extremely complex. This approach will help to develop more accurate models that will support business decision-makers to improve outcomes in a variety of industries and domains. In the future, generative AI will be used extensively in creating and managing the causal discovery process.

The Future of Causal Discovery

Causal discovery is a process in causal AI used to identify and understand the cause-and-effect relationships among variables. Causal discovery is intended to expose the underlying causal structure that generated the data. This can be useful for prediction, decision-making, and understanding the mechanisms underlying a system. While causal discovery itself is not new, there are new tools emerging to make causal discovery easier and more powerful. Leveraging generative AI, causal models can be developed to learn the underlying structure of the data and the relationships between different variables. Another important future trend is to include domain knowledge of experts in the discovery model to capture the complex relationships between different variables in systems. Combining domain knowledge with causal discovery will require combining Bayesian methods, deep learning, and other advanced techniques to develop more accurate and robust models of causal relationships. The bottom line is that combining these machine learning techniques such as generative AI will provide domain experts with an entry point for creating models that reflect the business problems being addressed. As causal discovery solutions are developed with the use of generative AI, researchers will be able to develop more accurate models of complex systems, which can be applied to complex problems in a variety of areas including healthcare, marketing, finance, and manufacturing. Causal discovery solutions can help codify knowledge that can help identify the most effective treatments for an illness or optimize a manufacturing production process.

The future of causal AI will include the causal discovery process combined with expert domain knowledge and various advanced ML methods. This will enable researchers to develop more accurate and robust models of complex systems and to apply these models to real-world problems in a wide range of domains, such as healthcare, finance, and manufacturing.

One key area of research that must develop is the ability to have scalable and flexible algorithms for causal discovery that can handle large and complex data sets, while also incorporating domain-specific knowledge and expertise.

Another area of research must be the development of decision support systems that leverage causal discovery and expert domain knowledge to provide actionable insights and recommendations. For example, these systems could be used to identify the most effective treatments for a patient, to optimize production processes in a manufacturing plant, or to identify the most promising investment opportunities in finance.

Overall, the future of causal discovery combined with expert domain knowledge is likely to involve the development of more sophisticated and integrated approaches to understanding complex systems and to leveraging this knowledge to drive better decision-making and improved outcomes in a wide range of domains.

The Emergence of Causal AI Reinforcement Learning Will Accelerate Model Training

In the future, reinforcement learning will become an important tool to support causal AI. Because reinforcement learning enables an agent to learn how to make decisions based on a rewards system (the ability to calculate a numerical indicator of how well an agent performed a task), it can help the causal AI system learn business policies to optimize outcomes. By combining causal AI with reinforcement learning, the agent in the reinforcement learning model can align its reward system with the required causal effects. In the future, DAGs will be combined with reinforcement learning so that developers can test unlimited numbers of different variations to make better decisions. However, to be effective, you must begin with a good hypothesis and apply domain knowledge to the process. Causal reinforcement learning is a hybrid approach that combines reinforcement learning with causal inference. This approach will enable causal AI agents to learn from both observational and interventional data.

Causal AI as a Common Language Between Business Leaders and Data Scientists

While in every generation of technological innovation, the claim is made that the innovation will help business and technology leaders collaborate. Why is causal AI different? The key to the differentiation is that visual modeling in the form of the DAG is designed to graphically indicate all variables and their relationships to each other. The DAG itself becomes that common language that enables business leaders to see the model. The process of creating the DAG begins by identifying and coming to a consensus about what problem the organization is trying to solve. By beginning with this visual framework, data scientists use the results of the DAG to create the complex underlying code to implement the organization's goals. For example, in a sales forecasting application, causal AI can be used to identify the causal relationships between different factors such as advertising spend, pricing, and inventory levels, and how these factors impact the sales. By providing a clear understanding of these causal relationships, data scientists can communicate the impact of different business decisions on the sales forecast, allowing business professionals to make more informed decisions.

By involving business stakeholders in the development of AI models, data scientists can better understand the business context and ensure that the models are aligned with business objectives. This will enable business leaders to make more informed decisions based on the insights provided by the models. One of the great benefits of causal AI is that it will have a direct impact on how valuable AI is to the business. A graphical DAG indicates what the variables are and how they relate to each other. This is in dramatic contrast to a black-box model that cannot be understood by business leaders. With a causal AI model, the team of data scientists and business professionals can focus their collaboration on understanding the cause-and-effect relationships in the model.

The details about the relevant problem being addressed can be communicated through a graphical model that focuses on the ability to explain the relationship between variables. Having a common visual representation of a hypothesis and the variables and data that are key to solving problems enables data scientists and business leaders to better understand and interpret the key factors in determining why problems are happening. For example, if a business user wants to know what factors are driving customer churn, a causal model can identify the key drivers of churn and provide insights into how to reduce it. Being able to provide transparency and interpretable models is imperative to getting to the heart of complex business problems.

The Emergence of Probabilistic Programming Languages

Understanding the cause and effect based on complex models can be difficult to interpret. Probabilistic Programming Languages (PPLs) are used to create flexible causal models. These languages are designed to help develop and test causal AI algorithms. They are especially useful in prototyping causal AI systems. PPLs can be used to construct complex probabilistic models that are more understandable and tractable ways. Therefore, PPL is an important trend that has the potential to speed up the development of causal AI solutions. One of the benefits of PPLs is that they are based on open-source libraries. These libraries provide a framework for expressing probabilistic models intuitively so they can be understood by data analysts and business leaders by making it easier to understand the behavior of the model and to perform inference over the model. For example, PPLs are increasingly being used in fields such as healthcare to better predict the outcome of treatments for diseases.

The Predictable Model Evolution Cycle

Leading AI practitioners know that the evolutionary cycle of nearly all models can be described in this manner. We start out by building models of varying sizes. We use trial and error to find the best-performing model. We then use trial and error to find the best data set to train the selected model. We ramp up the size of the data set to the largest possible amount of data that can be processed by the computers we can afford, or have access to, and then we experiment from there. This process works very well and has been used by all manner of AI professionals for decades.

At some juncture in the training of all models, we reach the point of diminishing return in the performance gains or the levels of accuracy of the model or both. It is at this moment that most AI practitioners know that adding more data is costly, produces marginal gains, and is, in the end, a waste of time, money, and resources.

The next trend we will examine is the broad and inexorable movement in computer science to make programming computers of all types easier and accessible by larger and larger parts of the general population. This trend is so endemic and so ingrained in the evolution of computer science that most people take it as a fundamental law, but it is not; it is a trend, just a long-running trend. Let's discuss and describe this elemental wave of change next.

The Emergence of the Digital Twin

While digital twins are not a new concept, it will be important for the success of causal AI. In many situations, a digital twin approach will help organizations that want to apply causal AI to solving problems without disturbing existing systems.

A digital twin is a virtual representation of a physical system or process; therefore, a digital twin is a copy of a physical system that is created using data and software. Overall, a digital twin can be a valuable tool for gaining insights into the behavior of a causal AI system and for testing and validating the performance of a system before it is used in the real world. In the context of causal AI, a digital twin can be used to gain insights into the behavior of a system by simulating it using data and software without changing existing systems.

For example, a digital twin of a manufacturing process can be used to simulate the process and identify potential problems or areas for optimization. This can be done by creating a model of the process using data on the inputs and outputs and then simulating the process using the model. The results of the simulation can then be used to identify potential problems or areas for optimization, such as inefficiencies in the process or ways to improve the quality of the output.

Another potential use of a digital twin is to test and validate the performance of a causal AI system before it is used in the real world. By simulating the system using data and software, it is possible to test the system in a controlled environment and identify any potential problems or areas for improvement. This can be especially useful for systems that are complex or have a high level of risk, such as in the case of medical devices or spacecraft.

By using a digital twin, researchers can test and evaluate the behavior of a system under different conditions and identify the underlying causal relationships that drive its behavior. Therefore, in the context of causal AI, digital twins can be used in counterfactual analysis to evaluate the effectiveness of different interventions and polices. Digital twins can help to reduce uncertainty and increase the accuracy of predictions. In addition, digital twins can be used to generate synthetic data, which can be used to augment or replace real-world data and can help to reduce the risk of privacy breaches or ethical concerns associated with the use of personal data.

Improving the Ability to Understand Ground Truth

For clarity, ground truth is information that has been observed to be real or true and proven empirically to be a fact by firsthand observation rather than taken to be true by inference.

The future of ground truth in causal AI is likely to involve the development of more sophisticated and accurate methods for identifying and labeling ground truth data. One possible approach is to use semisupervised learning techniques, such as self-supervised learning or co-supervised learning, to learn patterns and relationships in the data that can be used to improve the labeling process. These techniques can be used to learn features that are useful for identifying similar instances and can be combined with human expertise to refine the labeling process.

Overall, the future of ground truth in causal AI involves the development of more sophisticated and accurate methods for labeling the data that can be used to improve the accuracy and reliability of the models. By combining these approaches, it may be possible to develop more accurate and reliable models that can better capture the relationships between different variables in real-world systems.

The Development of More Sophisticated DAGs

The development of DAGs is a key innovation in being able to create visual models for a number of areas of AI, but specifically so for causal AI. In the future, the tools that create DAGs will evolve so that they will provide a more sophisticated and flexible way of representing causal relationships. This will be especially important when the underlying causal relationships are complex or difficult to characterize. There will be the development of more advanced algorithms and techniques that will make it easier for DAGs to learn from data and to create causal models directly from DAGs. This may involve incorporating deep learning techniques to identify the most likely causal relationships from complex and high-dimensional datasets. Over time, new techniques will include more sophisticated data visualization tools.

In addition to general advances in the development of new tools and techniques, there will purpose-built DAGs for specific domains and markets. These techniques will combine open-source libraries with industry-specific libraries that are combined with the graphical DAG models.

One key area of research is likely to be the development of more advanced methods for abstraction and generalization in causal AI models. This approach will be beneficial in situations where the underlying causal relationships are complex and difficult to characterize. There will be the development of new algorithms and techniques for identifying and abstracting the most important causal relationships in a system that will be designed to reduce the computational complexity of these models.

Visualizing Complex Relationships in the DAGs

The future evolution of DAGs in causal AI is likely to involve the development of more flexible and scalable models that can better capture the complex relationships between different variables.

One possible approach is to use more advanced techniques for modeling the relationships between different variables, such as deep learning or generative modeling. These techniques can be used to learn complex relationships between different variables and can be combined with domain knowledge to guide the modeling process.

Overall, the future evolution of DAGs in causal AI is likely to involve the development of more flexible and scalable models that can better capture the complex relationships between different variables. By combining these approaches, it may be possible to develop more accurate and robust models that can better capture the relationships between different variables in real-world systems.

The Merging of Causal and Traditional AI Models

In the future, a number of important techniques for both causal and traditional AI will begin to merge. We will therefore see causal inference techniques being combined with deep learning and generative techniques that will be used to create more powerful models that will be better able to capture the complex relationships between variables. One of the outcomes of this approach is that these techniques can learn complex relationships in domain-specific knowledge. One approach may enable a neural network to model complex relationships between different nodes in a graph. This approach could be used in complex situations such as controlling complex manufacturing processes or better understanding the behavior of an evolving or mutating virus.

The Future of Explainability

Explainability is emerging as one of the most important trends in AI because of its value in creating a common language for business and data scientists to collaborate. There has been progress in explainable AI (XAI) to help provide transparent and interpretable models that can help bridge the gap between technical and nontechnical stakeholders. However, this is only the beginning of the evolution of XAI.

XAI is an underlying premise that spans all subfields of AI, including causal, traditional, and generative. Explainable AI is an objective that will need to be developed, disseminated, and included in all commercial AI offerings and will become a requirement in AI systems that are to be implemented in regulated industries such as financial services, pharmaceuticals, and biopharmaceuticals.

The future of adding explainability into causal models is likely to involve the development of more sophisticated and flexible methods for understanding and interpreting the causal relationships in these models, particularly in cases where the underlying causal relationships are complex and difficult to characterize. For example, there may be more advanced methods for explaining the behavior of dynamic causal models. This may involve the development of new algorithms and techniques for generating explanations in natural language and visualization so that these models will be better understood by management teams.

Another area of research is likely to be the application of these methods to real-world problems in a wide range of domains, such as healthcare, finance, and manufacturing. These methods could be used to generate explanations of how medical treatments work, how financial markets behave, or how manufacturing processes are controlled, allowing users to better understand and make decisions about these systems.

The Evolution of Responsible AI

Gaining a deeper understanding of how to create responsible models and AI systems that are both accurate and unbiased is an important development that is underway. These types of systems and add-ons to AI systems involve the development of more sophisticated and powerful models that can better capture the complex relationships between different variables in real-world systems and can be used to analyze the potential impact of different policies on different groups of people.

Responsible AI systems are being developed today in a manner that provides for automated connections to governments and their policy-making functions and to academics and thought leaders and companies around the world. The new systems provide methods for business professionals, data scientists, and technologies to use current and accurate assets to test their system and model designs for compliance with relevant legislation and regulation. The systems also ensure that models can be validated and verified to be in alignment with multiple regulations in numerous geographies before those models are implemented either in test environments or in production.

The evolution of responsible AI will involve the development of new algorithms and techniques for measuring and comparing the implicit or unconsciously included bias of different data and models, as well as the use of causal graphs, such as DAGs, to identify and mitigate the sources of bias in these models. These new tools will be critical across many domains including healthcare, finance, and criminal justice. For example, these techniques can identify bias in the type of medical treatment approaches that are developed and ensure that responsible decisions are made in financial lending.

Advances in Data Security and Privacy

There will need to be extensive work done to ensure that causal AI systems and AI in general will be safe and secure. Individual data will have to be protected from fraud and inappropriate use. How will these systems be used to make decisions that will affect the well-being of individuals and groups? Will the data used to make these decisions be cleansed and evaluated to protect society from harm? While privacy and security are not new to the evolution of causal AI, the potential for "uncontrolled" AI is amplifying concerns among industry, governments, and social organizations. When causal AI is used to understand the cause and effect from data, it is critical that security and privacy be at the highest possible levels.

Integration Will Be Between Models and Business Applications

For example, we will see causal AI systems developing a set of parameters that will serve as inputs to a traditional AI system. One situation we encountered centered on the fact that a sophisticated traditional AI system was slow, expensive, and, in some cases, produced output that confirmed that the ground truth had not changed enough to warrant running the traditional model at that time. This is not what business managers and executives want. Waiting for, paying for, and receiving results that provide little to no value is not an optimal situation, but this is the state of the art. What was lacking was a means for determining when we should run these sophisticated systems.

Rather than guessing when to run the traditional AI model or system, the team experimented with building a causal AI model that explained why and when the traditional AI model should be run. The pairing of the two approaches worked well. The causal application and model was fast, easy to run on a regular basis, and inexpensive, and it provided a clear indication that the new set of environmental parameters would yield valuable insights from the traditional model.

We will see this chaining of models with increasing frequency. Causal models provide a view into why things happen. Traditional models help us understand the how and when of scenarios and situations, and generative AI provides a starting point for creating content or probable responses that we may want to edit to convey our views. These three technologies are made to work together.

The future of AI is an integrated future. Models feeding models. Subfields extending and refining our approach to delivering solutions and insights. Cross subfield integration of entire chains of applications helping humas to achieve new levels of performance and clarity. Very exciting.

Summary

The creation of causal AI software is a story that is decades in the making and millennia in the framing and refining. One still marvels at the story of pre-Socratic thinkers postulating that causality was a product of the mind and we as humans created causality in our perception of the world. Socrates and his teachers, contemporaries, and students were the ones to define causality as we know it and understand it today. The long and actual history of how we, as humans, have come to understand, codify, and finally harness causality is amazing. If you think about it, the pre-Socratic Greeks postulated that causality manifested only because humans thought things into existence as a product of our minds. Their view was that causality occurred because we observed it and created it with our mental activity. That would be incredible if it were true. It would be great to think things into reality, but this is not the case.

In general, people want to understand and fix problems plaguing their world. Once a phenomenon or force is understood, people want to measure it. Then people want to try to manage and mold the process to fit their view of what is optimal. As a species, humans have routinely built tools to help in this process. Software and computing are simply the most sophisticated tools that we have invented to date.

Given that causality is one of the most sophisticated and complicated processes that humans encounter on a daily basis, it makes sense that eventually, we would build software to define, record, examine, analyze, and manage causality; we have arrived at this point in time and history.

Some of society's most brilliant minds have dedicated themselves to creating the underlying models, software, and technology that we, as technologists and business professionals, can use and begin to dissect causality in every life and routine business processes.

The field of causal AI has emerged from pure academia into the segments of the business world where experimentation and early adoption are competitive advantages. While there are many advances in leveraging causal inference in many fields such as economics, healthcare, and manufacturing, the field is responsibility in models. We expect that the evolution of causal AI will be transformed in the coming years. For example, the ability to create models that are explainable and can indicate to all participants why a particular counterfactual is more advantageous will be a critical advancement. New techniques for data management, data integration, and cleansing are paramount to the success of causal AI. One of the most important advances in causal AI is to create a more sophisticated level of explainability, especially as generative AI emerges as one of the most important trends in the evolution of AI.

The market for causal AI will begin to accelerate as more businesses need to understand the cause and effect of complex problems in a variety of areas ranging from healthcare to marketing and finance. While many of the future innovations in causal AI already exist in other mature areas of data, packaged software offerings, and operational management, those functions and capabilities have yet to be adapted and implemented in the causal AI ecosystem. In addition, emerging innovations such as generative AI will begin to have a major impact on bringing causal AI into the mainstream of business.

Causal AI has arrived after a long journey that has been punctuated and characterized by periods of stagnation and, alternatively, by great innovation and acceleration. Luckily for us, we are in the most accelerated period of innovation and creation ever seen in this field. If you are a technologist, business executive or manager, or analytics professional, now is the time to start investigating the potential for causal AI to be one of the next tools that you add to your corporate arsenal to derive and protect your next source of competitive advantage.

Glossary

advanced analytics Advanced analytics refers to the use of sophisticated techniques and tools to analyze and interpret complex data sets, uncovering valuable insights and patterns that can inform business decisions and drive strategic actions.

algorithm This is a set of rules or instructions given to an AI, neural network, or other machine to help it learn on its own.

augmented intelligence Augmented intelligence, also known as intelligence amplification, refers to the integration of artificial intelligence (AI) technologies and capabilities with human intelligence to enhance human decision-making, problem-solving, and cognitive abilities.

backdoor criterion This is a method for identifying and controlling for confounding variables in a DAG, used in causal inference.

backdoor paths In causal inference, a backdoor path refers to a noncausal pathway between a treatment variable and an outcome variable that can introduce bias or confounding when estimating the causal effect. It occurs when there is an alternative route, or a set of variables, that connects the treatment and outcome variables without involving any variables that lie on the causal pathway. Controlling for or conditioning on variables along a backdoor path can help eliminate or mitigate the confounding effect and estimate the true causal relationship between the treatment and outcome variables.

bias (in machine learning) This is an error introduced in your model due to oversimplification of a machine learning algorithm or inadequate data sets. It can lead to underfitting, which happens when your model is too simple to capture all the features in the data set. Bias can also occur when the data itself is biased.

black-box model A black-box model is a type of machine learning or statistical model where the inputs and outputs are visible, but the internal workings of the model are not easily interpretable or understandable by humans. In other words, the model's decision-making process is not transparent or explainable.

Bayesian network   Also known as *causal network*, *belief network*, and *decision network*, Bayesian networks are graphical models for representing multivariate probability distributions. They aim to model conditional dependence, and therefore causation, by representing conditional dependence by edges in a directed graph.

big data   This refers to large and complex data sets that traditional data processing tools cannot handle. Big data typically includes data collection, data analysis, and data visualization.

causal AI   Causal AI is a solution based on causal inference. It provides a deeper understanding of the causal relationships between variables in a system and can help us identify interventions, predict alternative choices and actions, avoid bias, and make better decisions. Causal AI involves developing AI models and algorithms that can understand and reason about cause-and-effect relationships to make more informed and reliable decisions. Causal AI aims to go beyond traditional correlation-based approaches in AI, which focus on identifying patterns and associations in data. Instead, it seeks to uncover causal relationships and understand the mechanisms through which variables or events influence each other.

causal discovery   Causal discovery is the process of identifying underlying causal relationships between variables in a system. It involves the task of identifying the underlying causal structure of a system based on observational data.

causal inference   Causal inference refers to the process of drawing conclusions about cause-and-effect relationships between variables or events based on observed data. It involves determining whether a particular factor or intervention has a causal impact on an outcome of interest, beyond simple correlation or association.

causal library   A causal library is a software toolkit or collection of functions and tools that enable the implementations of algorithms and methods. Commonly used libraries include various forms of Do-Calculus including DoWhy and PyWhy. A causal library typically includes a set of prebuilt functions or classes that implement various causal inference techniques, statistical models, and algorithms.

causal pipeline   A causal pipeline is an end-to-end DevOps approach connecting causal AI methods to create a causal AI application or solution.

causality   This is the relation between cause and effect. In statistics and machine learning, causality refers to the notion that a particular event or action directly influences the occurrence of another event.

center of excellence A center of excellence (CoE) is a specialized department or organization within an organization that is dedicated to developing and promoting best practices, standards, and innovative solutions in a specific area of expertise. The purpose of a CoE is to create a central hub for knowledge sharing, expertise development, and innovation, with the goal of improving the overall performance of the organization.

chain diagram A chain diagram, also known as a cause-and-effect diagram or a chain-of-causes diagram, is a graphical representation of the relationships between events or variables in a system. It is used to understand the causal relationships between different elements in a system and to identify potential areas of intervention to modify the system.

In a chain diagram, the events or variables are represented as nodes, and the relationships between them are represented as arrows. The arrows indicate the direction of the relationship, and the strength of the relationship is represented by the width of the arrow. The chain diagram can be used to identify causal chains, which are sequences of events or variables that lead to a particular outcome.

colliders In causal inference, colliders refer to variables that are influenced by multiple causes and, when conditioned upon or controlled for, can induce spurious associations or modify the true causal relationship between other variables. Colliders are also known as *selection bias generators* because conditioning on a collider can introduce bias and distort the relationship between the variables involved.

confounder A confounder, in the context of research and causal inference, refers to a variable that is both associated with the treatment being studied and independently associated with the outcome of interest. It is a variable that can distort or confound the observed relationship between the treatment and the outcome, leading to a potential spurious association or misleading interpretation of causality.

Confounding occurs when the relationship between the treatment and the outcome is influenced or confounded by the presence of a third variable. This third variable acts as a common cause or a lurking variable that is related to both the treatment and the outcome but is not part of the causal pathway. If not properly accounted for or controlled, confounders can result in biased estimates of the true causal effect.

correlation Correlation refers to a statistical measure that quantifies the degree and direction of a relationship between two or more variables. It indicates how changes in one variable correspond to changes in another variable. In other words, correlation measures the extent to which two variables tend to move together or vary in relation to each other. A positive correlation means that as one variable increases, the other variable tends to increase as well. Conversely, a negative correlation indicates that as one variable increases, the other variable tends to decrease. Correlation values range from −1 to +1, with 0 indicating no correlation.

counterfactual   Counterfactual, in the context of causal inference, refers to a hypothetical scenario or condition that represents what would have happened if a particular event, treatment, or intervention had not occurred or had occurred differently. It involves reasoning about the unobserved or alternative outcomes that could have taken place under different circumstances. Counterfactual thinking allows researchers to compare the observed outcome with the hypothetical outcome, enabling the estimation of causal effects and understanding the impact of specific interventions or actions.

cross validation   Cross validation is a statistical technique used to evaluate the performance of a model or algorithm by dividing the available data into multiple subsets and using each subset to train the model or algorithm separately, while holding out the remaining subsets for testing. The performance of the model or algorithm is then evaluated by comparing its predictions on the testing subsets to the actual values.

Cross validation is a useful technique for evaluating the performance of a model or algorithm because it allows for a more accurate assessment of the model's ability to generalize to new data, rather than relying solely on the performance on the training data. By training the model or algorithm on different subsets of the data and evaluating its performance on different subsets, cross validation can help to identify potential sources of bias or error in the model or algorithm and to improve its overall performance.

data mining   This is the process of discovering patterns and knowledge from large amounts of data. The data sources can include databases, data warehouses, the Web, and other information repositories.

data set   This is a collection of data usually presented in tabular form. Each column represents a particular variable, and each row corresponds to a given record of the data set in question.

digital transformation   Digital transformation is the process of using digital technologies to fundamentally change the way a business operates and delivers value to its customers. It involves the integration of digital technology into all areas of a business, resulting in fundamental changes to how the business operates and how it delivers value to its customers. Digital transformation can involve the use of new technologies such as artificial intelligence, the Internet of Things, and big data analytics, as well as the adoption of new business models and processes. The goal of digital transformation is to improve efficiency, innovation, and customer experience, and to enable businesses to better compete in an increasingly digital world.

directed acyclic graph (DAG)   A directed acyclic graph (DAG) is a graphical representation used in causal inference and probabilistic modeling to depict the causal relationships between variables. It consists of nodes representing variables or events and directed edges indicating the causal connections or dependencies between them. The term *acyclic* means that there are no cycles or loops in the graph, ensuring a clear directionality of causality. DAGs provide a visual framework for understanding the causal structure and can be used to infer causal effects, identify confounders, and guide the selection of variables for analysis in causal modeling.

deep learning   The term *deep learning* is used to describe neural networks and the algorithms used for it that accept raw data (from which you need to extract some useful information). This data is processed by passing through the layers of the neural network to obtain the desired output.

direct effect   In causal AI, the direct effect is the causal effect of a treatment variable on an outcome variable that is not mediated or influenced by any intermediate variables in the causal pathway. It represents the specific impact of the treatment on the outcome that occurs independently of other variables or factors.

The direct effect is of interest because it allows us to isolate and quantify the unique contribution of the treatment to the outcome, independent of any other variables that may be affected by the exposure. By estimating the direct effect, we can gain insights into the direct causal relationship between the treatment and outcome, accounting for potential confounders and intermediate variables.

edge   In a graph, an edge indicates a direct cause-and-effect link between variables, and nodes. The orientation of the edge demonstrates the directionality of this causal connection. For example, an edge from A to B indicates that A causes B.

endogenous   Endogenous refers to any event or variable that is directly controlled by an observer or can be observed directly. It can be considered as "internal" or "within" the observer's internal state or pattern of behavior.

exogenous   Exogenous refers to any event or variable that is not directly controlled by an observer or can be observed directly. It can be considered as "external" or "extraneous" to the observer's internal state or pattern of behavior.

explainable AI (XAI)   Explainable AI (XAI) refers to the field of artificial intelligence focused on developing and implementing methods and techniques that allow humans to understand and interpret the decisions and behaviors of AI systems. XAI aims to provide transparency and explanations for the outputs, predictions, and recommendations generated by AI algorithms, making the decision-making process more understandable and interpretable for humans.

The need for explainability arises because many modern AI algorithms, such as deep learning neural networks, operate as complex black-box models, where the internal workings and decision-making process are not readily interpretable or explainable. XAI seeks to bridge this gap by providing insights into the factors, features, or reasoning that contribute to an AI system's outputs, helping users to understand the basis for the AI's decisions.

feature (in machine learning) A feature is an input variable—the attribute used by your model to make predictions. It's also known as an independent variable. Often, features are represented as columns in a spreadsheet.

fork A fork in causal AI is a situation where two or more variables are causally related to each other, but the direction of the causal relationship is not known. This can make it difficult to identify the true cause of an event, and it can also lead to inaccurate predictions.

Forks can be caused by a number of factors, including the following:

- **Confounding variables:** Confounding variables are variables that are correlated with both the cause and the effect of an event. This can make it difficult to isolate the causal relationship between the two variables.

- **Measurement error:** Measurement error is the difference between the true value of a variable and the value that is measured. This can also lead to inaccurate estimates of causal relationships.

- **Omitted variables:** Omitted variables are variables that are not included in a causal analysis. These variables can also affect the causal relationship between the variables that are included in the analysis.

forward chaining This is a method where AI looks back and analyzes the rule-based system to find the "if" rules and to determine which rules to use to find a solution.

Forward chaining is a reasoning method in artificial intelligence where inference rules are applied to existing data to extract additional data until a goal is reached. In this type of chaining, the inference engine starts by evaluating existing facts, derivations, and conditions before deducing new information. An endpoint (goal) is achieved through the manipulation of knowledge that exists in the knowledge base.

front-door path In causal inference, the front-door path refers to a causal pathway between two variables that involves an intermediate variable or set of variables, acting as a "front-door" mechanism. It is a pathway that allows the effect of a treatment variable on an outcome variable to be estimated, even when direct observation of the causal relationship between the treatment and outcome is unavailable or confounded. The front-door path involves three key steps: the treatment variable affects the intermediate variable(s), the intermediate variable(s) affects the outcome variable, and there is no direct causal relationship between the treatment and outcome variables. By understanding and analyzing the front-door path, researchers can gain insights into the causal relationship between the treatment and outcome through the indirect effect mediated by the intermediate variable(s).

generative AI Generative AI refers to a branch of artificial intelligence focused on creating models and algorithms that can generate new, original content or data that resembles real-world examples. Unlike traditional AI models that are trained to recognize or classify existing data, generative AI models are designed to generate new data instances that possess similar characteristics or patterns as the training data.

Generative AI models employ techniques such as deep learning, neural networks, and probabilistic modeling to learn the underlying structure and distribution of the training data. This knowledge allows them to generate new data samples that mimic the patterns, styles, or features observed in the training set.

ground truth Ground truth refers to the actual, accurate representation or measurement of a real-world event, condition, or system. It is the true or correct state or condition of an object, process, or system as it exists in the real world. The ground truth is used as a reference or basis for the testing, validation, or comparison of any information, models, or algorithms that are being used to correct or improve the real-world state or condition. The ground truth is usually obtained through direct observation, measurement, or testing, and is considered the "true" or "real" version of a particular state or condition.

hybrid team A hybrid team is a group of professionals representing the key constituents who contribute to the design and implementation of a causal AI model. The goal of a hybrid team in causal AI is to leverage the strengths of both human expertise and AI capabilities to solve problems more effectively and efficiently. For example, a hybrid team may use AI to analyze large amounts of data and identify patterns or anomalies that might not be visible to human experts. The human experts can then use this information to make more informed decisions or take more effective actions.

Hybrid teams can be used in a variety of fields, including healthcare, finance, and social services. They can be particularly useful in situations where there are complex problems to solve, large amounts of data to analyze, or a need for speed and accuracy. By combining human expertise and AI capabilities, hybrid teams can address these challenges and deliver better outcomes.

indirect effect   In causal AI, the indirect effect refers to the causal effect of a treatment variable on an outcome variable that is mediated or influenced by one or more intermediate variables in the causal pathway. It represents the impact of the treatment on the outcome that occurs through the changes or influence exerted by the intermediate variables.

The indirect effect is of interest because it helps us understand the mechanisms through which the treatment variable affects the outcome variable. It captures the indirect causal relationships and provides insights into the intermediate steps or factors involved in transmitting the effect of the treatment to the outcome.

Estimating the indirect effect requires understanding the causal pathways and relationships between the treatment, intermediate variables, and outcome. It often involves conducting mediation analysis, which quantifies the extent to which the relationship between the treatment and outcome is explained by the mediating variables.

intervention   In causal AI, intervention refers to the process of manipulating one or more variables in a system to observe the effect on other variables. It is a way of testing the causal relationships between variables by intentionally changing one or more variables and observing the effect on other variables.

Intervention can be either exogenous or endogenous. Exogenous intervention involves manipulating a variable that is not part of the underlying causal mechanism, while endogenous intervention involves manipulating a variable that is part of the underlying causal mechanism.

Intervention is a powerful tool for identifying causal relationships between variables, as it allows researchers to test the effect of manipulating one variable on other variables. However, it can be challenging to design and implement interventions in practice, as they require careful experimental design and control of confounding variables.

inverted form   Inverted form is a term used in causal AI to describe a situation where the cause of an event is not known. This can happen for a variety of reasons, such as when there are multiple possible causes for an event or when the cause is hidden or difficult to measure.

Inverted form can be a challenge for causal AI systems, as they are designed to identify and understand causal relationships. However, there are a number of methods that can be used to deal with inverted form, such as using causal graphs, controlling for confounding variables, and using sensitivity analysis. By using these methods, it is possible to reduce the impact of inverted form on causal AI systems and to improve their accuracy.

knowledge graph   A knowledge graph is a large-scale, structured knowledge base that represents real-world entities and their relationships. It is a powerful tool for understanding and reasoning about the world.

ladder of causality   The ladder of causality, also known as the causal hierarchy, is a conceptual framework that illustrates different levels or types of evidence used to establish causal relationships between variables. It provides a systematic approach for evaluating and assessing the strength of evidence supporting causal claims.

The ladder of causality typically consists of several levels, with each level representing a higher degree of evidence and certainty regarding causality. The levels often progress from lower levels of evidence, such as anecdotal observations or correlations, to higher levels that involve experimental designs and controlled studies.

machine learning (ML)   Machine learning is a subfield of artificial intelligence that focuses on the development of algorithms that can learn from data and make predictions or decisions based on that data, without being explicitly programmed. It involves training algorithms on large amounts of data to identify patterns and relationships and then using those patterns to make predictions or decisions on new data. Machine learning is used in a wide range of applications, including image and speech recognition, natural language processing, recommendation systems, and predictive modeling. It has become a key technology in many industries, including healthcare, finance, and marketing, and is driving the development of many new applications in areas such as autonomous vehicles, robotics, and smart homes.

model visualization   Model visualization is the process of creating visual representations of models used in scientific and engineering applications. These visualizations can take many forms, such as graphs, diagrams, images, or interactive dashboards. The goal of model visualization is to provide a clear, concise, and easy-to-understand representation of the model's behavior, parameters, or results. The visualization can help stakeholders understand the model's predictions, limitations, and potential implications and can be used for debugging, testing, and misunderstanding of the model's behavior. Model visualization is an important tool for the communication and understanding of complex models and is used in many fields, including engineering, physics, economics, and biology.

mediator variable Mediator variables can be useful in understanding the underlying mechanisms that link two other variables, and they can help to identify important factors that contribute to the relationship between them. They are often used in studies that investigate causal relationships and in the development of interventions to modify the relationship between two variables. In the context of time-series analysis, a mediator variable is a variable that acts as a bridge between two other variables. Specifically, it is a variable that affects the relationship between the two other variables. For example, if there is a relationship between two variables, X and Y, and a third variable, Z, is introduced that affects the relationship between X and Y, then Z can be considered a mediator variable. Understanding how the relationship between X and Y is affected by Z can provide insight into the underlying mechanisms driving the relationship between X and Y. In mediation analysis, the mediator variable is used to test whether the relationship between the two endogenous variables (X and Y) is indirect, through the mediator variable Z.

moderator variable In the context of statistical analysis, a moderator variable is a variable that affects the strength or direction of a relationship between two other variables. Specifically, it is a variable that changes the effect of another variable, known as the *independent variable*, on the dependent variable. For example, if there is a relationship between two variables, X and Y, and a third variable, Z, which changes the effect of X on Y, then Z can be considered a moderator variable. Understanding how the relationship between X and Y is affected by Z can provide insight into the underlying mechanisms driving the relationship between X and Y. In moderation analysis, the moderator variable is used to test whether the relationship between the independent and dependent variables is different when the moderator variable is present.

neural network A neural network is a machine learning model inspired by the structure and function of the human brain. It consists of layers of interconnected "neurons" or processing units, which process and transmit information. It is a type of machine learning algorithm that is used to recognize patterns, classify data, and make predictions based on input data. Neural networks are widely used in a variety of fields, such as image and speech recognition, natural language processing, and financial analysis. They are capable of learning from large amounts of data and can adapt to changing conditions, making them highly effective for many applications.

nodes The nodes in a causal graph represent variables, and the edges represent direct causal relationships between variables. The direction of the edge indicates the direction of the causal relationship. For example, an edge from A to B indicates that A causes B. In the context of graphs and networks, a node refers to a fundamental component or entity that represents a data point, a variable, an object, or an event. Nodes are interconnected to form a network or graph structure, where the connections between nodes represent relationships or dependencies.

outcome variables In research and statistical analysis, an outcome variable, also known as a *dependent variable* or *response variable*, is the variable of interest that is being studied or predicted. It is the variable that researchers seek to understand, explain, or model based on the influence or impact of other variables and is typically the variable that researchers measure, observe, or record to assess the effects or changes resulting from the manipulation or exposure to independent variables. It represents the result, consequence, or state of interest in a study or analysis.

passive observation Passive observation, or association, in causal AI refers to the process of identifying patterns or correlations in data without making any assumptions about causality. It is a form of unsupervised learning where the machine learning algorithm identifies relationships between variables in the data without any prior knowledge of the causal structure of the system. Passive observation is a method of discovering patterns or relationships in data that do not necessarily imply a causal relationship between the variables.

process model A process model is a mathematical or computational representation of a process or system, typically used to understand, analyze, and optimize the behavior of the process. Process models can be used to model different aspects of a process, such as the inputs, outputs, and interactions between different components of the process. Process models can also be used to predict the behavior of the process under different conditions or to design and optimize new processes. Process models can be developed using various tools and techniques, such as mathematical equations, simulation algorithms, or control systems theory and are often used in engineering, economics, and management to improve efficiency, reduce costs, and increase quality of a process or system.

propensity score A propensity score is a measure that can determine the probability of an individual or unit receiving a particular treatment, used in causal inference to reduce bias and account for confounding variables.

reinforcement learning (RL) Reinforcement learning (RL) is a type of machine learning algorithm that allows software agents and machines to automatically determine the ideal behavior within a specific context to maximize its performance. Reinforcement algorithms are not given explicit goals; instead, they are forced to learn these optimal goals by trial and error.

structural causal model (SCM) A structural causal model (SCM) is a statistical model that seeks to establish causal relationships between variables. SCMs are often represented as systems of equations with each equation expressing one variable as a function of its causes and some error term. It is common for an organization to first implement a visual DAG and then add a detailed statistical model to create the solution.

structural equation modeling (SEM) Structural equation modeling (SEM) is a statistical method used to model the causal relationships between variables in a system or process, often used in causal inference.

synthetic data Synthetic data is data that is artificially generated to mimic the characteristics and patterns of real data. It is data that is created using algorithms or statistical models, rather than being collected from real-world sources. Synthetic data is often used to replace real data in certain situations, such as when real data is not available or when it is not appropriate to use real data for various reasons.

Synthetic data can be used for a variety of purposes, including testing and validating systems, training machine learning models, and evaluating the performance of algorithms. It can be used to generate data that is similar to real data, but without the risks and limitations associated with using real data.

Synthetic data is becoming increasingly popular as a way to generate data for use in machine learning and other applications. It is particularly useful when real data is scarce or difficult to obtain or when there are concerns about privacy or security associated with using real data.

treatment (counterfactual) intervention Treatment (counterfactual) intervention is aimed at improving the outcomes of an individual or group of individuals who are already experiencing a certain condition or disease but not currently receiving any treatment. The goal of counterfactual interventions is to provide the best possible outcome for those individuals or groups of individuals, considering the current state of the disease, the individual's medical history and current condition, and any other relevant factors. This type of intervention is often used in situations where existing treatments are not effective or when other approaches are considered more likely to result in a better outcome.

Counterfactual interventions can take many forms, such as education, counseling, support groups, or other forms of intervention that aim to improve the individual's knowledge, behavior, or overall health. The specific nature and scope of counterfactual interventions can vary depending on the situation and the available resources and expertise. These interventions can be implemented in a variety of settings, including hospitals, clinics, community centers, and online platforms.

weights (causal strength) In causal AI, weights (causal strength) are a measure of the strength of the causal relationship between two variables. A higher weight indicates a stronger causal relationship, while a lower weight indicates a weaker causal relationship.

Weights can be estimated using a variety of methods, including the following:

- **Structural equation modeling:** Structural equation modeling is a statistical method that can be used to estimate the causal relationships between variables.

- **Machine learning:** Machine learning algorithms can be used to estimate the weights of a causal model.

- **Expert knowledge:** In some cases, expert knowledge can be used to estimate the weights of a causal model.

Weights can be used to make predictions about the future, to design experiments, and to make decisions. For example, if a company wants to increase its sales, it can use weights to identify the factors that are most likely to influence sales. The company can then focus its efforts on improving these factors.

Weights can also be used to identify the causal relationships between variables. For example, if a study finds that there is a positive correlation between smoking and lung cancer, this does not necessarily mean that smoking causes lung cancer. It is possible that there is a third variable, such as genetics, that is causing both smoking and lung cancer. Weights can be used to control for this third variable and to identify the causal relationship between smoking and lung cancer.

Appendix: Causal AI Tools and Libraries

This appendix is a supplement to Chapter 7. It is not an exhaustive list of every causal AI tool and library that you might encounter, but it is our attempt to help readers understand the types of tools that are emerging. The following table summarizes more than 30 popular tools, most of which are open source. The sites for these tools are found easily via a web search.

Tool	Category	Description	URL
Azua	Causal Inference Library	Azua is a project focused on observational decision-making approaches and processes in causal inference and counterfactual analysis. It was separated from the Causica project to specifically address observational decision-making.	https://github.com/microsoft/project-azua
CausalInference	Causal Inference Library	Causal Inference in Python (CausalInference) is an open-source project that implements various statistical and econometric methods used in the field of causal inference. It includes features for assessing overlap in covariate distributions, estimating propensity scores, and estimating treatment effects through matching, weighting, and least squares.	https://causalinferenceinpython.org

CausalML	Causal Inference Library	CausalML is a Python-based tool created by a development team at Uber for uplift modeling and causal inference. It supports various approaches to estimate and validate the Conditional Average Treatment Effect (CATE) or Individual Treatment Effect (ITE) from experimental or observational data. CausalML offers solvers such as S-Learner, T-Learner, R-Learner, X-Learner, Doubly Robust (DR) Learner, and Doubly Robust Instrumental Variable (DRIV) Learner, along with tree-based algorithms for effect estimation.	https://causalml. readthedocs.io/en/ latest/about.html
CausalPy	Causal Inference Library	CausalPy is a Python library designed to provide a comprehensive set of tools for estimating causal effects and discovering causal relationships in observational and experimental data. It includes algorithms for causal inference, sensitivity analysis, and result visualization.	https://github.com/ pymc-labs/CausalPy

(continued)

(continued)

Tool	Category	Description	URL
Causica	Causal Inference Library	Causica is a deep learning tool for end-to-end causal inference, including both causal discovery and inference. It aims to offer a scalable, flexible, real-world application for automating causal decision-making using observational data alone, combining causal discovery and inference steps in a single model.	https://github.com/microsoft/causica
EconML	Causal Inference Library	EconML is a Python-based tool for estimating heterogeneous treatment effects from observational data using machine learning techniques. It is part of the Automated Learning and Intelligence for Causation and Economics (ALICE) project at Microsoft Research, combining econometrics and machine learning to automate complex causal inference problems.	https://github.com/microsoft/EconML

IBM Research Causal Inference 360	Causal Inference Library	The IBM Research Causal Inference 360 package provides methods to estimate the causal effect of an intervention using observational data. It offers several meta-algorithms for plugging in complex machine learning algorithms for flexible causal inference modeling. A highlight is the evaluation module for model selection, parameter tuning, and selection of the causal meta-method itself. The philosophy behind it is to unify many causal models under one scikit-learn-inspired API and enable estimation on out-of-bag samples. It encourages extensibility and contribution from the community.	https://ci360.mybluemix.net
PyWhy	Causal Inference Library	PyWhy, formerly known as DoWhy, is a Python library for causal inference that provides a unified interface for estimating causal effects using a variety of methods and algorithms, including propensity score matching.	https://github.com/microsoft/dowhy

(continued)

(*continued*)

Tool	Category	Description	URL
SnowWhy	Causal Inference Library	SnowWhy is a Python library for causal inference and counterfactual reasoning developed by Microsoft Research. It offers a range of methods for estimating causal effects and conducting counterfactual analysis in various domains.	https://github.com/microsoft/SnowWhy
Cytoscape	Drawing and Visualizing Diagrams and Graphs	Cytoscape is an open-source platform for visualizing complex networks and integrating these networks with multiple data types. It was designed for biological research but is now a general platform for complex network analysis and visualization.	https://cytoscape.org
DAGitty	Drawing and Visualizing Diagrams and Graphs	DAGitty is a browser-based environment for creating, editing, and analyzing causal diagrams like DAGs, GCMs, SEMs, CIDs, or causal Bayesian networks. It is widely used in causal projects of various types.	www.dagitty.net

Gephi	Drawing and Visualizing Diagrams and Graphs	Gephi is an open-source tool for data analysts and scientists keen to discover, explore, and understand graphs and networks. It's a complementary tool to traditional statistics, as visual thinking with interactive interfaces is now recognized to facilitate reasoning.	https://gephi.org
ggdag	Drawing and Visualizing Diagrams and Graphs	ggdag is an R package based on DAGitty and is tidyverse-compatible with a focus on providing improved plotting functionality.	https://github.com/r-causal/ggdag
Graphviz	Drawing and Visualizing Diagrams and Graphs	Graphviz is open-source graph visualization software. It takes descriptions of graphs in a simple text language and makes diagrams in useful formats. It has many useful features for concrete diagrams, such as options for colors, fonts, tabular node layouts, line styles, hyperlinks, and custom shapes.	https://graphviz.org

(continued)

(*continued*)

Tool	Category	Description	URL
NetworkX	Drawing and Visualizing Diagrams and Graphs	NetworkX is a Python package for creating, manipulating, and studying complex networks. It provides tools for the study of the structure and dynamics of various networks, with interfaces to existing numerical algorithms and code written in C, C++, and FORTRAN.	https://networkx.org
PGF/TikZ	Drawing and Visualizing Diagrams and Graphs	PGF/TikZ is a language and a macro package for generating graphics. It is platform- and format-independent and works together with the most important TeX backend drivers. It comes with a user-friendly syntax layer called TikZ.	https://github.com/ pgf-tikz/pgf
shinyDAG	Drawing and Visualizing Diagrams and Graphs	shinyDAG is a web application that uses R and LaTeX to create publication-quality images of DAGs. The application also leverages complementary R packages to evaluate correlational structures and identify appropriate adjustment sets for estimating causal effects.	www.gerkelab.com/ project/shinydag

| TETRAD | Drawing and Visualizing Diagrams and Graphs | TETRAD is a free tool for analyzing causal systems, inferring "what causes what" given known data and causal manipulations. It contains tools for estimating parameters in causal systems, simulating data from causal models, and more. It supports Java, Python, and R. | https://cmu-phil.github.io/tetrad/manual |
| ALICE | Causal AI Platforms/ Projects | The Automated Learning and Intelligence for Causation and Economics (ALICE) project at Microsoft Research aims to combine state-of-the-art machine learning techniques with econometrics to bring automation to complex causal inference problems. It provides foundational components for causal-based AI applications and software, including A/B testing, effect estimation, causal inference, and interpretation. | www.microsoft.com/en-us/research/group/alice |

(continued)

(continued)

Tool	Category	Description	URL
gCastle	Causal AI Platforms/ Projects	gCastle is a Python-based tool developed by Huawei's Noah's Ark Lab for causal structure and AI learning. It includes a comprehensive collection of causal discovery and inference algorithms, providing a unified API for interacting with various causal models. gCastle utilizes a graph-based approach to identify causal relationships between variables, supports reinforcement learning approaches, and offers functionality for data generation, causal structure learning, and evaluation metrics. It primarily focuses on providing security services for organizations to secure their cloud infrastructure, applications, and data.	https://github.com/ huawei-noah/trust worthyAI/tree/mas ter/gcastle
Causal Discovery Toolbox	Causal Discovery and Visualization	The Causal Discovery Toolbox (CDT) is a Python package focused on causal discovery in observational settings. It provides algorithms for causal discovery, methods to discover dependences in the data, and tools for evaluating causal models.	https://fentechsolutions. github.io/ CausalDiscovery Toolbox/html/index. html

CausalNex	Causal Discovery and Visualization	CausalNex is a Python toolkit for causal reasoning leveraging Bayesian Networks and related probabilistic methods. It provides capabilities for structure learning, incorporating domain knowledge, building predictive models, visualizing causal graphs, and analyzing interventions.	https://github.com/quantumblack labs/causalnex
BETS (Bootstrap Elastic net regression from Time Series)	Causal Network Discovery Approaches and Tools	Bootstrap Elastic net regression from Time Series (ETS) is a Python package that infers causal networks from time-series data. Originally designed for genetic data, it applies regularized vector autoregression, permutation-based null, and False Discovery control to infer causal networks. It is useful for high-dimensional gene-expression time-series data but applicable to other data sets.	https://github.com/lujonathanh/BETS

(continued)

(continued)

Tool	Category	Description	URL
LiNGAM (Linear, Non-Gaussian, Acyclic causal Models)	Causal Network Discovery Approaches and Tools	Linear, Non-Gaussian, Acyclic causal Models (LiNGAM) is a method for estimating structural equation models (SEMs) or linear causal Bayesian networks. It is used for identifying causal models and deriving directed acyclic graphs (DAGs) and/or SEMs based on purely observational, continuous-valued data. This approach can discover and generate non-Gaussian linear causal models and includes functionality for different variations of the LiNGAM algorithm.	https://sites.google.com/view/sshimizu06/lingam
TiMINo (Time Series Models with Independent Noise)	Causal Network Discovery Approaches and Tools	Time Series Models with Independent Noise (TiMINo) is an approach using observations to infer the causal structure of the data generating system. By restricting the model class, it provides a general identifiability result, and if there	https://arxiv.org/abs/1207.5136

		are no feedback loops between time series, an algorithm based on nonlinear independence tests of time series can be applied. It is useful in situations where data are causally insufficient or the data-generating process does not satisfy the model assumptions.	
Applied Econometric Methods for Causal Inference	Estimations, Data Generation, and Validation Utilities	This repository is a resource for learning the fundamentals of causal modeling, including statistical techniques such as Controlled Regression, Regression Discontinuity Design (RDD), Difference-in-Differences (DD), Fixed-Effects Regression (FE), and Instrumental Variables (IV). It is useful as a learning guide, a tutorial, or for brushing up on math fundamentals.	https://github.com/ TeconomicsBlog/ notebooks/blob/ master/ CausalInference.ipynb

(continued)

(continued)

Tool	Category	Description	URL
DSA	Estimations, Data Generation, and Validation Utilities	Data-Adaptive Estimation with Cross-Validation and the D/S/A Algorithm (DSA) performs data-adaptive estimation through estimator selection based on cross validation. It defines candidate estimators using polynomial generalized linear models generated with the Deletion/Substitution/Addition (D/S/A) algorithm under user-specified constraints. It can be used for prediction or for data-adaptive estimation of propensity scores involved in the estimation of causal estimands.	www.stat.berkeley.edu/users/laan/Software
LtAtStructuR	Estimations, Data Generation, and Validation Utilities	LtAtStructuR is a SAS macro and R package that automates the processing of longitudinal electronic health record data from an observational cohort study. It transforms the data into a structured analytic data set suitable for evaluating	https://rdrr.io/github/romainkp/LtAtStructuR

the effects of time-varying treatment and monitoring interventions on a survival outcome. It supports techniques like inverse probability weighting and targeted minimum loss-based estimation.

Simcausal	Estimations, Data Generation, and Validation Utilities	Simcausal is an R package for simulating complex longitudinal data using structural equations, with a focus on problems in causal inference. It facilitates various steps of a standard data simulation workflow, including specifying interventions and simulating from intervened data generating distributions. It allows users to define and evaluate treatment-specific means, average treatment effects, and coefficients from working marginal structural models.	https://github.com/osofr/simcausal

(continued)

(*continued*)

Tool	Category	Description	URL
Stremr	Estimations, Data Generation, and Validation Utilities	Stremr is an R package that automates the implementation of various estimators of the effects of time-varying static, dynamic, and stochastic treatment and monitoring interventions on time-to-event outcomes. It provides estimation approaches such as inverse probability weighting, g-computation, and targeted minimum loss-based estimation, with the ability to adjust for observed time-dependent confounding using user-specified generalized linear models.	https://rdrr.io/ cran/stremr
Google Causal Impact	Time Series Causal Analysis	Google Causal Impact (CI) is an R package for causal inference employing Bayesian techniques for time-series modeling. It estimates the causal effect of a designed intervention on a time series by constructing a Bayesian structural time-series model. It requires the assumption of unaffected control time series and a stable relationship between covariates and treated time series.	https://google.github. io/CausalImpact/ CausalImpact.html

Selected Resources

Cunningham, Scott. *Causal Inference: The Mixtape*. Yale University Press, 2021

Hernan, Miguel A., and James M. Robins. *Causal Inference: What If*, Revised Edition. CRC Press, 2023

Huntington-Klein, Nick. *The Effect: An Introduction to Research Design and Causality*. CRC Press, 2022

Hurwitz, Judith, Marcia Kaufman, and Adrian Bowles. *Cognitive Computing and Big Data Analytics*. John Wiley & Sons, 2015

Hurwitz, Judith, Henry Morris, Candance Sidner, and Daniel Kirsch. *Augmented Intelligence The Business Power of Human-Machine Collaboration*. CRC Press, 2020

Molak, Aleksander. *Causal Inference and Discovery in Python: Unlock the secrets of modern causal machine learning with DoWhy, EconML, PyTorch and more*. Packt Publishing, 2023

Pearl, Judea. *Causality: Models, Reasoning, and Inference*, Second Edition. Cambridge University Press, 2009

Pearl, Judea, and Dana MacKenzie. *The Book of Why: The New Science of Cause and Effect*. Basic Books, 2018

Thompson, John K. *Building Analytics Teams: Harnessing analytics and artificial intelligence for business improvement*. Packt Publishing, 2020

Thompson, John K. *Data for All*. Manning Publishing, 2023

Thompson, John K., and Shawn Rogers. *Analytics: How to Win with Intelligence*. Technics Publications, 2017

Acknowledgments

Writing a book on a topic as complex as causal AI requires a tremendous amount of research. I read dozens of technical articles and books and had discussions with many experts who helped me to understand the nuances of causality. First, I'd like to thank the team at Wiley including Chris Nelson, our extraordinary editor; Pete Gaughan, senior managing editor; and Jim Minatel, associate publisher. I'd like to thank Dan Kirsch, head of community at Geminos, who contributed to the writing of this book, and Al Nugent, managing partner at Palladian Partners, who provided invaluable guidance and reviewed the manuscript for technical accuracy. I'd also like to thank key industry leaders: Judea Pearl, pioneer of causal inference, professor of computer science at UCLA, and author of many groundbreaking books; Paul Hunermund, assistant professor of strategy and information at Copenhagen Business School; Nick Huntington-Klein, assistant professor of economics at Seattle University; Scott Cunningham, president of Four Rivers Analytics and professor of economics at Baylor University; Ibrahim Gokcen, chief data and analytics officer at Aon; Aleksander Molak, chief educator and consultant at Lespire.io; and Dr. Candance Sidner, AI consultant. I'd also like to thank the team from Geminos Software including Stuart Frost, Owen Frost, Steve Eyre, Jerry Schuman, and Dan Kirsch.

—Judith Hurwitz

If you have read my previous books, you know that the only reason I ever wrote a word that became a book was because of the gentle, consistent encouragement of my wife, Jennifer. It was her idea that I write a book, then two, then three, and now four books. Of course, I enjoy writing, but I would have never discovered my passion for writing without Jennifer's urging and guidance. So, to you, Jennifer, the love of my life, my most sincere and continued love and gratitude for everything that you do for me, for our children, Kate and Zak, and for our family as a whole.

As I have started a new chapter in my professional journey as the global head of artificial intelligence for EY, my responsibilities and ability to have an impact on a global level have expanded significantly. What a great opportunity! I am so pleased to be part of this new team and to have the chance to make a difference in one of the most important developments in software and technology, the evolution of artificial intelligence. Amazing. Thank you to Mary Elizabeth Porray, Pablo Cebro, and Nicola Morini Biazino for bringing me into this team and group. Also, I want to thank Sam Wallace for introducing me to the EY team and this role.

Thinking back on my youth, much of it misspent after my father died when I was 12, I was searching for something, searching for guidance, searching for a mentor, searching for someone who could help by providing any kind of information on what I should or should not be doing. The two people who showed up were John Walker and Rick Partlo. Both were instrumental in keeping me moving in a direction, not always in the right direction, but moving forward. John was there as a surrogate father and Rick as a sage and a guide. Rick told me on a nearly daily basis that I was wasting my life working in that Ford dealership. He was right. I was destined for more than busting my knuckles working as a mechanic. My sincerest thanks go out to John for his support and love, and to Rick for showing me that education was the way forward. May both of them rest in peace.

—John K. Thompson

About the Authors

Judith S. Hurwitz is a technology strategist, consultant, thought leader, and author. A pioneer in anticipating technology innovation and adoption, she has served as a trusted advisor to many industry leaders over the years. Judith has helped these companies make the transition to new business models focused on the business value of emerging platforms. She is currently the chief causality evangelist at Geminos Software, a software company focused on causal AI software.

She was the founder of three consulting and research firms including Hurwitz & Associates (focused on AI, cloud, and data), CycleBridge (focused on life sciences software), and Hurwitz Group (focused on emerging software). She has worked in various corporations, including Apollo Computer and John Hancock. Judith has written extensively about all aspects of enterprise and distributed software. She has co-authored 10 books including *Augmented Intelligence: The Business Power of Human-Machine Collaboration* (2020), *Cognitive Computing and Big Data Analytics* (2015), and *Smart or Lucky? How Technology Leaders Turn Chance into Success* (2011). In addition, Hurwitz is a coauthor of seven For Dummies books, including *Cloud Computing for Dummies*, 2nd Edition (2020), *Machine Learning for Dummies*, IBM Limited Edition (2018), *Big Data for Dummies* (2013), and *Hybrid Cloud for Dummies* (2010).

Judith holds BS and MS degrees from Boston University. She serves on several advisory boards of emerging companies. She is also on the Dean's advisory board of Boston University's College of Arts & Sciences.

John K. Thompson is an international technology executive with more than 35 years of experience in the fields of data, advanced analytics, and artificial intelligence (AI).

John is responsible for the global AI function at EY. Prior to EY, he was responsible for the AI and advanced analytics team at CSL Behring, a leading biopharmaceutical company. John was an executive partner at Gartner, where he was management consultant to market leading companies in the areas of digital transformation, data monetization, and advanced analytics. Before Gartner, John was responsible for the advanced analytics business unit of the Dell Software Group.

John has published several previous books. *Data for All* (2023) is a consumer-oriented treatment discussing how the world of data works today and how it will work in the near future. It has been described as a primer for understanding your relationship with your data. *Building Analytics Teams* (2020) outlines how to hire and manage high performance advanced analytics teams. *Analytics: How to Win with Intelligence* (2017), which debuted on Amazon as the number-one new book in analytics, guides non-technical executives through the journey of creating an analytics function, funding initiatives, and driving change in business operations through data and applied analytical applications.

John's technology expertise includes all aspects of advanced analytics, AI, and information management including descriptive, predictive, and prescriptive analytics, artificial intelligence, analytical applications, deep learning, cognitive computing, big data, simulation, optimization, synthetic data, and high-performance computing.

One of John's primary areas of focus and interest has been to design and create innovative technologies to increase the value derived by organizations around the world. John has built startup organizations from the ground up, and he has reengineered business units of Fortune 500 firms to reach their potential. He is a technology leader with expertise and experience spanning all operational areas with a focus on strategy, product innovation, global growth, and efficient execution.

John holds a BS degree in computer science from Ferris State University and an MBA in marketing from DePaul University.

About the Contributor

Daniel (Dan) Kirsch is the head of community at the emerging causal AI startup, Geminos Software, where he is connecting customers who have a business need for causal AI with people who have both causal inference and the subject-matter expertise. Dan has spent nearly two decades helping organizations understand how disruptive technologies can propel their business forward and working with emerging technology vendors to position their technologies to meet business challenges.

Dan has launched and managed multiple analyst and consulting organizations. Dan was managing director and cofounder of Techstrong Research. At Techstrong Research, Dan launched a consulting, IT industry analyst, and thought leadership organization focused on how emerging technologies such as AI, machine learning, and advanced analytics are impacting businesses. As a member of the Techstrong Group's executive team, Dan delivered keynote speeches and trainings and led strategy workshops for both technology vendors and end-user groups.

Prior to Techstrong, Dan served as managing director at Hurwitz & Associates, an analyst and consulting firm where he led research in the areas of data and AI, modern software development, security, and multicloud computing.

Dan earned his BA in political science from Union College in New York and a JD from Boston College Law School, where he focused on emerging corporate strategies and intellectual property. As an attorney, Dan represented startups, cloud computing ventures, and early-stage startups as they sought funding. Dan is a coauthor of *Augmented Intelligence: The Business Power of Human-Machine Collaboration* (2020), *Cloud for Dummies* (2020), and *Hybrid Cloud for Dummies* (2012).

Index